The **RAILROAD** ENCYCLOPEDIA

The RAILROAD ENCYCLOPEDIA.

MBI Publishing Company

This edition first published in 2001 by MBI Publishing Company,
Galtier Plaza, Suite 200, 380 Jackson Street, St. Paul, MN 55101-3885.

Copyright © 2001 Eaglemoss Publications Ltd.
Based on *The World of Trains*.

MBI Publishing Company books are also available at discounts in bulk
quantity for industrial or sales-promotional use. For details write to Special
Sales Manager at: Motorbooks International Wholesalers & Distributors,
Galtier Plaza, Suite 200, 380 Jackson Street, St. Paul, MN 55101-3885.

Library of Congress Cataloging-in-Publication Data Available.

ISBN: 0-7603-1136-6

Printed in Dubai

10 9 8 7 6 5 4 3 2 1

Photographs: Front cover (top left) Millbrook House;
(top right) Onslow Auctioneers; (upper centre left) Rex Features;
(upper centre right) Robert Harding Picture Library;
(lower centre) National Railway Museum; (bottom) Salamander Books.
Page 7 Nils Huxtable (Steamscenes). Back cover Harold Edmonson.

Contents

Chapter 1
Loco Library

Liverpool & Manchester Railway (LMR) *Rocket* 0-2-2
Designer: Robert Stephenson
Built: Robert Stephenson & Co, Forth Street, Newcastle-upon-Tyne, 1829
Service: Built to compete in the Rainhill Trails, 1829. After winning the competition it was bought by the LMR and modified within 12 months. It later became a ballast engine until sold for use in the Midgeholm Colliery of Lord Carlisle
Livery: As built – white chimney, yellow boiler barrel and wheels, black frames, cylinder and boiler ends
Performance: It was recorded that 40 tons were pulled at 14mph on the level, 18 tons up a slope of 1 in 96 and 35mph as a light engine
Withdrawn from service: LMR 1835 and by Midgeholm Colliery 1844

Claiming credit
There have been many suggestions and emphatic statements that George Stephenson designed *Rocket*, but this was not so. It was solely the work of his son, Robert.

George did not see the locomotive once until it was delivered to Liverpool but he did frequently claim credit for his son's work. He was reprimanded in later years at a Parliamentary inquiry for doing just that.

A letter written by Robert and kept in the Devon County Record office, states 'I think it perfectly needless to go into the absurd and ridiculous stories which some writers have hatched up about my Father's conduct with *Rocket*. I had charge of the engine myself – whatever was done to the engine was done under my own eye and direction'.

▶ In 1979, a fully working reproduction *Rocket* was built under the auspices of the NRM, York, to take part in the 150th anniversary celebration of the Rainhill Trials. At the Trials, *Rocket*'s maximum speed was 29mph and its average speed was 16mph; the replica has run at speeds up to 27mph. When built, it had a gauge of 8ft 4in, the same as the original LMR, but this was later changed to 4ft 8½in.

Rocket *and* Planet

LIVERPOOL & MANCHESTER RAILWAY

Two of the most important events in the history of railway engineering are the development of Robert Stephenson's locomotives *Rocket* and *Planet*. These two designs contained the essential elements used in the majority of steam locomotives built after 1830.

In 1829, locomotive trials took place at Rainhill, Lancashire, to enable the directors of the Liverpool & Manchester Railway (LMR) to decide on two points – whether locomotives or stationary engines should provide the motive power for their railway; and, if it was to be a locomotive, what was the most suitable type. The trial was won by a locomotive called *Rocket*, which had been designed and built by Robert Stephenson at Newcastle-upon-Tyne.

Robert Stephenson returned to England from a trip to South America at the end of November 1827. His father, George, was busy with the construction of the LMR and this left Robert to concentrate on a new type of locomotive. This was needed, as up until then steam engines had only been designed for use within the confines of a colliery or to a canal or river wharf – not hauling freight and passengers between two cities. So the task facing Robert was to build the world's first intercity locomotive.

From the beginning of 1828, Robert became the managing partner at his father's factory at Newcastle-upon-Tyne. He engaged the services of a draughtsman, George Phipps, and a works manager, William Hutchinson. Work soon began on a series of prototypes and once sold to a customer, usually a colliery, the locomotive's performance was carefully monitored so that later designs could be improved. This was partly because there was no test track at the Stephenson's factory.

Rocket was one such prototype and was built with the forthcoming Rainhill Trials in mind. Work started on the locomotive around May 1829 and it underwent its first tests between 1 and 5 September; it was the nineteenth engine built by Robert Stephenson & Co. *Rocket* was light, fast and powerful and was the logical development of the locomotives Robert had designed and built in 1827 and 1828 when his stated aims were firstly to simplify the design of the steam locomotive and secondly to increase its power.

Essential elements

As early as 1803, Richard Trevithick, a close friend of Robert Stephenson, had introduced the essential elements for a successful steam locomotive, but *Rocket* was the first to combine them all. The most important feature of the locomotive was its use of the tubular boiler, a type which had been used on road locomotives for some time. Patents for railway locomotives using such boilers were taken out by Trevithick in 1815, W H James in 1821 and Marc Seguin in 1828.

TECHNICAL FILE

Rocket*
2 cylinders: (outside) 8in
diameter x 17in stroke
Driving wheels: 4ft 8¹/₂in
diameter
Carrying wheels: 2ft 6in
diameter (as built)
Boiler diameter: 3ft 4in
Boiler length: 6ft
Pressure: 50lb psi pressure
Number of tubes: 25
Diameter: 3in
Grate area: 5.16sq ft
Overall length: 11ft
Weight: 4 tons 3cwt
*engine was later modified

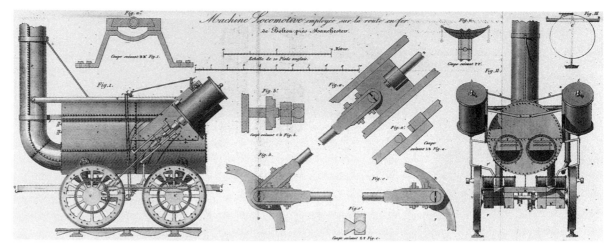

▼ By combining a number of successful ideas in one design for the first time, *Rocket* was an enormous advance over previous locomotive types. Although the key to its success was the multi-tube boiler, another vital factor was a water jacket around the firebox, which gave a greater heating area for the water. This was supplied from a tender built by Nathaniel Worsdell, a noted English coach builder.

Early Stephenson engines carried boilers with only a single flue. In 1828, some of these locomotives had been supplied to the St Etienne-Lyon Railway in France, but were unable to produce sufficient steam. The railway's engineer, Marc Seguin, then designed the multi-tubular boiler with its vastly increased surface area. The patent drawing of Seguin's boiler shows it to be identical to that used on *Rocket*, but with a different firebox.

The boiler on *Rocket* contained 25 copper tubes, 3in in diameter, and the firebox had spaces for water on the top and sides. The blast of the exhaust steam in the chimney helped increase the draw on the fire and its temperature. These features improved the boiler's ability to boil water and so produce more steam.

The boiler was supported, as on a previous Robert Stephenson-designed engine *Lancashire Witch*, on a wrought-iron frame made up of flat bars riveted and welded together with steel springs to each wheel. The two cylinders were mounted, again like *Lancashire Witch*, on the side of the

▲ *Rocket* was developed from previous Robert Stephenson designs. These included *Lancashire Witch*, built in 1828 for freight haulage on the Bolton & Leigh Railway. Unlike previous designs which had a single or return flue, this locomotive had two furnace-flues side by side leading into a common chimney. Although an inefficient arrangement, it produced sufficient power for the type of tasks demanded at collieries. The angle of the cylinders was also new, as previously they had been positioned vertically, causing the engine to shake considerably.

boiler at an angle of about 35° and drove the front wheels through a crosshead, supported by slide bars, directly. The bar frames and outside cylinders became a standard feature of American steam locomotives.

The availability of adequate steam with the light direct drive changed the speed of the locomotive from that of a cart horse to a race horse.

After a short time in service, *Rocket* was modified by the replacement of the original chimney, fixed directly over the tube ends at the front of the

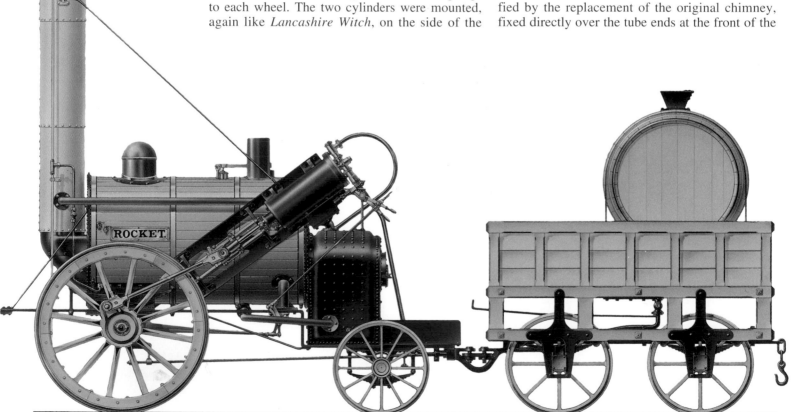

KEY FACTS

Liverpool & Manchester Railway (LMR) *Planet* 2-2-0
Designer: Robert Stephenson
Built: Robert Stephenson & Co, Forth Street, Newcastle-upon-Tyne, 1830
Service: The mainstay of the Liverpool & Manchester Railway for many years. For stiff gradients and goods trains, many were built as four-coupled 0-4-0 types
Performance: Typical, 25mph with 60 tons, on test: 15mph with 100-120 tons, and maximum speed light engine was 35mph
Withdrawn from service: In-service examples lasted until the 1850s

LOCO LIST

Following the success of *Rocket* at the Rainhill Trials, other locomotives soon followed. Most were named with an astronomical theme. *Meteor*, *Comet*, *Dart* and *Arrow* were built to the same general design but were more powerful. *Phoenix* and *North Star* were generally similar but somewhat larger.

Sixty-four locomotives of the Planet-type were built by Robert Stephenson & Co, and many others by other companies, such as Messrs Fenton & Murray, to Stephenson's drawings.

▶ On 26 February 1993, the reproduction *Planet* strolls across Swithland Viaduct, while undergoing trials on the preserved Great Central Railway in Leicestershire. In early locomotives, the boilers were usually fed with water by pumps driven by the engines themselves and it was necessary for the engine to be moving to work the pumps. To avoid this, the reproduction is fitted with an injector as well as a pump and this necessitates a boiler pressure of 100lb psi, rather than the original 50lb psi. The higher boiler pressure would, in turn, make the engine much more powerful and so the cylinder sizes are reduced to compensate. Steel has been used in the boiler and has replaced most of the other wrought-iron components. To conform with the modern safety requirements, this *Planet* has compressed air brakes, and modern buffers and couplings. Gauges and a device assist in reversing.

boiler, with a smokebox and the chimney on the top in the now familiar position. This allowed a more even suction through the tubes and the ashes could be cleared away more easily.

The cylinders were lowered to a nearly horizontal position, providing a steadier ride at speed, since the original position tended to cause considerable deflection of the driving wheel springs, making the engine shoulder and swing up and down and from side to side.

Rocket made the intercity passenger railway possible. There were six more engines built to the same basic design and then two bigger and more powerful Northumbrian types. These had different frames and the fireboxes were inside the boiler shell rather than attached at the back, as on *Rocket*.

The next stage

'Not content with what he had achieved, Robert Stephenson resolved on effecting further improvements and the *Planet* was the result of his renewed exertions', reported the proceedings of the Institute of Chartered Engineers.

While the Stephensons' factory at Newcastle-upon-Tyne was producing the earlier types of engines for the LMR, Robert Stephenson was working on the design for a more efficient machine called *Planet*. Trevithick had told him that the efficiency of a stationary engine he had rebuilt had been greatly increased by including a steam jacket which heated the cylinder on the outside. In *Planet*, Robert put his cylinders almost horizontally inside the smokebox to keep them hot and reduce condensation. This meant he then had to use a crank axle to drive the wheels.

Some years earlier in 1815, George Stephenson and his partner, Ralph Dodds, took out a patent which included rods to couple the driving wheels.

The rods were worked on cranks inside the wheels. This presented the unwelcome possibility of a crank failing in service. Although metallurgy and production methods had improved, they were not up to those of today. Robert had to design his new engine so that the risk of a crankshaft breaking was greatly reduced and if one did break then the wheels would remain in place and the safety of the engine and train would not be endangered.

The frames were designed and built with six timber members. The outside pair was strengthened with iron plates and each member carried a bearing for the crank axle. In this way, each wheel and each crank had a bearing on both sides. Although *Planet* had the same sized cylinders and boiler as *Northumbrian*, an earlier locomotive with outside cylinders, it was smoother running and the heated cylinders ensured that it was more economical to run.

In 1830, *Planet* and *Rocket* contained all the essential basic features that could still be found in new steam locomotives being built in China in the 1990s. New features included a firebox within the boiler shell. Between the frames, horizontal cylinders, with crossheads and slide bars, supplied power to a cranked driving axle. Horns, horn-guides and leaf springs helped to absorb the vertical forces and the effects of track inequalities.

Planet was completed at the Newcastle works on 3 September 1830 and missed the opening of the LMR by a few days only. On 4 December, it hauled its first train. This consisted of 18 wagons, carrying oatmeal and malt and 15 passengers, totalling 80 tons gross. The journey took just under three hours at an average speed of 12.5mph, and a top speed of 15.5mph. A month after delivery, *Planet* ran as a light engine from Liverpool to Manchester in one hour.

It proved to be far more economical than earlier

Where to see them

In 1844, *Rocket* was returned to Robert Stephenson & Co, Newcastle, for restoration and exhibited at the Great Exhibition in London. It was partly dismantled but no other work was done. Robert died in 1859 and, in accordance with his stated wish, the remains of *Rocket* were presented to the Patent Museum, the forerunner of the Science Museum, in London in 1862 where it can be seen today.

The original *Planet* was not preserved but *John Bull*, built for the Camden & Amboy Railway in America in 1831, has survived. It was a four-coupled engine similar in many ways to *Samson* and *Goliath* but has been much modified to suit American conditions. It is preserved at the Smithsonian Institute, Washington, USA.

TECHNICAL FILE

Planet
2 cylinders: 11in diameter x 16in stroke
Driving wheels: 5ft diameter
Carrying wheels: 3ft 1in diameter (as built)
Boiler diameter: 3ft
Boiler length: 6ft 6in
Pressure: 50lb psi
Number of tubes: 129
Diameter: 1⅝in
Total heating service: 407.66sq ft
Grate area: 6.5sq ft
Overall length: 12ft 9in
Weight: Approx 8 tons

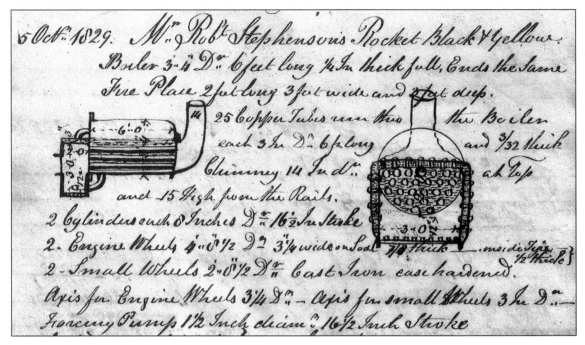

prototypes in terms of fuel consumption. When hauling four coaches, *Planet* consumed an average 19lb of coke per mile over 16 trips compared with the 27-28lb of previous engines.

Where steep gradients were found, it was necessary to provide more adhesion than *Planet*'s single driving wheels and so the small leading wheels were replaced by a second pair, the same size as the driving wheels, and coupled to them by outside coupling rods. Two of these engines, named *Samson* and *Goliath*, were delivered to the Liverpool & Manchester Railway in 1831.

The firebox of the Planet-type overhung the driving axle at the back and this caused the engines to swing from side to side at speed. This, together with the increased weights, caused concern. In later designs, an additional pair of wheels was positioned behind the firebox. After 10 years of service, *Planet* was withdrawn. A locomotive called *John Bull*, based on *Planet*, can be seen at the Smithsonian Institute, Washington, USA.

▲ The invention of the multi-tube boiler has often been attributed to Henry Booth, secretary of the Liverpool & Manchester Railway and co-owner of *Rocket* with George and Robert Stephenson. However, the boiler used on *Rocket* was similar to that designed by a Frenchman, Marc Seguin, who had developed it after becoming dissatisfied with the steam produced by two engines he had bought from the Stephensons for the St Etienne-Lyon Railway in 1828.

▼ The Planet-design was the prototype for the majority of locomotives built for British railways in the 19th century and the GWR used the same basic ideas on their City class of 1903. It is recorded in the proceedings of the Institution of Civil Engineers that the chairman, Rennie, stated 'Mr Stephenson has brought his engines to such perfection in construction that all questions appeared to be now a mere matter of detail arrangements'.

Ivatt Atlantics

GREAT NORTHERN RAILWAY

For over 30 years, Henry Ivatt's large-boilered Atlantics played a major part in express passenger train working over the Great Northern main line and, after superheating by Gresley, could keep time with heavy expresses normally hauled by Pacifics.

KEY FACTS

GNR and LNER Class C1
GNR Nos: 251, 272-301, 1300, 1400-1461 (including three four-cylinder compounds of which two were rebuilt as simples); 94 engines. 3000 was added to these numbers after formation of the LNER in 1923
Designer: H A Ivatt, superheated by H N Gresley
Built: 1902-10
Service: Main line passenger and fast perishable trains
Livery: GNR – two-tone green. LNER – apple green
Performance: In 1936, No 4404 (with a Gateshead crew having little previous experience with Ivatt Atlantics) averaged 57mph from Grantham to York, 82.7 miles, with 17 coach, 585 ton train
Withdrawn: 1945-50 (No 1300 was withdrawn in 1924)

When Henry Alfred Ivatt succeeded Patrick Stirling as Locomotive Superintendent of the Great Northern Railway (GNR) in 1895, its main line expresses were hauled, as they had been for the previous 25 years, by Stirling's single drivers in the form of outside-cylindered 8ft 4-2-2s and inside-cylindered 7ft 7in 2-2-2s.

As train loadings steadily increased, Ivatt directed the design of a more powerful outside-cylinder 4-4-2 and in July 1898, the prototype, No 990, was completed at Doncaster works. As it was built in the same year as the Canadian gold rush the class became known as the Klondikes. The locomotive's firebox and boiler were considerably larger than the Stirling 4-2-2, with the grate area increased by 30%; its adhesive weight on the coupled wheels was 75% greater.

Greater adhesive weight was an important factor in hauling heavier trains without the wheelslip problems experienced by the singles especially on greasy rails. However, existing track conditions on the GNR's main line were far from satisfactory –

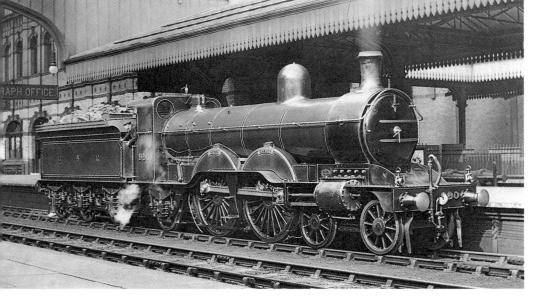

◀ In 1920, GNR Class C2 Atlantic No 990 *Henry Oakley* stands at Nottingham Victoria. This locomotive was the first of its type and was introduced at the time of the Klondike gold rush in northern Canada, giving the class its nickname Klondikes. Between 1900 and 1903, 20 more were built. On a test run with a 214 ton train, No 990 gave excellent results, averaging 57mph from King's Cross to Grantham.

▼ At the time of their first appearance, at Doncaster in December 1902, the large-boilered Atlantics created quite a sensation. Full advantage was taken of this by the GNR publicity department and someone commented that the locomotive 'with its large boiler leered from Great Northern advertisements on every hoarding'. In fact, Ivatt's large Atlantics were handsome engines with a neat, well balanced outline.

as Ivatt himself discovered after walking the whole of the 156 miles from King's Cross to Doncaster. Some sections were still laid with old 70lb per yard rail (most of the rail was 90lb per yard). This restricted the size of the boiler, as the axle loading had to be kept down to 16.5 tons, and the total engine weight was only 58 tons – little more than the 4-4-0s on other principal railways.

Larger boiler

A four-cylinder simple variant with the same boiler as No 990, No 271, was built in 1902, possibly as a means of reducing hammer-blow on the track. This engine proved to be over-cylindered in relation to boiler capacity and was rebuilt in 1911 with only two inside cylinders. However, by 1902 the track had been greatly improved. Ivatt was then able to develop fully his Atlantic type using a larger boiler, with diameter increased from 4ft 8in to 5ft 6in and a very wide, but short, firebox, with grate area increased by 17%.

With its relatively small 18¾in by 24in cylinders, 6ft 8in driving wheels and 175lb psi working pressure, as in the Klondikes, No 251's maximum

tractive effort was 15,670lb; only two-thirds that of Churchward's two-cylinder 4-6-0s and Atlantics running on the Great Western Railway (GWR). However, apart from the 1 in 105 start out of King's Cross, the steepest grade on the main line to York was 1 in 178 and in their early days GNR expresses were rarely more than 350 tons, so its locomotives seldom had to develop the same power outputs as the Churchward engines.

Unlike Churchward, who had adopted the latest American practice with long-travel, long-lap piston valves (to facilitate short cut-off working which allowed steam to expand more fully in the cylinders and so be used more economically), on No 251 Ivatt retained the conventional short-travel, medium-lap balanced slide valves of the small Atlantics. However, the direct steam ports and passages were of generous dimensions, allowing the Atlantics to run freely at speed.

Ivatt took the view that with relatively small cylinders, the drivers would have to use a wide regulator opening with longer cut-offs to obtain the required power output. This would avoid the steam throttling losses at the regulator which

Where to see them
Both prototype large- and small-boilered Atlantics, No 251 and No 990 *Henry Oakley*, have been preserved. However, it is probable that few original parts remain. In 1953, the engines double headed the Plant Centenarian specials to commemorate the centenary of Doncaster Plant works.

Both engines now reside in the National Railway Museum at York.

Compound special

After inconclusive tests between two four-cylinder compound prototypes and a standard large Atlantic in 1906, another large-boilered Ivatt four-cylinder compound Atlantic, No 1421, was built in 1907. This had larger low pressure cylinders, permitting a greater degree of expansion and power output in compound working. Although it reached 73mph on level track with a 305 ton train, Ivatt did not pursue compounding, feeling complications of four-cylinder drive with independent valve gears were not justified by small fuel economies in normal conditions.

Top offer
In 1909, there was an interesting locomotive exchange between the GNR's Ivatt Atlantic No 1449 and the London & North Western Railway's (LNWR) Precursor class 4-4-0 *Titan* on each other's railways. The Atlantic worked 26 trips between Euston and Crewe, while the Precursor ran from King's Cross to Doncaster. The Atlantic's fuel consumption was 8% less per ton/mile, probably due to burning its fuel more efficiently on a grate 37% larger. It is said that Henry Ivatt, who was on the footplate of the Precursor, offered the LNWR driver a new hat if he could pass Potters Bar summit in 20 minutes from the start at King's Cross – but this was never quite achieved.

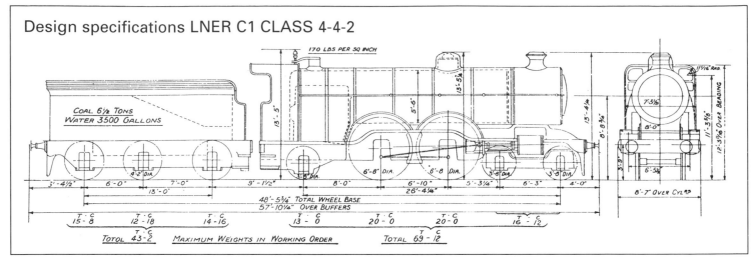

Design specifications LNER C1 CLASS 4-4-2

▲ In 1902, Ivatt redesigned his Klondike Atlantics with a larger boiler and firebox. This enabled the locomotive to meet fully Ivatt's dictum that the success of a locomotive was related primarily to its ability to boil water and produce sufficient steam. However, the frames, cylinder and valve layout of the earlier machine were retained; superheating was added later. These modifications totally transformed their performance.

TECHNICAL FILE

2 cylinders: 20in diameter x 24in stroke, with piston valves
Coupled wheel diameter: 6ft 8in
Maximum outside boiler diameter: 5ft 6in
Grate area: 31sq ft
Boiler pressure: 170lb psi
Tractive effort: 17,340lb at 85% working pressure with 20in cylinders
Water capacity: 3500 gallons
Coal capacity: 6.5 tons
Length over buffers: 57ft 10¼in
Weight in working order:
Engine: 69.6 tons*
Tender: 43.1 tons
*with 32-element superheater

▶Atlantic No 3279 was rebuilt with two outside cylinders, improved steam passages and long-travel, long-lap valves. This locomotive was the ultimate development of the Ivatt Atlantic with high degree superheat and modern valve setting, but it was completed only a year before the outbreak of war in 1939 and no further conversions were made. On 12 September 1938, classified C1, No 3279 waits at Spalding with a Grimsby – King's Cross express.

occur when running with a narrow regulator opening when steam is expanded without doing useful work. Thus Ivatt's large-boilered Atlantic could run fast and hard when necessary without any risk of its cylinders using steam quicker than the boiler could produce it. In 1904-08, 80 similar large Atlantics were built.

Superheaters

In 1909, Klondike No 988 was equipped with an 18-element superheater and, at Dr Schmidt's suggestion, 8in diameter piston valves. Despite working pressure being reduced from 175 to 160lb psi, to reduce boiler maintenance costs, results were excellent with fuel costs cut by 15%. In 1910, 10 further large Atlantics were built with superheaters and piston valves and pressure further reduced to 150lb psi.

However, it was found from tests that steam temperatures with the large superheated Atlantics were some 20% lower than on No 998 as, with the greater number of small tubes in the larger boiler, less hot gas passed through the large flue tubes which contained the superheater elements. To remedy this, Nigel Gresley, who succeeded Ivatt

in 1911, fitted five large Atlantics with 24-element superheaters giving 30% more heating surface and restored working pressure to 170lb psi, considerably improving their performance.

In 1917, towards the end of World War I, many express trains were cancelled and the remainder combined portions for destinations once served by up to three separate trains. The Ivatt Atlantics often tackled 500 ton train loads and the increased power of the superheated engines was most valuable. In 1918, pilot engines, usually Ivatt 4-4-0s, over the 12.7 miles from King's Cross to Potters Bar enabled trains of up to 600 tons to be worked by the Atlantics at an average of 50mph over the 63.7 miles on to Peterborough.

In 1918, Gresley fitted even larger 32-element superheaters which enabled steam temperature to be raised to a maximum of 800°F (427°C), giving an increase in steam volume of over 60% compared with an equal weight of saturated steam. While the production of this highly superheated steam required 20% more heat, the overall increase in maximum power output was found to be substantial.

This was the secret of the steep change upwards

in GNR large Atlantic performance capacity. Many were fitted with larger 20in diameter cylinders and piston valves, to take full advantage of the increased steam volume available; others retained their existing cylinders with balanced slide valves, but were fitted with mechanical lubricators to ensure adequate lubrication at these high steam temperatures. The smaller boilered Atlantics were fitted with 18-element superheaters, similar to No 988.

Even with coupled axle loading increased to 20 tons in the superheated large Atlantics, their limited adhesion made for slow starts with the heavy express trains – despite their ample boiler capacity. In 1919, America's New York Central Railroad had pioneered the use of the locomotive booster, with a two-cylinder auxiliary engine driving the trailing coupled axle under the cab. In 1922, Nigel Gresley fitted such a device to Atlantic No 1419, which increased its maximum tractive effort by 50%. When tested with an 18 coach, 535 ton train, No 1419 had no difficulty in restarting from a special stop on the 1 in 105 climb out of King's Cross, which would have been quite impossible without the device. At the same time, No 1419 was fitted with a double side window cab, similar to that of the prototype A1 Pacifics.

To the rescue

With the introduction of the A1s from 1923, the Ivatt Atlantics were gradually superseded on the heaviest trains over the Great Northern main line. However, they could still be found on many lighter expresses and the Pullmans. In emergencies they took over very heavy trains from Pacifics. On three known occasions, 16 and 17 coach trains of 540/585 tons were worked over the 82.7 miles from Grantham to York at an average speed of 57-58mph.

When due for heavy repairs in 1936, Gresley had No 3279, which had previously been rebuilt in 1915 as a four-cylinder simple, rebuilt again but with only two outside cylinders, an improved version of those of the K2 class 2-6-0s (later used in 1942 by Edward Thompson on his B1 class 4-6-0). The cab was extended to improve crew protection. However, World War II put an end to any further rebuilds.

The excellence of No 3279 (LNER numbering) was shown in 1944 during tests between it and new Thompson B1 No 8301. Both locomotives hauled semi-fast trains of up to 484 tons over the 79 miles from Peterborough to Grimsby with the heaviest train – by chance – being Atlantic hauled. No 3279's coal consumption per ton/mile was only 4% greater than the B1, whose working pressure was 38% higher and whose maximum tractive effort almost 50% more: no mean tribute to the Ivatt Atlantic design, perfected by Gresley. The last one, No 62822, was withdrawn in 1950.

▼ On 13 July 1926, C1 Atlantic No 4444 climbs past Belle Isle with the 10.45am King's Cross – Newmarket race special, formed of ex-SECR Pullman stock. The Atlantics in their final form were extremely powerful engines. On one occasion, No 4452 worked the Silver Jubilee streamliner from Doncaster to King's Cross at an average of 67mph. Performances by the high superheat Atlantics were on a level quite unimagined when the saturated steam No 251 was introduced 35 years earlier.

1906 compound trials
Following the success of compounding in France, tests were carried out in 1906 between a four-cylinder compound large Atlantic, No 292, with its pressure raised to 200lb psi, a standard Atlantic, No 294, and a four-cylinder compound Atlantic, No 1300, with a long narrow firebox. Although No 292 showed a 4% fuel economy over No 294, the total running costs, including repairs and lubricants, were virtually identical. Total costs for No 1300, which suffered from steam leakage at the pipe joints to the high pressure cylinders, were about 8% higher. However, No 292, which had very small high pressure cylinders, hardly exploited the potential economies of compounding in the same manner as the French engines, and further tests took place in 1907. (Ivatt intended that live steam from the boiler would be supplied directly to the low pressure cylinders when the engine was working hard – as in a simple – and function as a full compound only when working at moderate outputs.)

Pennsylvania K4

PENNSYLVANIA RAILROAD

The K4 was the most outstanding American Pacific ever to be produced in large numbers. Upgraded and modified throughout its life, this class blasted a legend across the tough mountains of Allegheny that is set to live on in the folklore of US railroads.

▼When the class first appeared in 1914, there was a rather turn of the century appearance about the design – with a square, encased oil burning headlight mounted high on the smokebox and a slatted wood pilot (cow-catcher). Contrary to the nickname, the pilot served to deflect any object, such as an automobile, from becoming snagged on the front coupling.

The locomotive that became the symbol of the Pennsylvania Railroad (PRR) was the K4. Introduced on the eve of World War I, in an era of hand firing, oil-lit headlights, manual reversing gear and wooden-bodied cars, the class stayed in production for 14 years to become a mechanically fired, power reversed workhorse.

Largest railroad

In the early 1900s, the PRR was considered the largest railroad in the US. What it lacked in route mileage, compared to some of the western US railroads, it more than made up for in track miles, numbers of cars and locomotives – 7667 by 1920 – and traffic density.

The PRR was a line with much high speed terrain: between New York, Philadelphia and Washington in the east and Chicago and St Louis in the Midwest.

On the Philadelphia to Chicago route, the back breaking obstacle was the 131 mile Allegheny Mountain section between Altoona and Pittsburgh. To keep the gradient to a maximum of 1 in 58 to the Gallitzin summit on the four-track main line

▶ The K4 went through numerous modifications in its 40 years of railroad service. A heavyweight pilot, made up from boiler plate, offered more protection than the original slatted one and helped to make the locomotive heavier at the front. At the same time the headlight was mounted on top of the boiler and the generator moved to the front of the smokebox.

PENNSYLVANIA

5498

required a series of tunnels and the world famous Horse Shoe Curve.

Although many US railroads built their own steam locomotives, none did so on a scale to compare with the PRR, whose workshops at Juniata, Altoona and at the adjacent stationary locomotive test plant were the largest in the world. In the early 1900s, PRR were looking for a new design to move passenger trains over the heavily graded section west of Pittsburgh. In 1906, with this in mind, the railroad tested an American Locomotive Company (Alco) built prototype Pacific, No 7067. Satisfied with the results, the PRR settled on the Pacific type, designated with the letter K.

From 1910-11, the PRR workshops at Juniata were busy turning out 215 Class K2 and K2a saturated Pacifics. These non-superheated locomotives struggled over Horse Shoe Curve, and were usually double and sometimes triple-headed to ensure a steady speed with heavy trains.

By this time, the Juniata works were busy developing and building the large-boilered, superheated E6 Atlantic 4-4-2, a gem of a locomotive capable of 2600 cylinder hp. This 83-strong class out-performed the non-superheated K2 classes on the level sections of the railroad.

To answer the pressing need for a more powerful locomotive, Alco delivered another prototype Pacific in 1911, Class K29 No 3395, with 6ft 8in driving wheels. This 4-6-2, with its large stoker-fired firebox, performed impressively and gave the PRR renewed impetus about the potential of a Pacific. Although never duplicated, No 3395, together with the highly successful E6 Atlantics, became reference points as the PRR started developing its own improved Pacific in 1913.

New technology

At one point, work on the new locomotive came to a halt. The engineers realized that the third pair of 6ft 8in driving wheels would not clear a conventional riveted joint between the rear ring on the boiler barrel and the firebox throatplate. To solve this problem, one of the first examples of one-piece construction in locomotive engineering was

▲When the streamlining era swept American railroads in the 1930s, PRR responded with aerodynamic shrouding designed by Raymond Loewy. In 1936, K4 No 3768 leaves Englewood on the first streamlined run of the Chicago – New York Trail Blazer express.

used. By producing a firebox throatplate and lower half of the rear barrel section flanged from a single plate, an extra $1^7/_8$in wheel clearance was gained.

The new K4 Pacific (also known as the K4s, the 's' standing for superheating), No 1737, rolled out of Juniata works in May 1914. The locomotive featured what was becoming the PRR trademark – a Belpaire firebox with a distinctive square corner outline. Previously, most locomotive fireboxes were round-topped and followed the circular barrel of the boiler. While more angular, the Belpaire firebox gave greater steam space at the top, where it was needed most.

No 1737 had a 3ft long combustion chamber (an extension to the firebox area in the rear of the

LOCO LIST

A total of 425 K4 locomotives were built. The original K4, No 1737, and 133 other locomotives, received numbers at random. The rest were allocated series production numbers depending on the year in which they were built:
1918 – Nos 3667-84 and 5334-49
1920 – Nos 3762-75
1923 – Nos 3800, 3805-07, 3838-89
1924 – Nos 5350-99
1927 – Nos 5400-91
1928 – Nos 5492-99

Brilliant machine

In 1939, K4 No 5399 was rebuilt with an enlarged steam flow circuit, Franklin oscillating cam activated poppet valves, bigger steam chests and superheaters and improved Kiesel exhaust. The previous limitations of the class due to restrictions in the steam flow circuit at full power, were overcome.

Cylinder hp was raised by 22% from 3500-4267 at 75mph, and by 47% from 2810-4130 at 100mph. No 5399 alone could handle many trains which would normally be double-headed on the Fort Wayne section. It once averaged 85mph for 79 miles, hauling a 13-car, 850-ton train. But the PRR did not rebuild the rest of the class.

with steel replacing wood in the body construction. The standard practice became to double-head with a Class K4, any train above eight cars on the hardest schedules, adding a front end helper such as another K4 or an L1 as far as Gallitzin.

In 1920, 50 more K4 locomotives were built. Modifications were made in the piping: a new pilot with horizontal metal slats – known as the hen coop – appeared; and a larger tender was employed, although with relatively small water capacity, as water pans (water troughs) were used by the PRR.

As the US experienced prosperity in the 1920s, the demand for more of the class was answered by building 57 in 1923, 50 in 1924 and 100 in 1927-28. An Alco power reverse gear was introduced in 1923, as was the round case electric headlight.

Improved design

In 1927 the PRR's rival railroad, the New York Central, brought out the 4-6-4 Hudson class, purchased from Alco, which pushed passenger steam locomotive design to new heights. In 1929, the PRR responded with an improved prototype Pacific, designated K5. This had 250lb psi and type E superheat for higher steam temperature and more power. Because of the recession, only two of the class were built.

boiler barrel) which gave an appreciably greater direct heating surface for the equivalent grate area than Alco's No 3395. Superheating had been adopted by PRR in 1912 and a Schmidt superheater was used on the K4. Walschaerts valve gear distributed steam to the cylinders, which had the generous dimensions of 27x28in. A screw-type manual reversing gear was used to set the cut-off – an advance on the lever reverse used previously. A large cast-steel trailing truck supported the end of the locomotive.

Initially, the progressive features of No 1737 were offset by the lack of a mechanical stoker, and although the boiler was an outstanding steam producer, it had a relatively modest pressure of 205lb psi. The boiler, trailing truck and certain other components were identical to those being installed on the contemporary Class L1 2-8-2, a successful and hard-working freight locomotive.

In service

Two years of service on the demanding Pittsburgh section convinced the PRR of the soundness of the design. In 1917, Juniata works produced another 41 locomotives, followed by 111 in 1918 and 15 in 1919. For a time Class K4 was able to maintain existing schedules up the 12 mile Horse Shoe Curve gradient, an average of 1 in 64, to Gallitzin without double-heading. But this became more difficult as trains grew longer and cars heavier,

▶ Standing on its home ground at Altoona on 12 April 1987, No 1361, one of two surviving K4 locomotives, waits after hauling its first road trip in preservation. In their heyday, the PRR workshops at Altoona were the biggest railway workshops in the world.

Design specifications CLASS K4 4-6-2

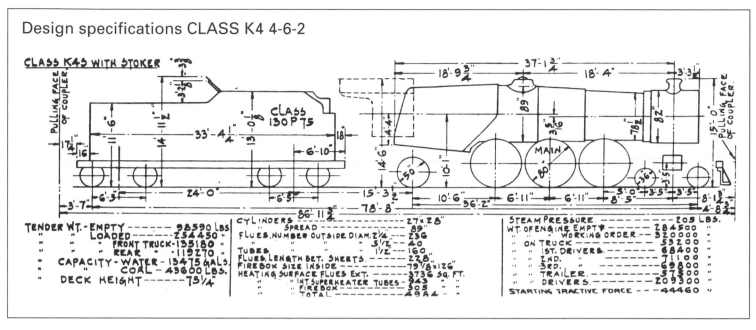

The K4 was not the largest, most powerful, or most modern Pacific in the US, but it was the best known. It coupled a high performance Belpaire firebox and large boiler with a modest boiler pressure and large cylinders, to provide rugged and dependable service for 40 years.

The PRR upgraded the K4s for working heavy trains at higher speeds. Mechanical stokers (a move made mandatory by the government), mechanical lubricators, table grates and improved exhaust nozzles helped to increase output from 3200 to 3600hp. A modified cab was introduced on the 1927-28 production locomotives.

Throughout their life, Class K4 was entrusted with all the top Pennsylvania express trains including Broadway Limited and Spirit of St Louis. Although the class is associated with the climb to Horse Shoe Curve, the locomotives gained a reputation for high speed running, especially over the 141 mile section between Fort Wayne, Indiana, and Chicago. Recorded timings showed maximum speeds up to 85½mph with an 11-car (850 UK tons) train and 97½mph with a 6-car train.

Further improvements

When the PRR electrified the lines from New York to Washington and Harrisburg in the 1930s, the K4s set the performance guidelines for the new P5a electrics, which took over K4 powered trains from Chicago at Harrisburg, 190 miles from New York.

The project released hundreds of steam locomotives, including the K4s, for service elsewhere. This was fortunate as the PRR became a principal player in moving freight and passenger trains during World War II (during the war the PRR actually had so many steam locomotives, some were kept in storage). Double-heading of Class K4 on heavy trains became the rule rather than the exception along the PRR's main lines, even east of Pittsburgh.

In the mid-1940s, the supremacy of the K4 was challenged by the new diesels. As they steadily took over after World War II, the first Class K4 was retired. The last run of a K4 in regular passenger service was No 5351 from Pemberton – Camden, New Jersey on 12 November 1957. Two of the class have been preserved, one in Strasburg and one in Altoona, Pennsylvania.

TECHNICAL FILE

2 cylinders: 27in diameter, 28in stroke
Coupled wheels: 80in diameter
Boiler diameter: 7ft 5in, tapering to 6ft 5in at front ring of boiler barrel
Grate area: 70sq ft
Boiler pressure: 205lb psi
Tractive effort: 44,460lb
Water capacity: 5831-13,475 UK gallons (depending on tender)
Coal capacity: 11¼-20 UK tons (depending on tender)
Length over buffers: 83ft 6in
Weight in working order: 533,000lb (pre-1935)

Where to see them
● **3750** Pennsylvania State Railroad Museum, Strasburg, Pennsylvania
● **1361** Stored serviceable at Altoona, Pennsylvania. In 1957, this locomotive was displayed alongside Horse Shoe Curve and removed in 1985 for restoration by the Railroaders' Memorial Museum. It made public trips in 1987-88, but organizational and mechanical problems have left the engine idle since.

A3 class 4-6-2

LONDON & NORTH EASTERN RAILWAY

The Gresley A3 Pacifics were a development on his earlier A1s and bore the brunt of express passenger working on the East Coast main line. In the 1930s these elegant and powerful race horses paved the way for the glamorous streamlined series that followed.

A3 Class 4-6-2
BR Nos: 60035-112 including rebuilds from original A1 class. 78 locomotives
Designer: Sir Nigel Gresley
Built: 1922-35, A1 conversions from 1927-48
Service: Express passenger and fitted freight trains
Livery: LNER apple green; wartime black; BR lined blue and later dark green
Performance: Newcastle – King's Cross, 268$\frac{1}{2}$ miles, at a net average of 72$\frac{1}{2}$mph with 290-ton train. 1939, Grantham – King's Cross 105$\frac{1}{2}$mph average of 63mph with 510-ton train
Withdrawn: 1959-66

In 1922, Gresley introduced his A1 Pacific. It had a boiler pressure of 180lb psi and relatively short-travel valves. The locomotives were capable performers and, if called on, could haul loads of 600 tons – a tonnage virtually unknown in Britain at that time for express passenger trains.

At the British Empire Exhibition in 1924, the London & North Eastern Railway's (LNER) A1

Pacific No 4472 *Flying Scotsman* was shown back to back with the Great Western Railway's (GWR) four-cylinder 4-6-0 No 4073 *Caerphilly Castle*, a slightly enlarged version of Churchward's earlier Star class. Although the maximum boiler capacity of the Castle was less than the Pacific, the GWR claimed that the Castle was the most powerful express locomotive in the country on the basis of its slightly higher nominal tractive effort.

Valve gear

A locomotive exchange between the two types on each other's home ground was suggested and took place in 1925 between King's Cross and Doncaster for a Castle, and between Paddington and Plymouth for an A1. In this, the smaller GWR locomotive generally showed better performance and greater fuel economy, due primarily to its lower rate of steam consumption with long-travel valves and steam lap. This feature allowed a greater volume of steam to be delivered to the

◀ In June 1962, No 60067 *Ladas* rolls into King's Cross with an express from the north. Late on in their lives, the A3s were rejuvenated by installation of Kylchap double blastpipes and chimneys. Because the new arrangement gave rise to a softer exhaust, German-style smoke deflectors were fitted. This type was chosen because it was a proven and inexpensive solution.

▲On 18 February 1961, No 60056 *Centenary* raises steam at Grantham shed. The A3s continued to haul top rank East Coast expresses right up to final withdrawal in 1966. In their last years, the class often replaced 2000hp diesels during their early teething troubles, working for up to 10 days on intensive diesel schedules.

cylinders at short cut-offs. In this, the piston travelled only a small part of its stroke before the supply of boiler-steam was cut off; the steam doing its work by expansion for the remainder of the stroke.

Gresley had previously fitted long-lap, long-travel valves to his K3 class 2-6-0s with excellent results. But there had been problems. A lack of rigidity in the mounting of the bracket providing the main pivot point of the valve gear conjugating levers, meant that the valve spindles could over travel at speed and cause damage to the inside steam chest covers.

While tests and redesign work to provide a more rigid centre pivot mounting were being carried out, the steam lap and valve travel of the K3s were reduced, with the Pacifics fitted similarly. After the 1925 trials, the design modifications were completed quickly to the proposals of Bert Spencer and Eric Windle, two members of Gresley's design team. After the Pacifics were equipped with longer travel and lap valves, the power required could be obtained at appreciably shorter cut-offs and their fuel consumption was reduced by about 20%.

However, during the 1925 trials Gresley's contention that ample boiler capacity was essential to

▼The A3s were first built new in 1928 and closely resembled the earlier A1s in external appearance. The A3s could be distinguished by a shallow curved casing on each side of the smokebox behind the chimney, which covered the ends of the larger superheater header.

rebuilt with higher pressure boilers, although the excellent design and long life of the 180lb psi boilers was such that the last replacement, No 2567 *Sir Visto*, was not made until 1948.

From 1928-30, following the rebuilding of five A1s, 18 new A3s were built and the final nine A3s were built from 1934-35. This batch of locomotives included some features Gresley used on his express passenger P2 class 2-8-2s. The main steam pipes from the dome to the superheater header were almost doubled in area, and the area of the branch pipes from superheater header to cylinders was increased by 23%. This followed Chapelon's practice, by improving the freedom of steam flow and reducing pressure drop losses; these features were incorporated in the boilers used in the later A4 Pacifics built in 1935. Also, like the P2s, perforated steam collectors, housed under a banjo-shaped cover, were also provided.

In service the A3s, and their 180lb psi forerun-

Exhaustive trials

One of the results of fitting long-travel valves to the A1s and A3s was a softer exhaust which tended to obscure the driver's view. The LNER's attempts to cure this problem included this modification to No 2751 *Humorist* in March 1933. This locomotive was the first A3 Pacific to be given a double Kylchap exhaust system in 1937. Although all of the class eventually received them – often only a few years before they were scrapped – had Gresley's intentions been carried out, this device would have been applied from 1941.

Where to see them
There is only one surviving A3, No 4472 *Flying Scotsman*. It is stationed at Southall and has often hauled excursions over BR.

Overheating problem
A myth has often been circulated that the A3s were constantly plagued by cases of overheated connecting rod middle big end bearings. In almost every case – and these were rare as in LNER days these locomotives averaged 75,000 miles between failures – this was caused by excessive tightening of the securing nuts and bolts for the two halves of the marine type big end which deformed the spacing piece (glut) between them. In the 1950s, harder metal was used for the spacing piece, which completely overcame the deformation problem and any associated overheating troubles.

locomotive performance capacity was borne out during the 1926 coal strike. His Pacifics were capable of near normal performance with low grade imported coal while the GWR 4-6-0s, with their small fireboxes and grates designed for high grade Welsh coal, were severely handicapped in performance.

Increased pressure

In 1927, Gresley was looking into ways of achieving greater improvements in the performance and efficiency of his locomotives. These were achieved in the A3s by using 43 element superheaters in place of 32 in the A1s, to take advantage of the greater volume of steam at higher temperatures and increasing the working pressure in the boiler from 180 to 220lb psi. Previously, Gresley had been reluctant to do this because his experience elsewhere with boilers working at higher pressures, where there was no effective chemical water treatment, had led to greater scale formation.

In the A3-type boiler, with 220lb psi pressure, the cylinder diameter was reduced to 19in compared with 20in for the previous 180lb psi engines, but nominal tractive effort was increased by 10%. The greater width of the header for the enlarged superheater in the A3s projected slightly through the smokebox sides just behind the chimney. This made the fitting of cover plates necessary – giving the class an obvious visual difference from the earlier A1s. The 180lb psi A1s were progressively

Conjugating mechanism
In the Gresley Pacifics, the actuating levers (equal motion and 2 to 1 levers) of the Gresley conjugating mechanism driving the inside valve spindle were located in front of the valves. Expansion took place in the outside valve spindles from which the drive was taken and an allowance was made for this when setting the middle valve. However, when starting cold before expansion had taken place, the exhaust beats were slightly irregular until the valve spindles expanded.

During the war, when it was impossible to obtain roller bearings for the two main pivots of the conjugating mechanism, these had to be replaced by plain bushes which wore rapidly. This resulted in irregular valve events and highly syncopated exhaust beats when severe wear occurred.

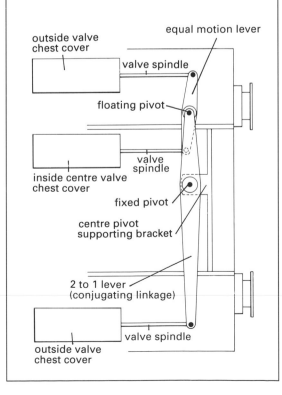

Design specifications A3 CLASS

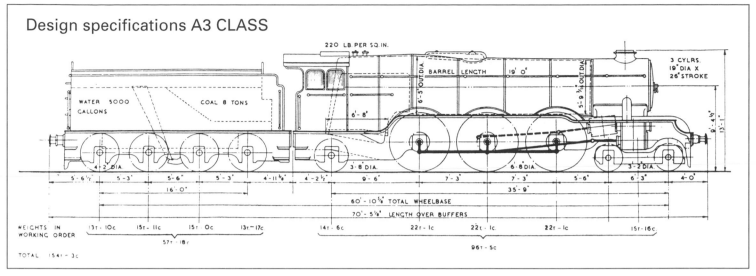

ners, did remarkable work against a background of continual acceleration of heavy express trains in the 1930s. The Anglo-Scottish Flying Scotsman express schedule of 1938-39 demanded an average speed of 60mph from Grantham to King's Cross with a load of up to 550 tons. In April 1935, No 2750 *Papyrus*, one of the 1929-built A3s, attained 108mph on a high speed run which proved the feasibility of a four hour London – Newcastle schedule for the Silver Jubilee express with an average speed of 67mph. Even more notable was the achievement in 1939 of No 2507 *Singapore*, with enlarged steam pipes, in hauling the 290-ton Coronation streamliner express from Newcastle to London, 268 miles in 222 minutes *net* – 15 minutes under the A4 worked schedule, at an average speed of 72½mph. During World War

II, the Gresley A1, A3 and A4 Pacifics worked expresses regularly of 20 coaches (700 tons gross) at average speeds of 50mph or more within a nominal 60mph speed limit.

Post-war service

In their final years, equipped with Kylchap double exhaust, the A3s did much notable work. In the late 1950s, during a period of 11 days, one of the class covered 4000 miles after making six return trips from London to Newcastle and two to Leeds – mainly on the fastest trains.

The development of the Gresley Pacifics was an important chapter in British locomotive history. It confirmed the necessity for large boilers and fireboxes to provide an ample margin of steam production capacity.

▲The A3s went through a number of changes and modifications throughout their lives. All of the class were eventually provided with perforated steam collectors, housed under a banjo-shaped cover. This meant that steam could be taken from the highest point above the water line in the boiler, passing to the dome through a number of slots in the boiler barrel to minimize the intake of moisture in the steam.

3 cylinders: 19in x 26in
Coupled wheels: 6ft 8in diameter
Maximum boiler diameter: 6ft 5in
Grate area: 41¼sq ft
Boiler pressure: 220lb psi
Tractive effort: 32,909lb
Coal capacity: 8 or 9 tons
Water capacity: 5000 gallons
Length over buffers: 70ft 5⅛in
Weight in working order:
Engine: 96¼ tons
Tender: 57.9 tons or 62.4 tons for corridor variety

◄By 1948, there were 78 A3 Pacifics in service on BR. Most of them, however, were converted from A1s. In August 1946, A3 Pacific No 2582 *Sir Hugo* waits at Grantham to take over a northbound express on its journey from London. In 1925, this locomotive was the last Gresley Pacific to be built as an A1 and was given its A3 boiler in 1941.

Class 9000 4-12-2

UNION PACIFIC RAILROAD

UP Class 9000 4-12-2
UP Nos: 9000-9087.
88 locomotives
Designer: A H Fetters/
American Locomotive
Company
Built: American Locomotive
Company, Dunkirk, NY and
Schenectady, NY
Service: Fast freight haulage
between Ogden, Utah and
Cheyenne, Wyoming (483
miles)
Livery: Plain black with
aluminium lettering
Performance: 4750 sustained
cylinder hp at 42mph
Withdrawn: 1953-56 (one
engine destroyed by boiler
explosion in 1948)

**The Class 9000s were built to haul mile-long
freight trains at the same speeds as passenger trains.
Not only were they the largest three-cylinder locomotives
ever constructed, but they were also the longest
non-articulated locomotives ever built.**

The Union Pacific Railroad (UP) at its peak had a total of nearly 10,000 route miles, which extended east from Kansas City and Omaha in the Midwest, and reached the west coast at Los Angeles and Seattle. Lying across the path of the railroad was the Rocky Mountain range. Most of this stood above the 6000ft contour and included the 8015ft summit at Sherman Hill, 31 miles west of Cheyenne, with an average gradient of 1 in 66. This was to become the stamping ground of the longest non-articulated locomotives ever built, the UP 9000 Class 4-12-2s.

Three-cylinder preference

In the 1920s, three-cylinder propulsion enjoyed a brief popularity in America. It was one of the few European design features to be incorporated into American locomotive practice. This was in contrast to the increasingly powerful influence of American design worldwide after 1900.

Three-cylinder propulsion was seen at the time as a solution to the problem of building increasingly powerful locomotives on rigid frames, when the prevalent boiler pressures were 220-230lb psi. To achieve higher power in two cylinders, locomotives would require large cylinders with heavy reciprocating masses (parts that go backwards and forwards such as pistons, piston rods and connecting rods). It is much easier to balance these masses without unacceptable dynamic arrangement (hammer blow) forces on the track in a three-cylinder locomotive. Three cylinders also allowed operation at earlier cut-offs, which led to lower fuel consumption.

◀ **UP Class 9000 No 9032 waits at Topeka, Kansas in 1952. The clutter on the front of the engine is largely made up of the air compressors which operated the train's brakes. The first of the class appeared in 1926, and construction continued for four years, during which time 88 locomotives were built. The last one was withdrawn in 1956.**

UNION PACIFIC   9000

▶In August 1952, a westbound evening freight train pulls out of Omaha, Nebraska. The Class 9000s were brought in to replace 25mph freight trains with mile-long trains (125 cars) hauled at passenger train speeds. The 4-12-2s could move their trains at 50mph and were 80% more efficient.

The American Locomotive Company (Alco) had obtained a North American licence for the Gresley 2 to 1 conjugated valve gear. This gave them an advantage over Baldwin, the principal competitor, in the three-cylinder locomotive market, as the Baldwin mechanism for operating the inside valve was far more complicated.

In August 1922, Alco converted two existing New York Central two-cylinder 4-8-2s to three-cylinder propulsion, with Gresley gear to operate the inside piston valve. This eliminated the inside eccentric and valve motion which were hated by American locomotive engineers. Encouraged by the highly satisfactory results obtained, Alco then made something of a speciality of three-cylinder designs, which although including a few 4-6-2s, more typically were eight-coupled – 0-8-0s, 2-8-2s, and 4-8-2s.

Heavier loads

In the early 1920s, it was recognized that heavy freight trains needed to run at faster speeds with greater fuel economy. At this time the American economy, and consequently the US railroads, were booming. Some, particularly in the Midwest, carried highly seasonal agricultural traffic with intense predictable surges. The UP president expressed his desire to work mile-long freight trains at passenger timings. The problem was to develop enough power at sufficient speeds. The solution was seen in three-cylinder locomotives.

In 1924, the UP Railroad took delivery of the final examples of traditional heavy-freight power in the form of compound 2-8-8-0 articulated Mallets, and two-cylinder 2-10-2s. The Mallets were used in the Wahsatch mountains but were quite unsuited to operating at any speed. This was because the leading engine unit had large low-pressure cylinders and inadequate lateral and vertical suspension controls. The 2-10-2s were

employed on less demanding grades at greater speeds. What was needed was a rigid-frame locomotive with the characteristics of both.

As a step in this direction, a three-cylinder 4-10-2 was designed in collaboration with Alco, and in April 1925 they delivered a prototype numbered 8000. Nine further engines were later delivered, becoming known as the Overland type. Tests with No 8000 demonstrated its ability to handle 20% more tonnage for 16% less fuel consumption – but the new design was still not powerful enough. Within an axleload limit of 59,000lb, a 12-coupled design – either a 2-12-2, a 2-12-4, or a 4-12-2 – was being looked at for early delivery during 1926. The design input by the railroad itself was considerable and the order for a prototype 4-12-2, No 9000, with 14 more to follow, was placed in October 1925.

Production series

No 9000 was completed in March 1926 and attracted a great deal of interest. The exceptional coupled wheelbase of 30ft 8in was eased round curves by the provision of 2in spring-controlled

> ### LOCO LIST
>
> A total of 88 UP Class 9000 4-12-2s were built, including the prototype, and were numbered 9000-87. They were built in five distinct batches, each with detailed differences. One batch had boosters on the tender, and the final 25 were provided with cast steel engine beds with integral cylinders.

▼Whereas 10-coupled engines accounted for a significant proportion of all the steam locomotives ever built throughout the world, 12-coupled examples were extremely rare – numbering fewer than 200 in total. Half of these were the remarkable UP Class 9000 4-12-2s, which were also the largest three-cylinder locomotives ever constructed.

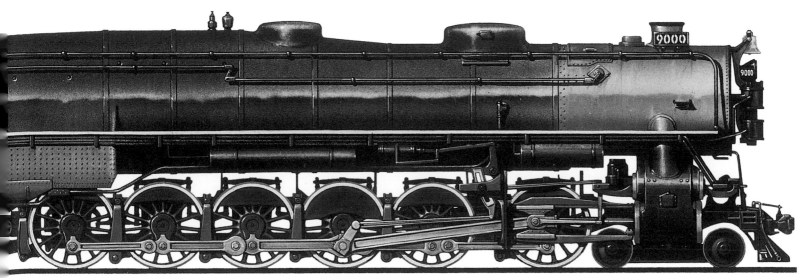

▲The long rigid wheelbase of the class gave great stability at speed, which often reached 60mph and was known to touch 65mph. But this did not suit the Gresley 2 to 1 valve gear, which was removed and replaced by a third set of Walschaerts gear on seven engines. Conversion to two cylinders only, as carried out on the earlier 4-10-2s during 1942-43, was considered but not acted upon.

lateral play on the leading and trailing axles. Coupled wheels of 5ft 3in diameter, the same as the 4-10-2s, would have sufficed for the 50mph maximum operating speed envisaged and recommended by Alco. But this had to be increased to 5ft 7in in order to provide the necessary track clearance for the inside big end (the end of the inside connecting rod attached to the crank pin), whose throw still had to be reduced to 15½in compared to the 16in of the outside crank pins with the inside piston stroke reduced by 1in.

The large wheel diameter reduced the space available above the rear pair of coupled wheels to accommodate the long and wide firegrate which was necessarily horizontal. The grate area was particularly large at 108sq ft, as it was required to burn Wyoming sub-bituminous coal at an adequate rate with a thin fire. This large grate extended behind the trailing coupled axle, the front 3ft 4in of the firebox being separated by a Gaines wall (partition) 12in high, in addition to the 88in com-

bustion chamber which extended into the boiler barrel. Unusually the trailing truck carried as high a loading as the coupled axles.

Paired with standard UP 12-wheeled tenders, the Class 9000s were built in five distinct batches, each with detailed difference: the earlier ones by the former Brooks plant at Dunkirk, and the later ones at Alco's main plant at Schenectady in New York State.

The final 25, of a total of 88 locomotives, were provided with cast steel engine beds with integral cylinders, which in themselves amounted to truly remarkable pieces of foundry work. At the time it was stated that these last engines were not needed, but the railroad wanted to take advantage of the operating economy demonstrated by the earlier engines – halving the coal consumption per ton-mile of the 2-8-8-0 Mallets. The long rigid wheelbase, assisted by the excellent Alco bogie with lateral control, conferred great stability at speed.

Out and about

When new, the Class 9000s were primarily employed between Cheyenne in Wyoming and Ogden in Utah, nearly 500 miles apart, where the UP main line crosses the Rocky Mountain range which includes the legendary Sherman Hill.

In early 1928, eight Class 9000s were initially delivered to the Oregon-Washington Railway & Navigation, a UP subsidiary, which numbered

Where to see them
No 9000 is preserved in static condition at Pomona, 30 miles east of Los Angeles, California by the Pacific Coast Chapter of the Railway and Locomotive Historical Society.

Wide applications
It is interesting to note that, worldwide, the Gresley valve gear found application on well over 1000 four-, six-, eight-, ten-, and twelve-coupled locomotives, in Europe, North and South America, Africa, Australia, New Zealand, China and Japan. The UP 4-12-2s inspired the Russians to build the world's only fourteen-coupled locomotive, the legendary 4-14-4, which in practice progressed no further than initial trials in 1934.

Design specifications CLASS 9000 4-12-2

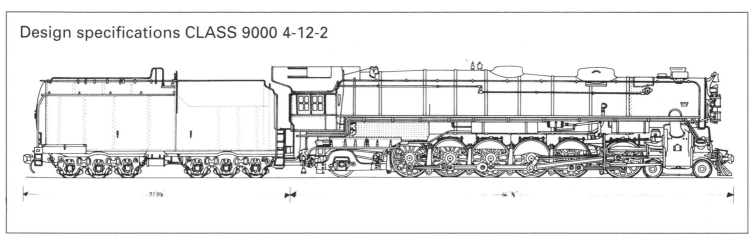

▲Unusually for an American locomotive, the Class 9000 incorporated British design practice in the shape of Gresley's 2 to 1 valve gear. This feature did not prove a success and was removed from seven of the locomotives and replaced by conventional Walschaerts gear. To balance the locomotive, the air compressors were moved from the smokebox to the left-hand running plate.

TECHNICAL FILE

3 Cylinders: 27in diameter 32in stroke (outside); 27in diameter 31in stroke (inside)
Coupled wheels: 5ft 7in diameter
Boiler diameter: 8ft 9in at dome ring with taper from 7ft 6in in second ring.
Grate area: 108.25sq ft
Boiler pressure: 220lb psi
Tractive effort: 96,650lb
Coal capacity: 18³/₄ tons (No 9000); 19¹/₂ tons (final series)
Water capacity: 12,525 gallons (No 9000); 15,000 gallons (final series)
Length over couplers: 102ft 6⁵/₈in
Weight in working order:
Engine: 221 tons (No 9000); 230 tons (final series)
Tender: 129 tons (No 9000); 139 tons (final series)

them 9700-7, but tight track curvature meant that they were sold back to the UP before the end of the year becoming 9055-62. These engines were provided with boosters on the leading tender trucks, of the Franklin type on the first six engines, and the Bethlehem variety on the seventh. These were removed when the locomotives rejoined the UP.

Fifteen of the final 1930 batch were delivered direct to another UP subsidiary, the Oregon Short Line (OSL) and were numbered 9500-14. They would otherwise have been UP Nos 9063-77, numbers which remained unused.

Compared with the earlier 2-8-8-0 compound Mallets, the 4-12-2s handled 80% more ton-miles per hour with halved fuel consumption per ton-mile. On easier sections they ran fast freights at an average speed of 35-40mph. Originally the speed was not intended to exceed 50mph. But these powerful, free-running machines commonly reached 60mph and were known to touch 65mph. At high speeds there were high inertia forces in

the heavy conjugating levers which increased wear. The Gresley gear was later replaced by a second set of Walschaerts valve gear on seven engines to operate the centre valve through a cross shaft. Conversion to two cylinders only, as carried out on the earlier 4-10-2s during 1942-43, was considered, but with the introduction of the new Challenger 4-6-6-4s on the higher speed heavy freight duties, this was not acted upon.

The UP took delivery of the first Alco Challenger 4-6-6-4s in 1936, and by 1944 over 100 had been built. Having the advantage of higher speeds and a greater permitted axleload of 65,000lb, these engines displaced the Class 9000s from many of their original duties. They were then transferred to heavy freight workings at lower speeds on the Idaho division and also on the Omaha – Castle Bluffs and Cheyenne – Kansas City lines.

The 4-12-2s continued to give excellent service on the slower fast freights. Diesels took over these trains in 1954.

▶The first batch of Class 9000s was fitted with standard UP 12-wheel tenders. These had a coal capacity of 18³/₄ tons and a water capacity of 12,525 gallons. The last batch received tenders of 19¹/₂ ton coal capacity and a water capacity of 15,000 gallons, which gave them a greater range. In 1952, UP 9000 No 9032 stands at Topeka, Kansas.

UP 4-12-2 No 9500 at Grand Island, Nebraska, in August 1955.
This was the first of the final 1930 batch of 15 locomotives which was
delivered to a UP subsidiary, the Oregon Short Line (OSL).

The length of the boiler is emphasized by this shot of UP 4-12-2 No 9500
at Grand Island, Nebraska in August 1955. Numbered 9500–14,
the OSL locomotives were built by Schenectady, New York.

A4 class 4-6-2

LONDON & NORTH EASTERN RAILWAY

**When *Mallard* broke the world rail speed record
on 3 July 1938 it set a mark which no steam locomotive
is likely to beat. But the world's most famous engine was only
one among a great class which hauled the premier trains
on the East Coast main line for 25 years.**

KEY FACTS

LNER Class A4 4-6-2
BR Nos: 60001-60034
Designer: Sir Nigel Gresley
Built: 1935-1938, Doncaster works
Service: Passenger services on the East Coast main line
Livery: 2509-2512 – pale silver grey, side valances in mid grey, nose in charcoal grey, lettering in silver white with dark blue shading, wheels in pale silver grey, external frames and cab roof in mid grey, tender buffer beam in signal red. Some engines painted apple green.

New livery introduced July 1937: Garter blue, nose in black edged with a fine red and a fine white line, cab roof and outside frames black, wheels rich Indian red with polished rims
Performance: 3 July 1938 – 126mph descending Stoke Bank: world speed record for steam traction
Withdrawn: No 4469 Sir Ralph Wedgwood June 1942 – after damage from enemy action. 60001-60034 displaced by Class 55 diesels 1962-1966

The streamlined A4s were the direct descendants of a line of locomotives that started in April 1922 when Nigel Gresley – knighted in 1936 – produced his first 4-6-2 express for the Great Northern Railway, No 1470 *Great Northern*.

Gresley was a devoted advocate of the three-cylinder locomotive with two outside Walschaerts valve gears and a simple conjugated valve gear for the inside cylinder. After trying this arrangement on the Class K3 2-6-0s in 1920, Gresley applied it to his new Class A1 Pacifics (engines with a 4-6-2 wheel arrangement) and was sufficiently satisfied to use it on almost every other locomotive he designed.

All cylinders drove on the centre axle, theoretically improving the balancing of the locomotive. The conjugated valve gear allowed a cylinder layout which gave minimal intrusion into the smokebox bottom. But it created further complications and was abandoned by the LNER on Gresley's death. The large boiler with wide round-topped firebox and 32-element superheater could produce ample steam. But steam temperatures were only

▼The A4s are known throughout the world as the fastest of all steam engines and No 4468 *Mallard* is the most famous because it holds the world speed record for steam. It can normally be seen at the National Railway Museum, York but still occasionally runs on main line excursions.

moderate and Gresley later adopted a larger super-heater.

Learning a lesson

But Gresley did have something to learn from other engineers. Comparative trials in 1925 between the GWR's Castle class No 4079 *Pendennis Castle* and Class A1 No 4474 *Victor Wild* showed the Castle's better fuel economy, attributed largely to its long travel valve gear.

It took Gresley two years of heart searching to apply the lesson, but from 1927 he modified the original valve gear of Class A1 No 2555 *Centenary* to provide freer steam flow. In July 1928 another A1, No 4480 *Enterprise*, was rebuilt to raise the boiler pressure from 180 to 220lb per sq in. Another experiment with No 2544 *Lemberg* raised the number of elements in the superheater from 32 to 43 to raise steam temperatures. All these modifications were incorporated into the first A3, No 2743 *Felstead*, which appeared in August 1928.

By mid 1930 there were 47 class A1 and 23 class A3 locomotives giving sterling service on the East Coast expresses from King's Cross to Leeds, Newcastle and Edinburgh. A further nine A3s were built in 1934-1935.

An interesting feature of some of these Pacifics was the provision for non-stop running between London and Edinburgh from 1928. As the 8¼ hour journey was too long for a single engine crew, special tenders were built with a corridor connection to the train – it was just 18in wide and 5ft high – so that enginemen could change over at speed between York and Northallerton.

The race for prestige

From 1932 higher speeds and accelerated services were needed to meet mounting competition from the London Midland & Scottish Railway. In 1934 an A1 established the first verified 100mph in

▶ Prestigious express services such as The Elizabethan, which ran non-stop between Edinburgh and London, were pulled by A4s until the introduction of Deltics in the early 1960s. The diesels were little faster than the Gresley Pacifics but they could work more intensive schedules.

▼No 4468 *Mallard* attained immortality on 3 July 1938 when it touched 126mph and stole the world record for steam traction from the German State Railway. *Mallard's* double Kylchap blastpipe gave improved steaming and an extra turn of speed that made it faster than single chimney A4s.

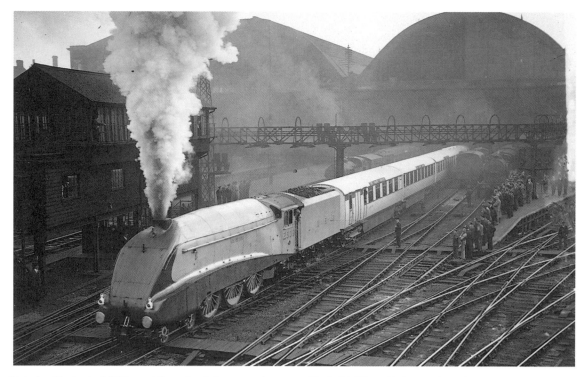

Britain. Early in 1935 an A3 pushed the record up to 108mph.

These outstanding performances prepared the ground for the A4s and the LNER's three high speed trains – the Silver Jubilee, Coronation and West Riding Limited – introduced in 1935 and 1937.

The A4 engines were a refined version of the A3s, with a slightly shorter boiler, higher pressure and smaller but improved cylinders. The streamlined casing had a wedge-shaped front end in which a large door opened upwards for access to clean out the smokebox. It soon became known as the cod's mouth.

The A4s quickly showed that 108mph was not the end of the LNER's record breaking performances. A trial run just before the Silver Jubilee service to Newcastle started in 1935 saw No 2509

▲No 2509 *Silver Link,* seen here leaving King's Cross, was built to haul the Silver Jubilee luxury express between London and Newcastle. The train touched 112$\frac{1}{2}$mph on its first trial run on 27 September 1935 and sometimes topped 100mph while it was in regular service.

Silver Link raise the record to 112$\frac{1}{2}$mph. This was beaten by an LMS Duchess in 1937, only to be recaptured by the 126mph run of No 4468 *Mallard* in 1938.

Mallard was one of four A4s built with double chimneys and Kylchap blastpipes, which improved the draughting. Not until 1957-1958, when coal quality was declining, were the remaining 30 engines similarly fitted.

The first four A4s – 2509-2512 – were painted silver grey to match the Silver Jubilee express,

Where to see them
Six A4s have been preserved.
● **Sir Nigel Gresley** is based at Bury, Lancs.
● **Dwight D. Eisenhower** is at the National Railroad Museum, Green Bay, USA.
● **Union of South Africa** is based at the Severn Valley Railway, Shropshire/Worcestershire.
● **Dominion of Canada** is at Montreal Railway Historical Museum, Canada.
● **Silver Link** (ex *Bittern*) is at the Great Central Railway, Loughborough.
● **Mallard** is at National Railway Museum, York.

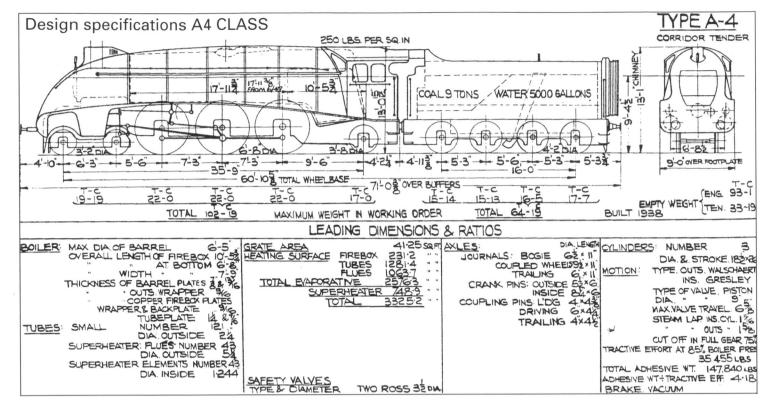

Design specifications A4 CLASS

TYPE A-4
CORRIDOR TENDER

250 LBS. PER SQ. IN

COAL 9 TONS   WATER 5000 GALLONS

BUILT 1938

LEADING DIMENSIONS & RATIOS

BOILER: MAX DIA. OF BARREL 6·5
OVERALL LENGTH OF FIREBOX 10·5½
" AT BOTTOM 6·8
" WIDTH 7·9
THICKNESS OF BARREL PLATES 1⅜·⅞
· OUTS. WRAPPER 9/16
COPPER FIREBOX PLATES
WRAPPER & BACKPLATE 9/16
TUBEPLATE 1·⅞
TUBES: SMALL NUMBER 121
DIA. OUTSIDE 2¼
SUPERHEATER: FLUES· NUMBER 43
DIA. OUTSIDE 5¼
SUPERHEATER ELEMENTS NUMBER 43
DIA. INSIDE 1·244

GRATE AREA 41·25 SQ FT
HEATING SURFACE FIREBOX 231·2
TUBES 1281·4
FLUES 1063·7
TOTAL EVAPORATIVE 2576·3
SUPERHEATER 748·9
TOTAL 3325·2

SAFETY VALVES
TYPE & DIAMETER TWO ROSS 3½ DIA

AXLES: DIA. LENGTH
JOURNALS: BOGIE 6½ × 11
COUPLED WHEELS 9½ × 11
TRAILING 6 × 11
CRANK PINS: OUTSIDE 5¼ × 6
INSIDE 8¼ × 6
COUPLING PINS: L'DG 4 × 4⅜
DRIVING 6 × 4¼
TRAILING 4 × 4½

CYLINDERS: NUMBER 3
DIA. & STROKE 18½ × 26
MOTION: TYPE. OUTS. WALSCHAERT
INS. GRESLEY
TYPE OF VALVE. PISTON
DIA. 9
MAX. VALVE TRAVEL 6⅝
STEAM LAP INS. CYL. 1⅝
" OUTS 1⅝
CUT OFF IN FULL GEAR 75%
TRACTIVE EFFORT AT 85% BOILER PRES
35,455 LBS
TOTAL ADHESIVE WT. 147,840 LBS
ADHESIVE WT ÷ TRACTIVE EFF. 4·18
BRAKE. VACUUM

with darker grey fronts and side valances. They were called *Silver Link*, *Quicksilver*, *Silver King* and *Silver Fox*.

The following engines were painted in LNER green until June 1937 when seven were turned out in Garter blue for the Coronation workings. All were sporting the Garter blue livery by September 1939.

The wartime workhorse

During the war the A4s handled prodigious loads. Trains of well over 20 coaches were taken out of King's Cross. Some were so long that they had to be loaded at two platforms and joined up for departure, by which time the engine would be out of sight in Gasworks Tunnel.

One A4, No 4469 *Sir Ralph Wedgwood*, was so

▲The A4s marked the peak of Nigel Gresley's career as chief mechanical engineer at the LNER. His basic design evolved from the A3 Pacific, which first appeared in August 1928. The streamlining was inspired by the Bugatti railcar, which first appeared on French railways in 1934.

badly damaged in an air raid on York in 1942 that it was scrapped.

The modernization of BR, in particular the introduction of the 3300hp Class 55 (Deltic) in 1961, began to push the A4s off their traditional work.

Scrapping started at the end of 1962, by which time most had run close on 1½ million miles each. The survivors were concentrated in Scotland to work the three hour Glasgow-Aberdeen expresses. The last A4 was withdrawn in 1966.

TECHNICAL FILE

3 cylinders: 18 ½in diameter, 26in stroke
Coupled wheels: 6ft 8in diameter
Boiler diameter: 6ft 5in
Grate area: 41.25sq ft
Boiler pressure: 250lb per sq in
Tractive effort: 35,455lb
Originally 32,500lb
Coal capacity: 9 tons
Water capacity: 5000 gallons
Length over buffers: 71ft ⅜in
Weight in working order:
Engine 102.95 tons
Tender 60.4/65.45 tons

Mallard's record run

No 4468 *Mallard* had been in service only three months when on 3 July 1938 Nigel Gresley approved an attempt on the British rail speed record. The engine was selected because it had already demonstrated that its Kylchap blastpipes gave it extra speed.

Mallard's regular driver Joe Duddington took the train south through Grantham and accelerated up to Stoke summit. The next 20 miles were downhill, and Duddington gave the engine its head. Four minutes later the British record belonged to *Mallard* but there was still an opportunity to go faster. Eventually the train touched 126mph but then problems developed in the engine and it was replaced at Peterborough. *Mallard* crawled back to Doncaster but no steam engine would ever go faster.

Hudson class 4-6-4

NEW YORK CENTRAL RAILROAD

**The J class Hudsons have become revered
as a classic by railway aficionados. Continually
improved throughout their careers, this magnificent fleet
of 275 locomotives hauled some of the fastest and
heaviest express trains in America.**

As the United States prospered after World War I, passenger traffic on the railroads boomed. Of the two railroads to serve New York City, the New York Central (NYC) system was second in size to its competitor, the giant Pennsylvania Railroad. But, thanks to express passenger trains such as the Twentieth Century Limited travelling the highly publicized Water Level Route to Chicago, the NYC was just as famous.

However, even on the generally gentle gradients of NYC, the line's main passenger power, the K3 Pacific, was capable of pulling only 12 heavyweight cars. At this time, sleeping car expresses,

which included lounge and dining cars, were proving so popular that trains made up of portions detached at different destinations were commonplace. As these trains grew heavier there was an obvious need for more powerful locomotives.

Previously, NYC had experience of a maximum capacity prototype 2-8-2 freight locomotive, No 8000 built by Lima, that was able to give a higher tractive effort at speed. This was achieved through a combination of a large firebox volume and grate area, and increased boiler pressure. A limited maximum cut-off gave more expansive use of steam and greater efficiency.

Pleased with the success of the 2-8-2, in 1924

KEY FACTS

NYC Hudson class 4-6-4
Designer: P W Kiefer/ American Locomotive Company
Built: American Locomotive Company, Schenectady, NY 1927-31, 1937-38; Lima Locomotive Works, Ohio 1931
Service: Express and general passenger service on NYC and B&A, Michigan Central and Big Four subsidiary railroads
Livery: Black with white lettering (non-streamlined locomotives)
Performance: Peak of 4900hp with enlarged blastpipe – as applied to all J3a types. Average start to stop speed of 70mph from Elkhart – Toledo, 133 miles, with 1000 US ton Twentieth Century Limited.
Withdrawn: 1953-56

J1b Hudson No 5217 thunders under a signal gantry with a mail train from Marion, Ohio. This locomotive was one of the original production batch which numbered 59. As a result of track stress studies, especially those by Kiefer of the British Bridge Stress Committee's report on the effect of locomotive hammer blow, from 1929-31 all the Hudsons, following No 5200, were dynamically cross balanced. This reduced total hammer blow which allowed the previous 70mph speed limit to be lifted and minimized stresses to the track.

▲In 1952, J3a Hudson No 5449 grinds over the points at Albany depot, New York. The Hudsons continued to be modified throughout their careers. Many received Worthington feedwater heaters (the square-sided protuberance on top of the smokebox in front of the stack) and Boxpok driving wheels to save weight. This basic type of wheel was used by Bulleid for the Southern Railway in Britain.

One stop tenders
To allow single locomotives to make the Harmon – Chicago run using water troughs and only one coaling stop, many J3s had PT long distance seven axle tenders from 1943-46. These held 40 tons of coal and 15,400 gallons of water.

Lima then carried these features much further in the Super Power 2-8-4 prototype Class A1. By extending the trailing truck to carry another axle, it was able to support more weight and this enabled the firebox and grate area to be enlarged considerably. The grate area of 100sq ft (25% more than No 8000) represented the first time this size of grate had ever been used in a non-articulated locomotive.

The A1 was tested on the NYC's Boston & Albany (B&A) subsidiary railroad against a standard 2-8-2 – both hauling 3000 US ton freight trains. The 2-8-4 started one hour later and overhauled the 2-8-2 on parallel track after only three hours' running. This impressive feat resulted in an order with Lima for a fleet of 2-8-4s for freight service on the B&A. They were designated Berkshires after the range of hills through which they worked.

More power
For passenger service, the NYC designers, headed by Paul W Kiefer, Chief Engineer of Motive Power and Rolling Stock, worked with Alco at Schenectady. They set about designing a locomotive of a higher tractive effort with a higher capacity boiler giving increased horsepower at speed, increased thermal efficiency and greater use than the K5b Pacifics, successors to the K3.

Their work produced a new design with 6ft 7in diameter driving wheels, two 25 x 28in cylinders with enlarged pipes and ports, and a working pressure increased from 200-225lb psi. The locomotive delivered a maximum tractive effort of 42,360lb.

Steam distribution was controlled by Walschaerts valve gear. A four-wheel Delta cast steel trailing truck, housing a booster engine geared to the rear axle, delivered an additional tractive effort of 10,900lb when in use, such as on the climb up the 1 in 65 gradient out of the river valley at Albany.

The enlarged firebox with a 20% larger grate area, based on results with the B&A's Berkshire 2-8-4s, needed a four-wheel trailing truck to support it. This created the world's first production run 4-6-4. In February 1927, Alco delivered the prototype locomotive, No 5200, for testing. The wheel arrangement received the designation Hudson from NYC president Patrick E Crowley in honour of the Hudson River.

Sub-classes
Called class J1a, No 5200 immediately demonstrated its capabilities in an elaborate testing programme. A 1696 US ton train of 26 cars was hauled at 75mph. With the boiler pressure raised temporarily to 250lb psi, a peak cylinder hp of 4295 was recorded at 67mph – the normal sustained maximum was 3900hp. The 4-6-4 delivered 13% greater maximum tractive effort (without its booster) and produced 27% greater cylinder hp at higher speeds than the K5bs.

From 1927-28, 59 more Hudsons were delivered and sub-classed as J1b. During the next production run of 1928-29, 30 more locomotives were produced. These engines, classed J1c, incorporated a number of modifications: one-piece cast steel frame beds with integral cylinders; Baker valve gear was also introduced (all the earlier Hudsons

NEW YORK CENTRAL

5417

LOCO LIST

Between 1927-38, 275 Hudsons were built and were the largest fleet of 4-6-4s owned by any railroad in the world. They consisted of several classes, all of which contained successive improvements.
J1a: No 5200
J1b: Nos 5201-49, 5345-54
J1c: Nos 5250-74, 5355-59
J1d: Nos 5275-314, 5375-94, 5360-74 (Nos 5311 and 5313 operated on the Toronto, Hamilton & Buffalo Railroad as Nos 501 and 502)
J1e: Nos 5315-44, 5395-04
J2a: Boston & Albany Railroad Nos 600-619
J3a: Nos 5405-54

Lost replica
All the Hudsons went to the scrap heap in the 1950s – in spite of an attempt to buy one for preservation. However, such was the appeal of the Hudsons that in the 1960s plans to have a full-size working replica were initiated. A viable quotation was received from a Japanese locomotive builder. Unfortunately the main backer of the project died before the contract could be signed.

▼The asymmetrical appearance of the Hudsons was a design criterion and the result was a masterpiece of pleasing curves and balanced proportions. In front of the locomotive's chimney can be seen the booster exhaust stack.

Streamlined classic
On 24 February 1940, streamlined Hudson No 5450 rolls by with the Twentieth Century Limited. NYC was in the forefront of the 1930s streamlining fad. In 1934, streamlining was applied to J1e Hudson No 5344 which was named *Commodore Vanderbilt* after NYC's former president. The casing was heavy and was often referred to as an inverted bathtub. In 1938, the industrial designer Henry Dreyfuss re-styled the streamlining for the Twentieth Century Limited, encasing the last 10 J3a types (Nos 5445-54) in a simple grey dress. The locomotive's natural lines were enhanced by adding a vertical fin over the bullet nose to the angular firebox covering. The cylinders and driving rods and wheels were left exposed to ease access for maintenance. After World War II, the front end streamline casing was removed following a crossing collision with a heavy truck. The remaining shrouding was removed piecemeal, over many months.

were fitted with Baker valve gear retrospectively; most also got cast frames).

Seventy-five locomotives of sub-class J1d, delivered from 1929-30, featured minor improvements, including roller bearings on the leading and trailing trucks. The class was completed in 1931, with 40 J1e Hudsons, making a total of 205. For the heavily graded B&A Railroad, Alco, in 1928, and Lima, in 1931, each built 10 Class J2 Hudsons with smaller driving wheels of 75in – later modified to 76in. Square sandboxes were also provided, and mounted on the boiler.

In service, the Hudsons routinely handled 16- to 18-car trains over long distances without change: from Harmon, 33 miles from New York at the end of the electrified section, to Buffalo, (403 miles); Cleveland, Ohio (585 miles); Toledo, Ohio (693 miles). In 1938, on secondary heavy express trains, a typical Harmon – Chicago run over 926 miles with 27 stops, including one engine change, averaged 20 hours and 50 minutes; the crack Twentieth Century Limited, a 1000 US ton

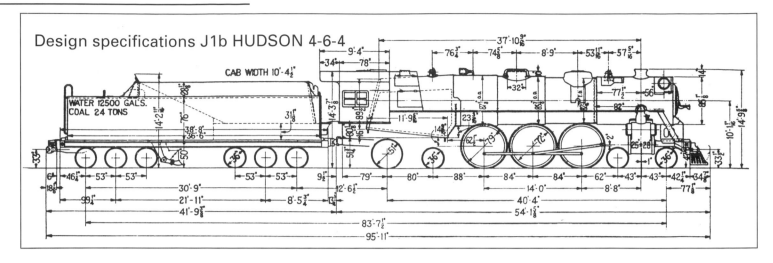

Design specifications J1b HUDSON 4-6-4

TECHNICAL FILE

J3a Hudson Nos 5405-54
2 cylinders: 22½in diameter, 29in stroke
Coupled wheels: 6ft 7in diameter
Grate area: 82sq ft
Boiler diameter: 7ft 7½in maximum outside diameter, tapering from 7ft
Boiler pressure: 275lb psi
Tractive effort: 43,440lb at 85% boiler pressure; increased by 12,100lb when booster in operation
Coal capacity: 27 tons
Water capacity: 14,000 US gallons*
Length over couplers: 95ft 11in
Weight in working order:
Engine: 360,000lb
Tender: 314,300lb (12 wheel type)
* original smaller tender

express with six intermediate stops took 15 hours 15 minutes, averaging 61mph. Pleased by the manner in which Hudsons were doing heavier work more economically than older and smaller Pacifics, NYC ordered a further 50 4-6-4s.

Peak performance

In 1935, Alphonse Lipetz, Chief Consulting Engineer for Alco, went to France to study the work of the engineer André Chapelon. Lipetz was particularly impressed by the Chapelon compound Pacifics which, having only 60% of the boiler capacity of a J1 Hudson, produced 90% of its maximum power. When he returned to America, Lipetz recommended to Paul Kiefer that the J1s would be considerably improved by higher boiler pressure and greatly enlarged steam pipes, ports and passages.

In 1937, Kiefer and his team tested J1e Hudson No 5339 extensively, using its performance characteristics as a bench mark for improving the design. By the end of the year, the result was manifested in steel with 40 examples of a new class –

▲The Hudsons became a symbol of the NYC. The term Hudson came from the Hudson River and referred to the wheel arrangement. Although these locomotives were the world's first production run 4-6-4s, Gaston du Bousquet of the French Nord produced two 4-6-4 prototype compounds 16 years previously.

the J3a, embodying Lipetz's recommendations. These locomotives gave a 21% increase in cylinder horsepower (4725hp) and a 20% improvement in drawbar pull above 12mph compared with the J1s. They also consumed less fuel and water for similar work. These 40 were followed the next year by 10 streamliner versions.

While maintaining the classic Hudson appearance, the J3a type was distinctive. The straight-top carbon steel boiler was supplanted by a nickel-steel conical type with a larger diameter tapered third course and a combustion chamber firebox extension, which enabled evaporation to be increased by 10%. Half of the locomotives had Boxpok drivers (oval openings) and half had Scullin disc drivers (round openings).

Mechanical improvements included roller bearings on all axles and on lightweight main and side rods and a special device, called a valve pilot indicator, in the cab to help engineers adjust cut-off in relation to speed to achieve maximum acceleration. Cylinders 22½in by 29in matched with an increase in boiler pressure to 275lb psi – this was later reduced to 265 to reduce stresses in the driving rods.

The Hudsons were partially displaced by the arrival of the Niagara 4-8-4s from 1945 and diesels soon afterwards. Nevertheless, most of the 150 daily steam runs at a start to stop average speed of 60mph and over in 1946 were still hauled by Hudsons. In 1953, the first was withdrawn. By 1955, only one first class train was pulled by a Hudson. By 1956, the last one was gone.

◄ In February 1952, J1d Hudson No 5280 takes the Empire State express through Dunkirk, New York. The Hudsons had a clean appearance by contemporary US standards. At the top of the smokebox, the cylindrical feedwater heater was largely recessed so only the round ends showed. The air compressor and feedwater pump, mounted on the cow-catcher beam, were covered by graceful shields.

Challenger 4-6-6-4

UNION PACIFIC

Union Pacific's Big Boys achieved fame far beyond United States borders, but it was the 105 Challengers that were the backbone of the railroad. One of these, preserved No 3985, is today the world's largest operating steam locomotive.

During the 1930s, the US was suffering through the Great Depression. At the same time, however, some of the most significant developments took place in steam locomotive design, as the railroads sought to control costs and remain competitive through the introduction of more powerful, faster and more fuel efficient locomotives.

Articulated locomotives

In 1936, two lines of locomotive development merged with the Union Pacific's (UP) introduction of the first 4-6-6-4 Challenger type. One of these themes was the principle of articulation. This used a hinged connection between the rear fixed frame unit, on which the boiler and firebox were mounted, and the leading truck unit, so providing it with free lateral movement. The articulated locomotive made plausible a large boilered and more powerful double engine which could easily negotiate curves.

Most early articulated locomotives were of the Mallet compound type, which were often slow, ponderous machines.

The second line of development was Super Power. This combined a large firebox and grate area with a high capacity boiler to provide continuously the ample steam needed to sustain a locomotive operating at high power outputs. UP's early version of Super Power, which normally was

▼ The UP's Challenger class of 4-6-6-4 locomotives is one of the most powerful steam engine designs ever built. In their heyday, they swept westwards through Wyoming and over the Blue Mountains of Oregon towards the coast. In 1981, the solitary active member of the class, No 3985, stands at Green River, Wyoming. Today, this locomotive is the goodwill ambassador of the UP's historical programme and has visited the far reaches of the UP system, including areas not travelled in steam days.

KEY FACTS

Union Pacific 4-6-6-4 Challenger
Designer: The early locomotives were a joint effort by Union Pacific and the American Locomotive Co under the direction of Arthur Fretters. Later engines were designed under the direction of Otto Jabelmann
Built: Alco 1936, 1937, 1942, 1943, 1944
Service: Main line freight and passenger
Livery: Black with aluminium leaf; some assigned to passenger service were painted black, two tones of grey, with white or yellow striping
Performance: Designed to operate continuously under maximum horsepower output up to 70mph. Had a tonnage rating of 4290 tons across most of Wyoming and over Sherman Hill via the lower gradient (1 in 122) 1953 route. Could haul 7000 tons on a level gradient
Withdrawn: Displaced by diesel traction 1956-59. The last six locomotives operated through the seasonal agricultural rush during the summer of 1959 but were later withdrawn due to a steel strike

◀ A number of Challengers were converted to run from oil fuel and 10 of the 1943 and eight of the 1944 batch were so converted and renumbered 3700-3717. One of these, No 3710, was later fitted with smoke deflectors and in August 1955 hauls its vast bulk over a street crossing at Salt Lake City. Upon its retirement from the UP in 1960, this locomotive was used for snow melting services in North Platte Yard, Nebraska and later preserved on a plinth.

LOCO LIST

The Challengers were built in various batches and all contained various detail differences:
1936: 3900-3914
1937: 3915-3939. Renumbered 3800-3839 in 1944
1942: 3950-3969
1943: 3975-3999. 3975-3985 converted to oil in 1952 and renumbered 3708-3717
1944: 3930-3949. Seven of this batch were converted to oil and renumbered 3700-3707; some of the conversions were briefly returned to coal firing and numbered in the 3900s again

Where to see them
Of the 105 UP Challengers, two have been preserved:
● **3710** public park, North Platte, Nebraska
● **3985** private site, Cheyenne

embodied in the 2-8-4, 4-8-4 and 2-10-4 wheel arrangements, was quite unorthodox by US standards – a three-cylinder Class 9000 4-12-2 with an extremely long frame and rigid wheelbase.

The American Locomotive Company (Alco) and UP, under the direction of General Mechanical Engineer Arthur Fretters and research administrator Otto Jabelmann, conceived the articulated 4-6-6-4 type as a way to maintain the high adhesive weight and tractive effort of the 4-12-2s with a more flexible wheelbase for working high speed freight trains.

In 1936-37, Alco delivered 40 4-6-6-4s, Nos 3900-3939; these would become known as the little Challengers when the later 3900s were built. The locomotives were divided into two groups with a number of differences between them. The 1936 group had cast-steel bar frames and fabricated pilots (cow-catchers) with silico-manganese steel boilers (later found to be prone to cracking around the rivet holes), while the 1937 group had cast-steel frames and weighed slightly more. All were built as coal burners, but in 1937, UP converted six to fuel oil and a further five, Nos 3935-3939, were converted to oil for passenger service as they were received from Alco. In 1944, the entire class was renumbered 3800-3839.

With 69in driving wheels and 97,400lb tractive effort, the little Challengers quickly proved their worth in both freight and passenger service. Initially, they worked the main line across the state of Wyoming, but following conversion to oil they soon became the mainstay of the line to the Pacific Northwest over the Blue Mountains of Oregon as well as the line down to Los Angeles, California, where they were used routinely on passenger trains.

The little Challengers finished their days hauling freight trains across the prairies of Nebraska between North Platte and Omaha. Modifications were made during their careers: some frames were welded while other front-unit frames were replaced with cast-steel frame beds with integral cylinders. All the group received carbon-steel boilers and wound up as oil burners.

Second batch
The experience gained with these 4-6-6-4s was used by Jabelmann, now Vice-President of Research, and Alco to develop the UP's 820 series FEF class 4-8-4 passenger locomotives and, in 1941, the famous Big Boy 4-8-8-4s. The burgeoning traffic demands of World War II resulted in the development of a new Challenger series, numbered 3950-3969 and delivered in 1942.

Although the basic overall dimensions were retained, the 20 new 3900s were markedly different in appearance from their predecessors. The new group featured a smooth smokebox (displaying only the number shield), cast-steel pilot with deck mounted headlight, encased double chimneys, rectangular sandbox enclosures, integral cast-steel frames and cylinders.

The locomotives employed many of the appliances and styling characteristics, plus similar 14-wheel high capacity centipede tenders, of the Big Boys with a leading four-wheeled truck and five

UNION PACIFIC 3977

◄ The Challengers are divided into two main categories. The first group, built in 1936-37, were known as little Challengers. Unlike the later version, this group had single chimneys and separate frames and cylinders. All had been converted to oil burning by the end of 1943 and were renumbered from 3900s to 3800s on 1 April 1944. In August 1955, No 3826 undergoes servicing at Grand Island Nebraska. One of the Class 9000 4-12-2s is seen on the right.

Rough riders

In their early days, the Challengers were beset by poor riding. The solution was found in combining the leading bogie and the Alco lateral-motion spring control device on the first and second coupled axles of each engine group with an articulation hinge. This had only minimal working clearance. The front end of the boiler was supported by a precision flat-plate. This greatly improved the ride stability of the front engine unit and the Challengers rode superbly well at 80mph.

rigidly mounted axles. The weight on the front driving wheels was increased to correct a slipping problem occasionally encountered with the first series. Both the bogies and driving wheels (but not the rods) were equipped with roller bearings.

The boiler pressure was raised from 255lb psi to 280lb psi and the cylinder bore size was reduced correspondingly from 22 to 21in, with 32in stroke, maintaining virtually the same tractive effort (97,530lb). The boiler barrel was shortened by 2ft and the combustion chamber extended. The firebox length remained the same while the grate area was increased from 108.2sq ft to 132.2sq ft by moving forward the Gaines wall and lengthening the ashpan. The Gaines wall prevented coal being spread over the entire area of the ashpan, but nevertheless increased the heating surface of the firebox. These modifications greatly improved combustion when burning

soft Wyoming coal with only 11,800 British Thermal Units (BTU) content per lb from the railroad's own mines.

Multiple bearing crossheads, Walschaerts valve gear and Boxpok semi-disc type driving wheels were fitted. Special attention was given to provision of large steam pipes, passages and ports to minimize throttling and power losses. The cab, unusually for the UP, was not supported by the main frame, but was attached to the mud ring – increasing the comfort of the crew by greatly reducing the vibration transmitted from the running gear. The cab had two seats on each side and vestibule doors which could be closed to protect against Wyoming winters. At least five oil-burning 4-6-6-4s were painted in two-tone grey for passenger service.

In 1943, 25 more 4-6-6-4s, Nos 3975-3999, were delivered. Finally, in 1944, 20 additional

▼ The Challengers were built to replace the rigid-wheelbased Class 9000 4-12-2s. The articulated 4-6-6-4 type was seen as a way to maintain the high adhesive weight and tractive effort of the Class 9000s, but with a more flexible wheelbase for working high speed freight trains. This was important to the UP, as much of its traffic consisted of perishable goods, such as fruit and vegetables grown in California that had to be quickly transported to the markets in the eastern US.

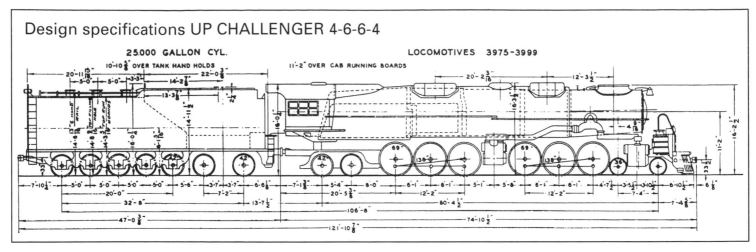

Design specifications UP CHALLENGER 4-6-6-4

25,000 GALLON CYL.   LOCOMOTIVES 3975-3999

▲ The second batch of Challengers, Nos 3950-3969, were constructed as a consequence of World War II, and the increased demands on the UP. Modifications to the boiler and firebox greatly improved combustion when burning soft Wyoming coal from the railroad's own mines. Power losses were minimized by the provision of large steam pipes, passages and ports. A larger tender was later provided.

TECHNICAL FILE

3900 class 4-6-6-4
2 simple expansion
cylinders: 21in diameter x 32in stroke
Coupled wheels: 5ft 9in diameter
Maximum boiler diameter: 94¹¹/₁₆in
Grate area: 132.2sq ft
Boiler pressure: 280lb psi
Tractive effort: 97,530lb (at 85% working pressure)
Water capacity: 20,900 gallons
Coal capacity: 25 tons
Length over buffers: 121ft 10⁷/₈in
Weight in working order:
Engine: 279.9 tons
Tender: 185.3 tons

▶ In 1993, there was only one working Challenger, No 3985. Its return to service in 1981, by a group of UP volunteers, was helped by the fact that it was given a major overhaul shortly before being retired from service. In 1990, the locomotive was converted to burn oil fuel, using the oil tank from the tender of another preserved Challenger, No 3710. In 1993, new smoke deflectors were commissioned, with the intention that the appearance of the Challengers that had them could be reproduced if desired.

Challengers, Nos 3930-3949 (using numbers vacated by renumbering the little Challengers to 3800-3839), were built, bringing total UP 4-6-6-4 ownership to 105 – by far the largest Challenger fleet. During World War II, over 100 Challengers based on the UP pattern were delivered to five other railroads. Additional number juggling took place later as 10 of the 1943 and eight of the 1944 batch were converted to oil and renumbered 3700-3717.

Draughting problems

Previously, UP had encountered draughting problems with their modern steam locomotives and to some extent this led to difficulties in sustaining maximum power. This was attributable mainly to the relatively low grade coal – and UP experimented with many different smokebox nozzle arrangements.

Finally, in the last 65 Challengers (as well as Big Boys and later 4-8-4s), these problems were overcome by using a double chimney design derived from the Chapelon Kylchap. In this, the twin exhaust streams from the nozzle blastpipe mixed with the exhaust gas in intermediate petticoats before it was discharged through the chimney. As a consequence of this new arrangement, the exhaust blast was now softer and smoke deflectors had to be fitted to the oil burners, and some coal burners, to lift steam and smoke clear of the boiler and so provide the crew with a clear view ahead.

Designed to conquer mountain grades without helpers, UP nevertheless did not hesitate to doublehead Challengers when necessary to maintain the fast schedules of perishable goods trains. The last Challenger to see service ran between Cheyenne and North Platte, Nebraska in 1959.

FEF 800

UNION PACIFIC RAILROAD

The FEFs were the world's first 4-8-4 passenger locomotives designed to haul trains at speeds of over 90mph. These carefully designed and successful engines were the last steam locomotives to be delivered to the Union Pacific Railroad.

A select number of locomotives have achieved international fame. High on this list is Union Pacific's (UP) No 844, representing the railroad's excellent FEF 800 4-8-4 class and owning the singular US distinction of never having been retired from the active locomotive roster.

On the UP in 1936, the demand for a modern, fast passenger locomotive was quickly becoming apparent. Only 14 years earlier, the American Locomotive Company (Alco) had delivered the 4-8-2 Mountain class, but their capabilities were being taxed by increasingly long passenger trains. During the same year, Lima locomotive works was developing the super power concept.

In 1922, Lima had rolled out the first of two demonstrator locomotives – No 8000, a 2-8-2 – and three years later produced the A-1, a 2-8-4. Both engines combined a high capacity boiler with a feedwater heater, superheated steam and a large firebox with a mechanical stoker. These features made for a comparatively fast freight locomotive with high horsepower. The basic concept was quickly applied by Alco to an even larger locomotive, built for the Northern Pacific Railroad, that could pull longer passenger trains and eliminate expensive double-heading.

Passenger debut

In 1926, the first 4-8-4 was introduced and other railroads soon adopted the wheel arrangement.

▼**In the summer of 1952, Union Pacific 4-8-4 No 813 takes an evening passenger train northwards from Denver, Colorado. The FEFs astonished the locomotive world by proving that the 4-8-4 wheel arrangement was ideal for hauling heavy passenger trains, whereas before it had been considered exclusively for freight haulage.**

Where to see them
● **814** – Council Bluffs, Iowa
● **833** – Salt Lake City, Utah
● **838** – Cheyenne
● **844** – Operational at Cheyenne, Wyoming

Sole survivor

The vast majority of US steam locomotives not scrapped were retired to museum or park display, mainly in the 1950s, and examples now being returned to steam have been plucked from these refuges. But when UP put its Big Boys, Challengers and 4-8-4s out to pasture in 1958 and 1959, No 844 was maintained at Council Bluffs as a snow melter with steam pipes added to the pilot. In late 1960, it was moved to Cheyenne, Wyoming for use on public excursions and company specials. No 844 celebrates its 50th birthday in 1994, with well over two thirds of those years serving the railroad after the general disappearance of steam.

▼**The FEFs formed the backbone of the Union Pacific's passenger motive power. They took over from the earlier Mountain type 4-8-2s and performed duties single-handedly which had once needed two engines. The FEFs were both fast and rugged: qualities that were not necessarily associated with the 4-8-4 wheel arrangement prior to their introduction.**

◀ **When introduced, the 800s suffered a number of teething problems. Several designs of superheater were fitted and different smokebox front ends were tried before UP decided on its own Labyrinth design. In October 1958, FEF-2 No 829 shows off its impressive front at Grand Island depot, Nebraska, shortly before withdrawal.**

The UP referred to their 4-8-4s as 800s, or the more stilted classification letters, FEF, standing for four eight four.

By 1936, most 4-8-4 designs were seen primarily as freight locomotives or mountain division passenger locomotives, as the balancing of their driving rods was deemed unsuitable for sustained high speed operation. This notion was successfully challenged by the 800s.

Working closely together, UP, under the direction of Otto Jabelmann, Assistant Superintendent of Motive Power, and Alco designers reached a new plateau of steam performance. The 800s combined a number of new design features: new tandem (articulated) rods, dividing the heavy piston thrusts between two crankpins on each side; long-

valve travel; large port openings for exhaust; extensive use of roller bearings on all axles (but not rods), and force fed lubrication. These features were incorporated in a machine mounting a 300lb psi boiler over eight 77in Bokpok drive wheels on a cast frame, with integral cylinders and air brake reservoir. The balancing of piston rods was also greatly improved. The UP 800s were designed for continuous maximum horsepower output at 90mph and a maximum speed of 110mph. Tender capacity was 25 US tons of coal and 20,000 US gallons of water.

Passenger service

Following running in duties with freight trains, the 800s began entering passenger service in late 1937, pulling such heavyweight trains as the Challenger and Overland Limited. Soon they were averaging over 14,000 miles per month and saving about $300,000 a year – or twice their purchase price – in running costs, compared to a 4-8-2.

In late 1938, the Association of American Railroads (AAR) decided to test modern steam designs to see what power was required to move a 1000 US ton passenger train at 100mph on level track. Two freshly shopped K4 Pacifics failed to reach more than 91mph on the Pennsylvania Railroad. Next, on the Chicago & North Western, brand new 4-6-4s with 7-foot driving wheels and 300lb boiler pressure achieved a maximum which fell short of the ton by 6mph.

When the tests moved to Nebraska, UP, short of motive power and to the chagrin of the AAR, could spare only a grimy, one year old Class 800, No 815, which was due for overhaul. Yet No 815 reached a top speed of 102.4mph and stayed above 100mph for six miles on slight falling grades of 1 in 500 to 1000, with 89mph up a comparable slight rising grade. The maximum cylinder power was 5043hp, despite the use of relatively low grade

UNION PACIFIC

844

◄ FEF-2, No 826, waits by the coaling chutes at Grand Island, Nebraska in October 1958. During their last years of service the class was converted to oil burning as coal supplies were frequently threatened by miners' strikes. This was one reason for steam's abrupt replacement by diesel in America throughout the 1950s.

1958 was the last year that the 800s were in everyday service; within a few weeks of this picture being taken, the majority of the class were waiting their call to the scrapyard.

Locomotive tests

Towards the end of 1938, the Association of American Railroads (AAR) wanted to see what power was required to move a 1000-US ton passenger train at 100mph on level track. The AAR went to a number of different railway companies which offered up their finest engines – but without success.

When it came to the turn of the UP, it was short of motive power and could only spare a run-down FEF, No 815. Yet this engine reached a top speed of 102.4mph and stayed above 100mph for six miles.

Wyoming coal.

In the following year, an order was placed and completed for a second series of 15 engines, Nos 820-834, and these were designated Class FEF-2. UP designers were able to incorporate improvements learned through extensive testing of the first group. Larger 80in drivers (wheels) resulted in a 4% higher speed capability for a given rpm. An increase in cylinder diameter from 24½in to 25in, together with modest increases in length and engine weight, produced an increase in tractive effort from 63,500lb to 63,800lb. Hollow piston rods were employed, a single cover enclosed the steam dome and sandbox, and the cab was larger. Tenders of 14 wheels with 23,500 US gallons water capacity were constructed.

The volume of passenger and troop traffic during World War II placed new demands on the railroad, and a final batch of 4-8-4s, Nos 835-844, arrived in 1944. These Class FEF-3 locomotives were similar to the Class FEF-2s, but featured a special twin stack arrangement. This was developed by A L Lipetz of Alco and was derived from the French Kylchap type. Each exhaust nozzle was divided into four jets and two intermediate gas entraining petticoats were placed between these and the chimney. This arrangement had previously been applied to the Challenger 4-6-6-4s, on which it had appreciably reduced exhaust back pressure and increased power output. A modified pilot (cow-catcher) casting more appropriate for 90mph protection was also added; it was later fitted to

LOCO LIST

45 locomotives were built from 1937-44. They formed three distinct sub-classes:
1937: FEF-1 800-819
1939: FEF-2 820-834
1944: FEF-3 835-844

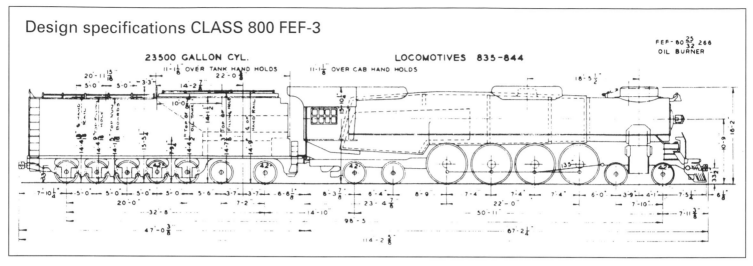

Design specifications CLASS 800 FEF-3

23500 GALLON CYL.   LOCOMOTIVES 835-844

▲The FEF 800s were built in three batches. The second and third batches were almost identical to one another, both having larger wheels, cylinders and tenders than the first batch. The third batch also benefited from a Kylchap style exhaust system. Although this increased power output, the soft exhaust necessitated the fitting of smoke deflectors.

TECHNICAL FILE

Class FEF-3
Cylinders: 25in diameter, 32in stroke
Coupled wheels: 6ft 8in diameter
Boiler diameter: 7ft 16in
Grate area: 100.2sq ft
Boiler pressure: 300lb psi
Tractive effort: 63,800lb
Fuel capacity: 6000 US gallons
Water capacity: 23,500 US gallons
Length over buffers: 114ft 8in
Weight in working order:
Engine: 486,340lb
Tender: 421,550lb

▶ On 15 May 1989, the only operational member of the Class, No 8444, storms through Hilgard, Oregon. It is painted in the old Greyhound livery of the late 1940s, to complement the livery of the non-streamlined passenger trains. In May 1989, the locomotive celebrated the 50th birthday of the Los Angeles Union passenger terminal by hauling a major excursion from Cheyenne. Afterwards the locomotive received its old 844 number which had been changed to avoid confusion with diesels.

some earlier 800s.

The 800s were not immune to teething problems, and different types of superheater were tried. Smoke drifting that obscured vision was a problem, especially with the softer blast of the double chimney. Eventually, all 45 received smoke deflectors.

Iron masters

The 800s ruled the main lines of the UP, operating 507 miles from Omaha, Nebraska, to Cheyenne, Wyoming, a layover point and the major maintenance and overhaul base; they continued on for 307 miles to Green River, Wyoming, and then either Salt Lake City, Utah or Huntingdon, Oregon. Western-based 800s hauled passenger trains between Los Angeles and Salt Lake City, while at the eastern end the 4-8-4s also worked to Denver and Kansas City.

Following World War II, the locomotives received a two-tone grey paint scheme with white, and later yellow, striping to complement the livery of non-streamliner passenger trains. When coal supplies became disrupted by miners' strikes, the 800s were converted to oil fuel.

By the mid-1950s, the 800s were relegated to express mail and fast freight services. The class distinguished themselves in Nebraska Division freight service between Council Bluffs, Iowa and North Platte, hauling the same length trains as previously allotted to 4-12-2s and 4-6-6-4s. Occasionally the class was used as helpers on diesel streamliners over Sherman Hill west from Cheyenne. These duties reaffirmed the merit of the 4-8-4 as both a passenger and freight hauler.

The 800s were stored following the autumn of 1958 and were never reinstated. The exception, No 844, was retained as a snow clearer and renumbered as No 8444 in 1962 to avoid conflict with diesel numbering.

FT and F3 diesels

GENERAL MOTORS ELECTRO-MOTIVE DIVISION

When launched in 1939, the F-series diesels amazed US railroad officials with their haulage power. These engines ran on American railroads for fifty years, heralding the start of the diesel age which swept steam from the railways of the world.

KEY FACTS

EMD FT Bo-Bo
Manufacturer: General Motors Electro-Motive Division
Built: 1941-45
Introduced: 1941
Prototype built: 1939

EMD F3 Bo-Bo
Built: 1946-49

Service: General freight and passenger service
Livery: Many individual railroad variations

Few events changed the face of railways like the 11-month, 83,764-mile demonstration tour over 30 US railroads of a 5400hp freight diesel, called the FT, in 1939-40.

Since 1934, diesels had been successfully powering lightweight streamlined passenger trains in the US, but their suitability for freight work was unknown. By hauling heavy freight services in a demonstration tour, Electro-Motive Division's pioneer FT No 103 showed the power and reliability of the new diesel engines to an audience of sceptical railroad officials. During World War II, the FT class would become the mass-produced locomotive which proved the superiority of diesel over steam in daily service. After the war, the improved F3 class among others sent nearly 50,000 steam locomotives to the scrapheap and assured Electro-Motive Division's position as the world's foremost diesel manufacturer.

Small beginnings

EMD's story began in Cleveland, Ohio, in 1922, when the small Electro-Motive Engineering Company began assembling components such as petrol engines, generators, traction motors and car bodies bought from other manufacturers, into gas-electric doodlebugs (railcars) for passenger service on branch lines. In 1930, the car manufacturer General Motors invested heavily in Electro-Motive and the Winton Engine Company. Six years later GM moved the firm, now Electro-Motive Corporation (EMC), to LaGrange, Illinois and absorbed it as the Electro-Motive Division (EMD) in 1941.

After looking at the new diesel technology, GM developed the Winton 201A, eight-cylinder inline

▼A line-up of three examples of the North American diesel which dominated the US railroads in the 1950s and '60s, makes an imposing sight. The famous nose profile became standard on all EMD car body freight and passenger locomotives from 1941. Although the locomotives were mass produced, a special styling section at EMD allowed the railroads to create their own colourful livery.

600hp engine and installed it in a Budd-built, stainless steel, lightweight train called the *Zephyr*. This train made a non-stop dawn to dusk Denver – Chicago run in 1934 and almost overnight launched railroading into the streamlined age.

While the *Zephyr* and later diesel passenger locomotives provided the glamour, the 201A engine was fitted in a switcher (shunting locomotive), where it showed its power at low speeds. However, switchers were used mostly in cities where smoke abatement was an issue. When it came to pure muscle, steam was still regarded as supreme.

The 201A was intended as a general purpose engine for railroad, marine and stationary applications. EMC's engineers set out to prove that a diesel engine could also provide muscle, by correcting the 201A's faults and redesigning it for railroad use only.

The new engine – the Vee configured two-stroke 567 (referring to cubic inch displacement in each cylinder) – became a masterpiece of reliability and easily changeable parts. In 1938, a 12-cylinder 1000hp version was tried in a switcher and two passenger locomotives, and a six-cylinder switcher application followed in 1939. But the engineers wanted the more powerful 16-cylinder 1350hp model to show the diesel's true potential and one of these was fitted into the new FT 103 design.

Classic locomotive

The FT – freight (F) and twenty-seven hundred horse power (T) – was described as a two-section locomotive: a cab section and booster section, each with a 1350hp engine, joined by a heavy drawbar to form one 2700hp locomotive. The joined sections – or units as they became known – were given a single number. This applied even when two 2700hp A-B locomotives (A referring to

▶ On the Gulf Mobile & Ohio Railroad, a freight train is hauled by a variety of F-type diesels. On US railroads, individual diesel units are often joined (lashed) together until there is enough power to haul a heavy train. The F-series locomotives were the first diesels in the world to haul freight trains with greater success than steam.

Where to see them
Only one FT, 2203, is operational. 104 F2s were built in 1946 and none has been preserved.
FT:
● EMD 103 (ex-Southern Railway 6100) – Kirkwood, Missouri
● Ferrocarri Sonora Baja, California 2203 (ex-Northern Pacific 6010-D, 5410-D) – Sonora, Mexico
F3:
● Bangor & Aroostook 502 – Northern Maine Jct, Maine
● Anthracite Railroad (ex-BAR 46) – Jim Thorpe, Pennsylvania

◀ In 1939, the performance of FT103 took the US railroad systems by storm. In 1989, volunteer workers at EMD celebrated the fiftieth anniversary of this pioneer diesel, now in the US National Museum of Transport, by cosmetically restoring it to its original appearance. Because the original booster unit no longer exists, a former FT unit was acquired from another museum.

the cab section and B referring to the booster section) were coupled back to back to form a 5400hp A-B-B-A locomotive to rival the 5000+hp ratings of the latest 4-8-4 steam locomotives. This designation was adopted partly in anticipation of union interpretation of the sections as separate locomotives – each requiring a fireman.

Not only did the new prime mover last (with certain improvements), but also the car body styling of the FT became a classic. Conceived and built in just 10 months, the body design looks as fresh today as it did five decades ago. EMC had developed the car body concept on early passenger locomotives, including boxcab models using two V-12 201A engines in 1935 and streamlined versions with long slant noses in 1937.

For the FT, the nose in front of the cab was gracefully rounded, tapering at a slight angle down to the pilot. This nose soon became standard on all EMD car body freight and passenger locomotives. The outer shell, or car body, was joined to the underframe with support members and became part of the structural framework.

During its 1939 demonstration tour, FT No 103 handled freight trains with half as much tonnage again as the steam locomotives on the same routes

– and in less time. Where gradients were steep, the FT shunned the assisting engines the steam locomotives needed and time-wasting stops for coal and water were no longer necessary. These factors had important implications for future costs of labour and fuel transportation. Compared with steam, the diesel was cheaper to run. Throughout the tour the FT achieved remarkable reliability; No 103 never missed a call for mechanical reasons.

Production series

In October 1940, the Santa Fe Railroad ordered the first production FTs. These introduced dynamic braking, where the gearing of the axles and traction motors could slow the train on long downhill sections; the traction motors were turned into generators and the heat dissipated by fans through grids, housed in a box-like structure on the roof. Dynamic braking saved wear and tear on the air brake system and brake shoes, allowing smoother handling.

During World War II, the US War Production Board ruled that only EMD could build freight diesels. The FT played an important role in moving goods trains, especially through districts where

LOCO LIST

FT: 555 cab and 541 booster units sold to 23 US railroads. Three US and one Mexican railroad bought second-hand units
F2: 104 were built, 28 units delivered to Mexico
F3: 1111 cab and 696 booster units built, six units delivered to Canada

▼The shape of the FT was conceived and built in 10 months and it is hard to believe that this modern looking design is over 50 years old. It was the coming of the diesel in America that sounded the death knell of steam throughout the world. Until 1939, US diesels were used only for shunting or hauling lightweight passenger trains.

Design specifications EMD FT-SERIES

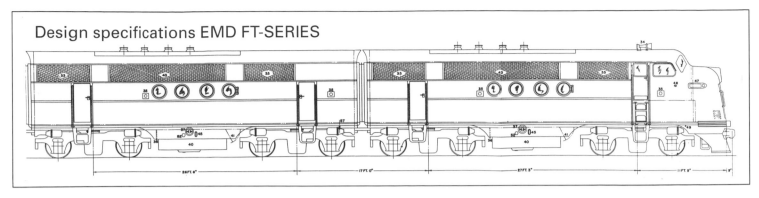

▲The various F-series types have many subtle differences in side-panel portholes, air intakes and grill work. The individual sections are called units and a single locomotive can be made up of a number of units coupled together. Units fitted with a cab are given the letter A and the driverless second units are called B, or booster units.

TECHNICAL FILE

EMD F3
Length: 50ft 8in
Distance between bogie centres: 30ft
Bogie wheelbase: 8ft 10in
Wheel diameter: 40in
Diesel engines: One 567B 16 cylinder 2-stroke rated 1500hp
Transmission: D12 main generator, 4 D17 traction motors
Maximum speed: 100mph
Fuel capacity: 1500 gallons
Weight: 230,000lb

water was either not suitable or scarce. Between 1940 and 1945, 1096 production units were built, some in drawbar-linked 4050hp A-B-A sets. Santa Fe, which ordered the largest FT fleet at 320 units, specified couplers between all units in its A-B-B-A formations. Some FTs were built with steam generator boilers to provide train heat for passenger service.

Because railroad companies were used to buying customized steam locomotives, a special styling section at EMD helped them choose one of the elaborate liveries – complete with pinstripes and flowing bands of colour – that came to typify the era and distinguish one railroad from another.

The FT was not completely without faults. It relied on manual transition, in which the engineer had to match throttle settings with ampere readings. There was also a manually controlled cooling system with a cumbersome arrangement of mechanically driven cooling fans employing shafts, pulleys and belt drives. At the end of World War II, an improved locomotive was developed with a 567B engine and a new main generator, the D12, permitting an increase to 1500hp. When faults developed in the generator, the older D8 was used in production, creating the interim F2

version of which 104 were built in 1946.

Finally, in late 1946, EMD began marketing the 1500hp F3 with the improved D12 generator. Redesigned dynamic brakes, new electrical cooling fans, couplers between units and improved arrangement of engine room components – allowing better access and space for high capacity steam generators – made the F3 an instant sales success. By 1949 when it was replaced by the 1750hp F7, 1111 cabs and 696 booster units had been built.

The last FT operated in the US on the Burlington Northern in 1970. Later, rebuilt F3s served on commuter service into the early 1990s. The US Southern Railway, which had purchased the FT demonstrator set, donated the lead cab unit to the National Museum of Transport in 1960. In 1992 another locomotive, No 2203, was rebuilt by Ferrocarri Sonora Baja, California, for use on special trains.

▼In 1952, the skyscrapers of Chicago tower over Santa Fe Railroad's Super Chief as it slides over the tracks at the start of another journey. Santa Fe ordered the largest FT fleet out of all the US railroads – 320 units. All its locomotives were made up of four units in A-B-B-A formations.

**The revolution in front-end design between the classic EMD and the longer bonnet
of more recent locomotives is evident in this shot taken at Dearbourn Street
station, Chicago.**

Classes M3 and M4

DULUTH, MISSABE & IRON RANGE RAILWAY COMPANY

For almost 20 years, these massive locomotives hauled some of the heaviest trains to be found anywhere in the world and played their part in the grand finale of US steam power, taking iron ore trains of up to 16,000 tons from mine to port.

KEY FACTS

M3 and M4 class Yellowstone 2-8-8-4 locomotives DM&IR
Designer: George Bohannon, Missabe Road; Ralph P Johnson, Baldwin works
Service: Heavy iron ore trains
Performance: 30mph on level track with 16,000 ton train. Fraser – Proctor, 55 miles at start-to-stop average of 22mph with 190 cars, 15,700 tons
Withdrawn: 1958-61

LOCO LIST

The 18 Yellowstone 2-8-8-4s were built in two batches. Eight were Class M3 and numbered 220-227. A further 10 similar locomotives were constructed as Class M4 and these were numbered 228-237.

▶With an overall height of 16ft 3in, over 3ft more than an LMS Coronation class Pacific of Great Britain, the M3s were most imposing machines. Like other American steam locomotives, they were equipped with a cow-catcher, bell and front spot lamp. In August 1957, No 224 shows off its impressive front end at Highland on the Iron Range Division.

▼ The M3s and M4s were coupled to high capacity 14-wheeled tenders, with a leading two-axled truck and five rigidly mounted axles. The water tank capacity of 21,000 gallons enabled the 80 mile run from Ely in the Vermilion Range and 65 miles from Virginia in the Misabe Range to Two Harbors on Lake Superior to be made without taking water. The bunker capacity of 23.5 tons was sufficient for round trips taking 12 and 10 hours respectively.

The Duluth, Missabe and Iron Range Railway Company (the DM&IR; also known as the Missabe Road), was formed in 1930 by a merger of two companies: the Duluth & Iron Range Railway (D&IR) moved the first ore mined from the Vermilion Iron Range in Minnesota in 1884 and the Duluth, Missabe & Northern Railway (DM&NR) which first moved ore from the 100 mile long Mesabi Range in 1892.

From 1901, both railroads were owned by the United States Steel Corporation and the DM&IR carried the largest part of its iron ore. This amounted to 49 million tons in 1953 and was wholly steam hauled. The most severe grade against loaded ore trains on the Missabe Division was four miles at 1 in 333. However, the much lighter empty ore trains had to climb 6½ miles at 1 in 45 from Duluth docks up to Proctor freight yards.

In 1910, the DM&NR had introduced eight 2-8-8-2 Mallet-type saturated steam compounds which, when fitted with mechanical stokers, could handle 85 empty ore cars (1250 tons) up Proctor Hill. Large 2-10-2s hauled the ore trains from Proctor over the 60-70 miles to and from the mines in the Mesabi Range and 0-10-0 shunters with two booster driven tender axles were used in Proctor yards.

In 1928, following the successful conversion by the neighbouring Great Northern system of compound Mallets to simples for faster running, the DM&NR rebuilt its four superheated 2-8-8-2s as simples. They proved capable of hauling 35% heavier trains than the 2-10-2s over the main line section.

Heavier loads

On the D&IR, the other constituent of the Missabe Road, 1 in 160 ruling grades against loaded ore trains from the mines to Two Harbors limited the maximum tonnage hauled by their large booster equipped Mikados to 3600 tons. After the 1930 merger, the DM&NR's rebuilt simple expansion 2-8-8-2s were used here, allowing 60% heavier trains.

During 1939-41, ore tonnage handled by the

Missabe Road rose from 18 to 37 million with the increased production of steel to meet the flood of war material sent by the US to Britain. George Bohannon, the Missabe's mechanical engineer, was therefore directed to prepare specifications for a much more powerful Mallet-type locomotive to haul 8000 ton trains over the Iron Range Division – 25% more than handled by the 2-8-8-2s. In 1941, following thorough design studies, the Baldwin Locomotive works delivered eight M3 class 2-8-8-4s of great power. The very high maximum tractive effort of 140,000lb was greater than that of the Union Pacific's Big Boy 4-8-8-4s.

The 2-8-8-4 Mallet-type was introduced in the United States in 1928 with a remarkable prototype machine built by the American Locomotive Company (Alco) for the Northern Pacific Railway

(NP), to haul 3600 ton trains over a difficult 216 mile route with 1 in 90 grades through North Dakota and Montana in the Yellowstone Division, which skirted the Yellowstone River.

This locomotive had the largest firebox ever used on a steam engine, 22ft long and 9ft 6in wide, enabling low cost, low grade, semi-lignite coal from the company's own mines to be burned – its heat content per pound was little more than half that of good bituminous coal. With this very long firebox, fed with up to 18 tons of coal per hour by mechanical stoker, the additional weight at the rear of the locomotive made it necessary to use a two-axle trailing truck instead of the single-axle truck of the preceding 2-8-8-2s.

Following the success of the prototype, 11 more locomotives were built by Baldwin in 1930

▲ The last Yellowstone hauled ore train, with M3 No 222, ran on 5 July 1960 – even later than the last steam hauled Norfolk & Western mineral train – and on 4 July 1961, Nos 224 and 227 worked final passenger steam specials on which No 224 is seen at Duluth, Minnesota.

During the oil crisis of 1973, the DM&IR considered returning Nos 225, 227 and 229 to service. It decided that these three would be enough to work the Iron Range side of the railroad with the current traffic. However, the cost of servicing them on a system now equipped for diesel traction was too great and oil supplies soon stabilized.

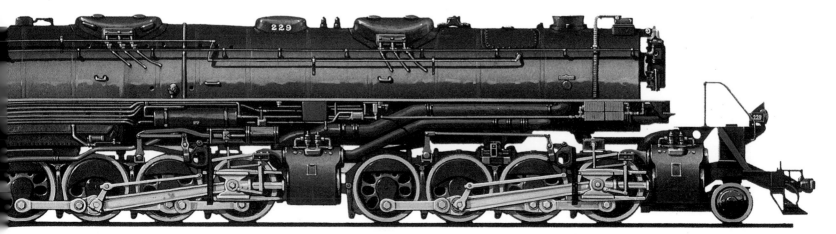

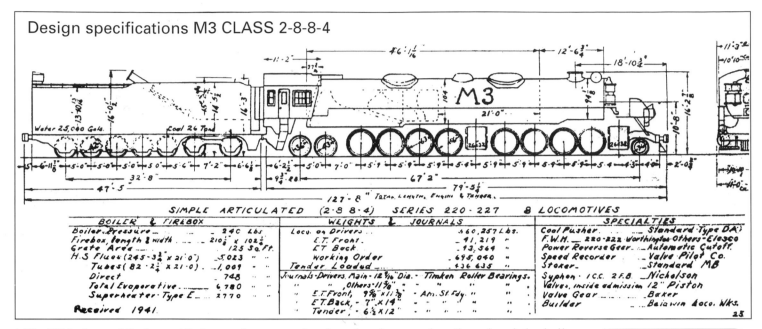

Design specifications M3 CLASS 2-8-8-4

Water 25,000 Gals.   Coal 26 Tons   M3   21'0"

SIMPLE ARTICULATED (2·8·8·4) SERIES 220-227 8 LOCOMOTIVES				
BOILER & FIREBOX		**WEIGHTS & JOURNALS**		**SPECIALTIES**
Boiler Pressure	240 Lbs	Loco. on Drivers	560,257 Lbs.	Coal Pusher — Standard Type DA
Firebox, length & width	210½" x 102½"	E.T. Front	91,219 "	F.W.H. — 220-222 Worthington-Others-Elesco
Grate Area	125 Sq.Ft.	E.T. Back	13,564 "	Power Reverse Gear — Automatic Cutoff
H.S Flues (245·3½ x 21·0")	5,023 "	Working Order	695,040 "	Speed Recorder — Valve Pilot Co.
Tubes (82·2¼ x 21·0)	1,009 "	Tender Loaded	436,635 "	Stoker — Standard MB
Direct	748 "	Journals-Drivers, Main·12⅜" Dia.· Timken Roller Bearings.		Syphon · I.C.C. 2.F.B. — Nicholson
Total Evaporative	6,780 "	" Others·11⅜"		Valves, inside admission 12" Piston
Superheater· Type E	2770 "	" E.T.Front, 9⅝"x11⅞" · Am.St.Fdy. "	"	Valve Gear — Baker
Received 1941.		" E.T.Back, · 7"x14" · " " "	"	Builder — Baldwin Loco. Wks.
		" Tender, · 6½x12" · " " "	"	25

▲ The M3 had one of the longest fireboxes of any steam locomotive – 17ft 6in long and 8ft 6in wide. The front 2ft 6in of the grate was separated by a Gaines wall which, in effect, extended the 7ft long combustion chamber. The grate area of 125sq ft was three times more than that of a Gresley Pacific and used up to eight tons of coal per hour.

(having undercut Alco's tender price). Classified as Z5 and known as Yellowstones, these 12 2-8-8-4s replaced 28 Mikado machines and ran for 25 years, allowing large operating economies.

Baldwin thus already had wide experience in the design and building of 2-8-8-4s for the NP and the Southern Pacific (SP). However, the Missabe's M3 design was largely based on the huge 2-8-8-2s, built in 1931-38 for the Western Pacific Railroad (WP), but with lengthened cab and main frames and two-axle trailing truck. In the M3, the com-

bustion chamber was lengthened and the boiler barrel was shortened by 2ft, compared to the WP's 2-8-8-2, thereby improving steaming, and the superheating surface was increased by 25%. A large radial ported single blastpipe was provided, similar to those used on the N&W Railway.

The boiler of the M3 was virtually equal in length and diameter to that of the NP Z5 Yellowstone, but as the bituminous coal burned was of much higher heat content there was no necessity for such a long firebox and grate to ensure an economical rate of combustion. Four thermic syphons from the firebox and combustion chamber crown sheets assisted boiler water circulation.

The one-piece cast-steel frame for the main and front truck units also incorporated the cylinders, buffer beam, cab supports and articulation hinge by which the front truck unit was connected to the

TECHNICAL FILE

4 simple expansion cylinders: 26in diameter x 32in stroke
Grate area: 125sq ft
Boiler diameter: 9ft ¹¹⁄₁₆in, outside (maximum)
Driving wheels: 5ft 3in
Maximum tractive effort: 140,000lb
Boiler pressure: 240lb psi
Length over couplers: 127ft 8in
Height: 16ft 2⅞in
Length of tender: 47ft 5in
Coal capacity: 23.5 tons
Water capacity: 21,000 gallons
Weight in working order:
Locomotive: 310.3 tons
Tender: 195.7 tons

Where to see them
Three Yellowstones have been preserved. Currently none is in running condition.
●**225** – Proctor, Minnesota
●**227** – Lake Superior Museum of Transportation. Duluth, Minnesota
●**229** – Two Harbors, Minnesota

◄ The need for the M3 and M4 came about with the rapid growth of steel production from 1940, to meet the demands of war supplies. The tonnage of iron ore carried by the DM&IR doubled in two years and required more powerful locomotives to haul much heavier trains. In August 1957, No 229 passes No 226 at Highland, Minnesota, on the Iron Range Division en route to port at Two Harbors.

main frame unit. The weight of the front of the boiler was transferred to the front truck unit through a sliding shoe type bearing with centring control device. To ensure smooth negotiation of curves, the Alco lateral motion device, allowing limited side-play under spring control and reducing the rigid coupled wheelbase, was applied to the first and fourth coupled axles of the leading truck unit and the first coupled axle of the main frame group.

Franklin automatically adjusting axlebox wedges virtually eliminated play between axleboxes and horn guides of the coupled axles. This was essential in a locomotive such as the M3 with maximum piston thrusts of about 50 tons, which would result in rapid wear and destructive axlebox knock unless this provision was made.

Steam distribution was through piston valves 12in in diameter using long-travel Baker valve gear (widely used in North America). This was preferred because it eliminated the wear between the die block and expansion link experienced in the Walschaerts gear. Boiler feed when running under power was by a feedwater heater and pump delivering up to 45 tons per hour, giving an economy of about 10% compared with the live steam injector also provided. To provide maximum crew protection against the severe winter conditions in Minnesota, the very large cab was totally enclosed with vestibuled connection to the tender front.

Greater haulage capacity

Michael Sullivan, DM&IR's Superintendent of Motive Power & Cars, said that the new M3s were broken in hauling practically the full rated tonnage and were released for general pooled working after only three supervised trips, with no teething troubles and only minor adjustments.

A further 10 virtually identical 2-8-8-4s, of Class M4, were built by Baldwin in 1943 for the Missabe Division. Here, they enabled maximum ore train loadings to be increased to 16,300 tons. The M4s only differed from the M3s by the wartime substitution of carbon steels for alloy

▲ The reign of the M3s and M4s lasted almost 20 years, during which they hauled iron ore trains of up to 190 cars, 16,000 tons, probably the world's heaviest loads at that time. These ran from the ore mines in northern Minnesota to ports on Lake Superior for shipment to ports serving steelworks along the Great Lakes. M3 No 226 shows its grimy flanks as it plods past the camera at Highland, Minnesota.

steels in certain components. In their first winter, when as usual Lake Superior was frozen over and ore shipments ceased, the M4s were loaned to the Denver & Rio Grand Western Railroad where they were a great success hauling and banking heavy trains over the 10,240ft Tennessee Pass of the Continental Divide. The Rio Grande told the Missabe they were the finest steam power ever to operate over their railroad.

These 18 2-8-8-4 engines, also known as Yellowstones, were later backed up on lighter main line trains by 18 large 2-10-4s displaced by diesels from the Bessemer & Lake Erie, another US Steel railroad. The Yellowstones handled the DM&IR's enormous iron ore traffic until the late 1950s. Nine of the unique 0-10-2s, with booster equipped tenders from the Union Railroad, took over working from the old 2-8-8-2s on Proctor Hill. The performance of the Yellowstones was outstanding and their maintenance costs low. Their tonnage ratings were 25% higher than those of the simple expansion 2-8-8-2 Mallets previously used.

With its top rank steam motive power doing an admirable operating job on the DM&IR, Motive Power Superintendent, Michael Sullivan, argued forcibly that there was no urgent case for dieselization, and this was put off until the cessation of production of specialized proprietary equipment for steam locomotives, such as feedwater heaters, injectors and air compressors, left little alternative. Dieselization was completed in 1959-60, quickened by the fall in ore tonnage handled to only half that of 1953. The last M3 was withdrawn in 1961.

4-8-8-4 Big Boy

UNION PACIFIC RAILROAD

**Cheyenne, Laramie, Union Pacific – the names
evoke memories of Indian country, the exploits of Butch
Cassidy and cattle rustling. In the 1940s arose another legend –
a fleet of steel leviathans appeared on the scene and
the West became Big Boy country.**

The Union Pacific Railroad formed part of the first transcontinental route across the United States. The final connection was made in April 1869 at a point west of Ogden, Utah. The line has remained one of the most important routes between the Mid West and the Pacific coast ever since.

The main line starts at Council Bluffs, Omaha and runs west through Cheyenne and Ogden to Los Angeles over the Rocky Mountains. It climbs from Cheyenne at just over 6000ft (1829m) above sea level to the top of the Wasatch range at 6799ft (2072m) before dropping to 4298ft (1310m) at Ogden.

The 2501ft (762m) fall into Ogden is 65 miles (105km) long with an average gradient of 1 in 137. A second track for eastbound journeys was added between 1916 and 1923 with 25 miles (40km) of 1 in 88, a formidable challenge.

These gradients made the line over the Wasatch range difficult to operate and a second locomotive was needed on most trains, particularly heavy freight.

From 1909 these helpers were articulated 2-8-8-2s and 2-8-8-0s, which were ponderous and powerful but quite incapable of anything more than moderate speeds. With customers demanding quicker deliveries for their goods, something faster was necessary.

The American Locomotive Company (Alco) was a leader in the development of the most powerful steam locomotives capable of higher speeds. It had pioneered the use of a trailing two-axle truck providing space and support for very large fireboxes. From 1927 Alco introduced machines with 4-6-4, 2-8-4, 4-8-4 and 2-8-8-4 wheel arrangements for many US railways which needed increased power and the ability to move freight at

▼The extraordinary length of the Big Boys – 132ft 9in (40.5m) – meant that the turntables in the locomotive yards on their route from Cheyenne, Wyoming to Ogden, Utah had to be enlarged to 135ft (41m) diameter. Curved track on the main line was realigned to increase the distance between passing trains because of the amount of overhang on the cab and smokebox.

▶The massive smokebox of Big Boy was large enough to allow a man to stand upright inside. Union Pacific regulations insisted that the door had to be opened and the interior inspected when the engine reached the shed at the end of each run. Despite its size and weight, the smokebox front could be opened by one man in 30 minutes.

▲The giant 4-8-8-4s were designed to move huge freight trains without assistance over the stiff gradients of the Wasatch range of the Rocky Mountains. Even though the trains frequently weighed more than 3000 tons the locomotives rarely slipped.

60mph (97km/h) or more.

In 1936 the Union Pacific went to Alco for a simple four-cylinder articulated engine, suitable for moving freight tonnage and passenger trains at speeds up to 70mph (113km/h), with good riding qualities. The result was the 4-6-6-4 Challenger with 5ft 9in coupled wheels. By 1944, 105 Challengers had been built.

But with war in Europe and further growth in traffic, even the Challengers could not satisfy the Union Pacific's needs. Alco was approached for an even bigger locomotive, purely for freight haulage but good for 60mph (97km/h) and able to haul 3600 tons unassisted over the Wasatch range.

In 1941 Alco created the first (and only) 4-8-8-4 design. Before the first of the class emerged from the works at Schenectady someone, clearly impressed by the sheer bulk of a locomotive and tender nearly 133 feet (40.5m) long and

weighing over 530 tons in working order, chalked 'Big Boy' on the smokebox front. The name stuck and quickly became official.

530 tons of power

The name was entirely justified. The boiler worked at 300 pounds per square inch while its barrel had an outside diameter of 8ft 11in (2.72m). Because of the stresses involved in transferring weight on to the leading engine, the barrel plates were 1³⁄₈in (3.49cm) thick.

The enormous firebox, sitting over the last two coupled axles in the trailing truck, was necessarily shallow. The grate, 8ft (2.44m) wide and 19ft 7in (5.97m) long (bigger than many rooms), had an area of 150sq ft (13.94sq m), while the front of the firebox continued into a combustion chamber more than 8ft (2.44m) long. Seven transverse circulators were fitted which also carried the brick arch.

Coal was fed by a mechanical stoker and a consumption of nine tons per hour was quite normal. Draught was provided by a double multiple-jet blastpipe and double chimney, while a steam operated smoke deflector hood over the double chimney was used when working hard in tunnels to protect the tunnel roofs from the fierce blast.

The two chassis units were one-piece steel castings incorporating the cylinders, a form of construction almost universal in the USA since 1930; they were masterpieces of the steel foundryman's art. All axles ran in roller bearings. The cab was fully enclosed – the plains of Wyoming in winter can be like the arctic.

The tender alone weighed 191 tons and was carried on seven axles, five rigid and the leading two in a truck – little wonder that the type was called a centipede. It held 24,000 gallons of water (25,000 in later examples) and 25 tons of coal, which was reckoned ample to get a 3600 ton train the 40 miles (64km) from Ogden to Echo before refuelling. Weather affected fuel consumption and the tender was filled close to the top in adverse conditions. In good weather it needed to be only three quarters full.

Before long the bunkers were extended upwards to hold another 3¹⁄₂ tons. Soon after World War II, during a mining strike, No 4005 was converted for oil firing but reverted to coal later.

These 25 remarkable locomotives took over most of the freight working between Ogden and Cheyenne. But when traffic peaked they might still be seen with a 2-8-2 or 2-10-2 helper, even though their tonnage rating over Wasatch was

Big Boy arrives

The first Big Boy, No 4000, reached Union Pacific's Omaha depot on the evening of 5 September 1941. A large crew set to work immediately to prepare it for the first run. When they came to fill the giant firebox, the front corners were so far away that one man had to climb inside to spread the coal that others fed to him. Once the men were satisfied with the coal levels, the mechanical stoker was started.

A few days later No 4000 pulled its first 3500 ton train eastwards over Sherman Hill. People were parked along the highway to see the show. The word was out that Union Pacific had a new king of the road.

▼The clouds of black smoke were a trade mark of the Big Boys because the exhaust contained large quantities of particles of unburnt coal. Water from the tender could be sprayed on to the following cars if red hot cinders threatened to set light to them.

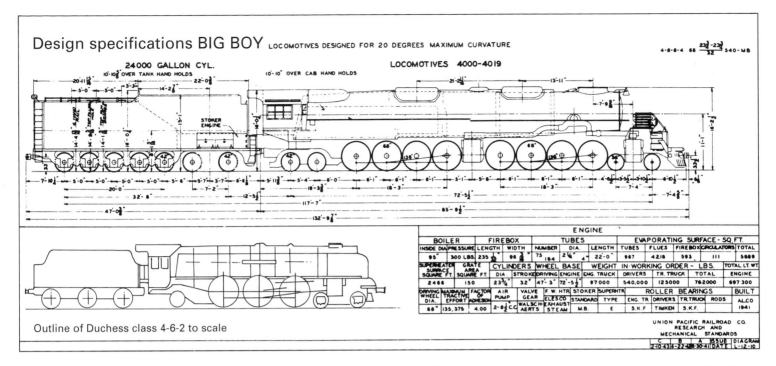

Design specifications BIG BOY
LOCOMOTIVES DESIGNED FOR 20 DEGREES MAXIMUM CURVATURE

24000 GALLON CYL. — LOCOMOTIVES 4000-4019

4-8-8-4 68 $\frac{23\frac{3}{4}-23\frac{3}{4}}{32}$ 540-MB

Outline of Duchess class 4-6-2 to scale

BOILER		FIREBOX		TUBES			EVAPORATING SURFACE - SQ.FT.				
INSIDE DIA	PRESSURE	LENGTH	WIDTH	NUMBER	DIA.	LENGTH	TUBES	FLUES	FIREBOX	CIRCULATORS	TOTAL
95"	300 LBS.	235	96	75 / 184	2¼" / 4"	22'-0"	987	4218	593	111	5889

SUPERHEATER SURFACE SQUARE FT.	GRATE AREA SQUARE FT.	CYLINDERS		WHEEL BASE		WEIGHT IN·WORKING ORDER – LBS.				TOTAL LT. WT
		DIA.	STROKE	DRIVING	ENGINE	ENG. TRUCK	DRIVERS	TR. TRUCK	TOTAL	ENGINE
2466	150	23¾"	32"	47'-3"	72'-5½"	97000	540,000	125000	762000	697 300

DRIVING WHEEL DIA.	MAXIMUM TRACTIVE EFFORT	FACTOR OF ADHESION	AIR PUMP	VALVE GEAR	F.W. HTR	STOKER	SUPERHTR	ROLLER BEARINGS				BUILT
								ENG. TR	DRIVERS	TR.TRUCK	RODS	
68"	135,375	4.00	2-8½ C.C	WALSCH AERTS	ELESCO EXHAUST STEAM	STANDARD M.B.	TYPE E	S.K.F	TIMKEN	S.K.F		ALCO 1941

UNION PACIFIC RAILROAD CO.
RESEARCH AND
MECHANICAL STANDARDS

stepped up, first to 4200 then to 4400 tons. During the heavy California fruit season, spare Big Boys arriving at Cheyenne were sometimes sent back westbound as helpers. The sight of a long freight with two Big Boys at its head was impressive indeed.

The cost of power
There was considerable wastage inherent in the performance of Big Boys. The high rate of combustion, combined with the thin fire normal with mechanical stoking, led to prodigious loss of unburnt fuel up the chimneys. There was even provision on the tender back to spray the leading wagons in order to douse burning cinders.

Cinder cutting of superheater flues was so heavy that the firebox ends needed renewal at intervals of 44,000 miles (70,000km). Provision was made for the blastpipe nozzles to be turned regularly to present a new side to the abrasive gas flow. It was a brutal way of producing power.

Before changing completely from steam to diesel, the Union Pacific indulged in a lengthy dalliance with gas turbine locomotives, starting in 1952, as they tried to replace the Big Boys. It was hardly surprising that these newcomers were christened 'Big Blows'. But they were not entirely successful and their availability and economy were not good.

In the 1960s Union Pacific abandoned the gas turbines – but the writing was on the wall for the Big Boys because the company had turned to diesels. Withdrawal started in mid-1961 and by July 1962 all had been withdrawn. The locomo-

▲Assisted by staff from Union Pacific, four teams at the American Locomotive Company designed Big Boy. It weighed three times as much as an LMS Duchess and was almost twice as long. Even the tender was enormous and held 24,000 gallons, six times the capacity of a Duchess.

tives had covered between 818,000-1,064,000 miles (1,316,000-1,712,000km) each.

At maximum firing, the Big Boys in their usual four hour trip up Sherman Hill would consume 20 tons of coal and 12,000-13,000 gallons of water. The engines were restricted to 35mph (56km/h) in general service when new and when after shopping. Although the engines could have quite a turn of speed they were used on passenger trains only in emergencies. This was because of a preference to use the Challenger types which were also available at this time.

TECHNICAL FILE

4 cylinders: 23¾in diameter, 32in stroke
Coupled wheels: 5ft 8in diameter
Boiler diameter: 8ft 11in outside maximum
Grate area: 150 sq ft
Boiler pressure: 300lb psi
Tractive effort: 135,375lb
Coal capacity: 25 tons*
Water capacity: 24,000 gallons. 25,000 gall tenders on Nos 4019-4024
Length over buffers: 132ft 9⅞in
Weight in working order:
Engine 340-344.8 tons
Tender 191-195 tons
*Increased to 28½ tons

▶ Each cylinder had such a large surface area that all four were fitted with lubrication lines on top, at the bottom, back and front and on each valve bush to ensure that they never dried up. The large pipe carried steam from the boiler to the rear cylinder.

Big Boy No 4003 was captured at Cheyenne, Wyoming, in October 1958, four years before the last of the class was withdrawn. Although eight have been preserved, none is currently in operation.

Class J 4-8-4

NORFOLK & WESTERN RAILWAY

The Class J was the last steam locomotive design to be built for express passenger work in the US and was one of the most powerful types ever. They ran high mileages with low maintenance costs – largely through mountainous terrain.

From the late 1920s, the small, busy and prosperous Norfolk & Western Railway (N&W) was totally committed to building its own steam locomotives – unlike most US railroads which relied on the big three commercial locomotive builders: Alco, Baldwin and Lima.

By 1939, the N&W was planning a new express locomotive to supplant its 15- to 25-year-old 4-8-2s which were in charge of main line passenger trains. An extended version of the N&W's biggest 4-8-2, with a four-wheel trailing truck, had once been on the drawing board and so the logical wheel arrangement for the new locomotive would be the popular 4-8-4, with its ample boiler and firebox capacity.

High tractive effort

Five 4-8-4s, numbered 600-604 and designated Class J, were rolled out of N&W's Roanoke, Virginia (Va) works from October 1941 to January 1942. The Class J was given comparatively small driving wheels for express passenger duty, of 5ft 10in. When this feature was combined with high boiler pressure and large cylinders, it provided high tractive effort for operation over the N&W's 1 in 66 ruling grades (with one section at 1 in 50). The small wheels also provided clearance for an exceptionally large boiler to provide ample steam production for sustained high power outputs.

Not only did the riveted boiler have a maximum outside diameter of 8ft 6in, but the grate area of 108sq ft matched that of the giant Santa Fe oil-burning 4-8-4s. It was only exceeded by the 115sq ft of the Northern Pacific 4-8-4s, necessitated by the low British Thermal Unit (Btu) heat content of Montana coal. Even more significant was the Class J's large combustion chamber extension to the firebox. At 8ft 6in, it was the longest of any 4-8-4 – resulting in a total firebox direct radiant heating surface of 578sq ft.

The Class J was destined to receive acclaim for both performance and appearance. In the early

KEY FACTS

Norfolk & Western Railway Class J 4-8-4
Designer: N&W Motive Power Department, Roanoke, Va under R G Henley, general superintendent of motive power
Built: 1941 (4); 1942 (1); 1943 (6); 1950 (3); N&W Roanoke works, Roanoke, Va
Service: Express passenger trains; local freights at end of career
Livery: Black with band of Tuscan red trimmed with gold and gold lettering
Performance: Averaged 4700 drawbar hp on test, reaching a peak of 5100 drawbar hp at 40mph. In 1946, No 610 attained 110mph with a 915 UK ton test train on level track on the Pennsylvania Railroad.
Withdrawn: 1958-59

▼The N&W was the second largest coal-hauling railroad in the US, but it did run a number of passenger trains of luxurious modern stock. One of these, the Powhatan Arrow, is hauled westbound by Class J No 605 in September 1951. This express ran the 676 miles between Norfolk, Va and Cincinnati, Ohio. Nowadays, former N&W lines carry freight only.

▶ **A Class J 4-8-4 could run 1300 miles before its lubricating oil reservoirs required refilling. At the clean modern servicing depots, the various grades of oil or grease were supplied by different hoses, each of which had its own special sized connector. Mechanical lubricators fed lube oil under pressure to 220 separate points – a further 72 points had pressure grease lubrication. N&W principal steam locomotive servicing depots were the world's most modern – inspection and servicing, ash disposal, coaling, watering and refilling the lubricators of a Class J 4-8-4 normally took one hour, far less time than other US railroads.**

1940s, streamlining was still fashionable in a country not yet affected by war. Instead of commissioning one of the famous industrial designers (Henry Dreyfuss had shrouded the New York Central's Hudsons while Raymond Loewy had styled Pennsylvania steam and electric locomotives), the Class J was very much an in-house design.

The streamlined cow-catcher housed a retractable coupler. A large curved shell, or bullet nose, enclosed the smokebox door. A skyline casing ran from the front of the boiler to the cab, covering the Worthington feed-water heater, chimney, sandbox and steam dome. The outside motion was tastefully left exposed – thus minimizing any tendency for overheating – and was accentuated by a graceful running-board skirt, displaying a band of Tuscan red trimmed in gold that was continued across the tender. This contrasted with the overall black livery of the locomotive.

Additions and variations
The first five members of Class J initially carried a boiler of 275lb psi and produced 73,300lb tractive effort. One locomotive, No 602, also had a booster. This device was later deemed unnecessary when the working pressure was raised to 300lb psi and was removed in 1945.

Progressive railroads judiciously applied roller bearings to their locomotives. After intensive studies by the bearing manufacturers, Timken, the N&W made a comprehensive application to the Class J – driving axles, rods, wrist and crank pins,

valve gear, locomotive and tender trucks – totalling over 60 applications per locomotive. Cylinders, crosshead guides and motion plates were cast integral with the one piece frame bed.

Very thorough design studies were made of the running gear, which included lightweight pistons and rods, also excellent counter- and cross-balancing. Franklin automatically adjusting axlebox wedges eliminated axlebox knock due to uncontrolled wear – a destructive and quite unacceptable factor in very powerful two-cylinder locomotives.

The lowest possible proportion of the reciprocating masses – pistons and driving rods – was balanced to minimize both the rotating out-of-balance forces resulting from these components and vertical hammer-blow forces on the track. The partially balanced reciprocating parts could create a yawing motion at speed and to overcome this tendency the bogie and trailing trucks were provided with a stiff lateral suspension which gave a strong centring action.

LOCO LIST

The 14 members of Class J were constructed in batches between 1941 and 1950 in the following order:
1941 Nos 600-603
1942 No 604
1943 Nos 605-610
1950 Nos 611-613

Where to see them
No 611, the only J preserved, is based at Norfolk Southern's steam shops at Irondale yard, outside Birmingham, Alabama, and from April to November pulls excursion trains at many points on the NS and other systems.

BR interest
N&W's advanced steam locomotive designs – especially the J – and modern servicing depots were featured in the company's notable film made in 1950 advocating modern steam traction. This created a considerable impression on some BR engineers, especially Stewart Cox, Executive Officer Design, and Roderick Harvey, Chief Motive Power Officer, who had modernized the Polmadie depot in Glasgow. The 1955 BR Modernization Plan included £10m for improved steam depots, but this was not fully implemented, only one new depot being built at Thornaby.

This, combined with both an excellent steam flow circuit and layout of the Baker valve gear, enabled the Class J to run freely at unheard-of top speeds for a locomotive with 5ft 10in diameter driving wheels. There were only a few stretches on the N&W suitable for really high speeds, where the Class J easily reached 80mph, but on test on the Pennsylvania Railroad in 1946, No 610 recorded 110mph on level track with a 15-car train weighing 915 tons.

The next six locomotives, including No 610, were delivered in 1943 – at the height of World War II. Because of material shortages, these locomotives, temporarily classified J1, initially did not have the streamlined shroud and lightweight rods with roller bearings. Alligator two-bar crossheads – to be repeated on the final production run – replaced the multiple-bar type used on Nos 600 and 604. After road tests, when 5100 drawbar hp was developed at 40mph with pressure increased to 300lb psi, this was applied on all the class. It raised the maximum tractive effort to 80,000lb – the highest for any non-booster-fitted 4-8-4.

Passenger finale
Most of the N&W's traffic was coal and out of all the major US railroads, it was the company that resisted wholesale dieselization the longest. In 1950, Roanoke works produced the last three passenger steam locomotives to be built for a US railroad – Class J Nos 611-613.

The fleet of 14 Class Js accounted for over 80% of N&W passenger train miles (22 K2 class 4-8-2s, now streamlined in a manner similar to the 4-8-4s, were used on secondary trains and lines too restrictive for the Class J). The Class J hauled trains such as the streamlined Powhatan Arrow on the 676-mile daylight Norfolk, Va – Cincinnati, Ohio run, the overnight Pocahontas and the through Tennessean and Birmingham Special, which were operated jointly with the Southern Railroad (SR).

▼In the 1940s, streamlining was still very much in fashion, but instead of commissioning one of the famous industrial designers to style the Class J, the N&W relied on its own staff. Frank Noel, a tool room supervisor at Roanoke works with a flair for industrial design, was responsible. He touched up one proposal that was rejected as too plain and then made a proposal that was deemed too fancy; the third was considered magic.

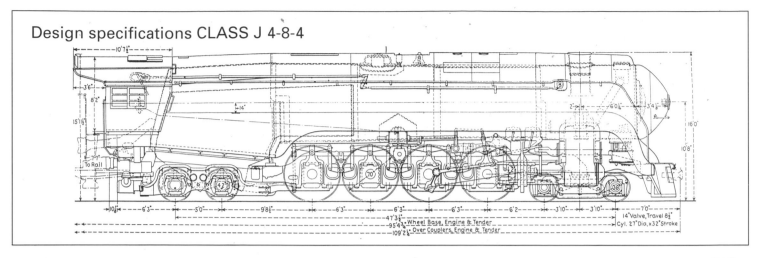

Design specifications CLASS J 4-8-4

▲The Class J was designed by two N&W mechanical engineers, G P McGavoc and C P Harris, who combined their own experience with the latest research data to create a state-of-the-art machine that had high performance, low maintenance costs and high utilization. In fact, maintenance costs for the Class J 4-8-4s were 26% less per mile than for preceding 4-8-2s, which had been used on much less arduous duties, over a similar three year period, when the Js ran 63% more mileage. They required minor shed attention, one-sixth of the days of the 4-8-2s.

This work put the Class J on precise weekly cyclic engine diagrams, resulting in diesel-like monthly mileages of 15,000. This was despite necessarily moderate average overall speeds due to severe grades and curvature over the mountain sections traversed. Roanoke, Va to Cincinnati, Ohio and back, 849 miles, was a regular daily Class J roster. The first 11 Class J locomotives averaged a lifetime mileage of over two million each in a working life of 15 to 18 years.

Although N&W's principal main lines were almost wholly steam operated as late as 1958, new management then dieselized with a vengeance – even scrapping locomotives which had recently completed costly general overhauls at Roanoke works. That year, the company leased passenger

diesels to replace the Class J, a few of which went into local freight service. In October 1959, No 611 was rescued from probable scrapping to pull two farewell steam excursions. The locomotive was later donated to the city of Roanoke for exhibition at the Roanoke Transportation Museum, where it remained a static exhibit.

Steam enthusiast Robert B Claytor became president of the Norfolk Southern (NS) (the Norfolk & Western combined with the Southern Railroad in 1982) and speculation centred on the return of No 611 to operable condition. In October 1981, the locomotive had been towed already to the Southern Railway's steam shops at Birmingham, Alabama, and given a thorough inspection. Complete overhaul followed and in the summer of 1982 the locomotive became the mainstay of the newly merged Norfolk Southern's steam excursion fleet.

At the beginning of the 1990s, No 611 joined a small but growing list of locomotives that have spent more years in excursion service than in regular service. Another overhaul in 1992 primed No 611 for many more years of pulling excursions from major US cities in the East, Midwest and South. A fitting reminder of an outstanding class, one much admired by British engineers.

TECHNICAL FILE

2 simple expansion cylinders: 27in x 32in
Coupled wheels: 5ft 10in diameter
Boiler diameter: 8ft 6in
Grate area: 107.7sq ft
Boiler pressure: 300lb psi
Tractive effort: 80,000lb
Water capacity: 16,700 gallons
Coal capacity: 31.25 tons
Length over couplers: 109ft 2¼in
Weight in working order:
Engine: 494,000lb
Tender: 378,600lb

Driven off the rails
The stiff lateral suspension, necessary to ensure good riding, occasionally resulted in derailments on sharp curves in yards. On 23 January, 1956, No 611 jumped across one track and landed on its left side in the Big Sandy River, after the driver, who was killed, had became disoriented during a storm and entered a 30mph curve at 50mph. Although No 611, now used on excursions, is capable of speeds in excess of 100mph, the locomotive is today limited to 40mph. This is due to different track configurations and reduced super-elevation of curves on Norfolk Southern for freight only operation in the diesel era, with no provision for faster passenger trains.

◀ In 1985, No 611 was pronounced a National Historic Mechanical Engineering Landmark by the American Society of Mechanical Engineers. On 1 November 1982, the locomotive heads eastbound with an excursion from Bluefield, W Va to Roanoke, Va.

When J class No 611 was withdrawn from regular service in 1959, it hauled two special excursions.
Before No 611was donated to Roanoke, the famous railroad photographer O. Winston Link offered to buy
the machine, seen here at Kings Mountain, Noth Carolina, on its penultimate run in steam, in 1994.

Kriegslok 2-10-0

DEUTSCHE REICHSBAHN

The Kriegsloks were one of the most numerous types of locomotive ever. Built in their thousands at factories all over Europe, they became the motive power of the Nazi war machine. Many still survive today but with tourists, not tanks, as their passengers.

The German 2-10-0 Kriegsloks (War Locomotives) of World War II, comprised three classes. The 3000 Class 50s, introduced in peacetime, were simplified while in course of production and the final units were reclassified as Class 52. Over 6000 were built in 1942-5; 473 were built in one month. A larger version of the Class 52, the Class 42, was also built.

Under the supervision of Richard Wagner, Chief Engineer of the Central Design Office at the Locomotive Standards Bureau, the Deutsche Reichsbahn (DRG) had introduced a range of standard locomotives between the wars. Unlike contemporary British locomotive designers, Wagner did not give great priority to a high power-to-weight ratio. More power meant more stress and Wagner wanted locomotives that were reliable, cheap to maintain, and longlasting. In the 1920s,

▼ **Class 52s built by Henschel in 1943-44, Class 52 KON, had condensing tenders enabling up to 90% of the exhaust steam to be condensed to water and re-used in the boiler. This increased the maximum distance between water stops to 1000km (620 miles). During the Russian campaign, many watering points were destroyed by Soviet partisan groups and in many cases only German troop and hospital trains hauled by Class 52 KON locomotives could get through.**

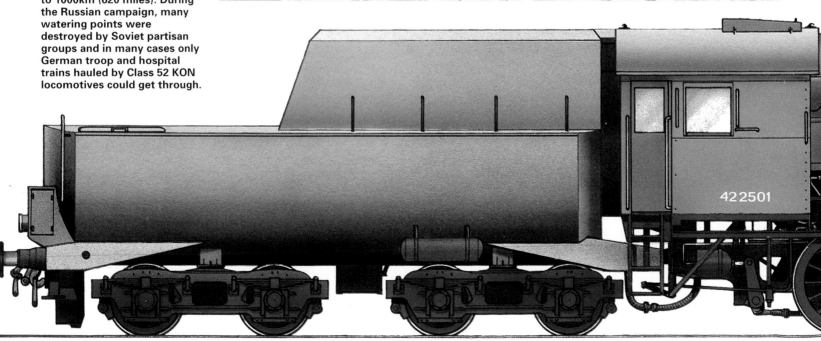

LOCO LIST

Most units kept their 52 and 42 prefixes, which became 052 and 042 for those that survived into the computer age. In Russia, the Class 52 became the TE Class and the 042 the TL, the 'T' signifying 'Trophy'. In Austria those locomotives having bar frames were reclassified as 152. The Class 52 was known as the 150Y in France, Class N in Denmark, Class 63a in Norway, the 555 in Czechoslovakia, the 30 Class in Yugoslavia, the 15 Class in Bulgaria, and the 26 Class in Belgium. In Poland the 52 became the Ty2, but those built after the war were Ty42s.

his design office worked on the principle that power outputs above 1000hp were unnecessary and expensive.

Wagner's most numerous design was the Class 50 freight 2-10-0, which, with its very low axleload (15 tons), could be used on most routes and haul 40% more tonnage at the same speed than the Prussian 0-10-0s it replaced. Construction began in 1938 and was overtaken by World War

◀ The original caption to this 1943 publicity photograph states that 'A batch of Kriegsloks are leaving the factory at Erschienen'. However, it is probably simply a posed photograph of as many 2-10-0s as could be mustered.

II. To suit war conditions, various changes were introduced to simplify its construction and maintenance, and the design gradually became the Class 52, which was specifically produced as a war locomotive, or *Kriegslokomotiv*.

The Class 52, too, was a design that was never really finalized, several variations being introduced during the years of its construction. Principal dimensions were the same as the Class 50, with the 52 being some two tons lighter.

The Class 52 first appeared in 1942, a year after Germany invaded Russia. For the Russian campaign, Hitler had envisaged a minimal use of railway transport and a maximum use of highways. This was soon to be a cardinal error and the

Where to see them
In Germany and Austria Class 52 units appear frequently on excursions. Others are at museums and tourist lines. Two are in the UK – one at Bressingham, Norfolk and the other on the Nene Valley Railway.

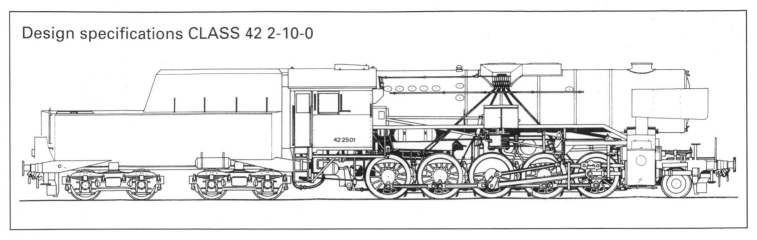

Design specifications CLASS 42 2-10-0

▲ The Kriegsloks were given wholly enclosed cabs so that the crew had all-round cover. The main lubricator was moved to the cab, enabling the crew to keep the engine oiled without venturing out. The 2-10-0 wheel arrangement gave a light axleloading enabling the locomotive to have a wide route availability.

TECHNICAL FILE

Classes 50 and 52 (Class 42 in brackets)
2 simple expansion cylinders: 23³/₅in diameter x 26in stroke (24⁴/₅in x 26in)
Coupled wheels: 4ft 7in diameter (4ft 7in)
Maximum boiler diameter: 5ft 7in (6ft 3in)
Grate area: 42 sq ft (50.6 sq ft)
Boiler pressure: 227lb psi (227lb psi)
Tractive effort: 50,025lb (55,240lb) at 85% working pressure
Water capacity: 7,000 gallons (7,000 gallons)
Coal capacity: 13 tons (13 tons)
Length over buffers: 77ft 3in (75ft 5in)
Weight in working order:
locomotive: 85.5 tons (Class 50), 83.3 tons (Class 52), 95 tons (Class 42)
tender: 61 tons (61 tons)
Axleloading: 15 tons (18 tons)

▶ On 9 April 1985, a Class 52 locomotive, No 56552, attached to a bathtub tender, stands in Usak shed yard in Turkey. Many of these locomotives were used on secondary duties and tender-first running was a frequent feature avoiding the necessity of using turntables.

Class 52 was developed with Russia in mind. There was not only a growing military traffic towards Russia, but also inside occupied Russia, where the main lines had been re-gauged. As things turned out the Class 52 would see service not only in Germany but also in most of German-occupied Europe.

The Class 52 was intended to avoid the use of materials in short supply and was simplified so that unskilled labour could provide most of the workforce; in due course, what was later known as slave-labour was allotted to the locomotive building works. Of the 6000-odd components that were assembled to make the earlier Class 50 engine, a thousand were dispensed with for the Class 52 and another 3000 simplified, often to make them suitable for stamping and welding instead of casting and rivetting.

The Class 50 needed seven tons of copper, but the Class 52 made do with 128lbs. Like the Class 50's, feedwater heaters and pumps were replaced by injectors. One sandbox instead of two, and glass wool insulation for boiler and cylinders were also features of the Class 52.

There were three types of tender; one type, known as 'bathtubs', had a semi-cylindrical tank, while another had a clever device that changed the pressure exerted by the tender brakes in accordance with the changing weight of the tender as coal and water were consumed. Another tender design offered sleeping accommodation for the crew, a very valuable feature for service behind the lines, when trains might take days to break through to their destination.

The Class 52 was produced with several variations. The earlier units had bar frames but many of the later batches were designed for plate frames. All in all, the Class 52 was a very versatile and trouble-free locomotive, with sufficient power to handle most freight trains and a maximum permissible speed of 80km/h (50mph) – enough for most passenger trains in wartime Europe. However, although it was undoubtedly a heavy-duty locomotive, the Germans realised that there was a need for heavier and more powerful locomotives where track and bridges could take them.

Until 1943, this need was met by the heavy three-cylinder Class 44 2-10-0, but its construction was extravagant in man hours and materials so a heavier version of the Class 52 was built. This was

the Class 42, a Kriegslok, and which combined the Class 52 chassis with a shortened 44-Class boiler, with a small increase in cylinder dimensions. It had an 18-ton axleload and 837 were built in 1943-5.

Because so many of the Kriegslok locomotives were built, in so many different places, and with large numbers being transferred from country to country, a definitive figure for the number built has never been obtained, but there were probably 6700 of the Class 52 and 900 of the Class 42. The number of locomotive works building this one design may be a record, but the Class 52 total of 6700 units is, perhaps surprisingly, not a record, because two Russian locomotive designs were built in even greater numbers.

German works built most of the engines, Borsig being the pioneer with Henschel, Jung, Krauss-Maffei, Orenstein & Koppel, Schichau, Schwartzkopff and Esslingen joining in. The Graffenstaden Works in Alsace also participated. One Polish works built considerable numbers, and so did Skoda in Czechoslovakia and the Vienna Locomotive works. The four big Belgian locomotive works also built them, but somehow contrived to delay completion of their units until after the war. Many other works built boilers. In addition, a works in the Soviet Union assembled Kreigsloks from spare parts and damaged locomotives overtaken during the Red Army's westward offensives.

For a few years after the war, the Kriegsloks, both in East and West Germany and much of Europe as well, were the mainstay of services on the war-torn railways. Many of the Class 42s were acquired by Soviet and Polish railways, together with hundreds of Class 52s. Russia acquired about 2000 engines and used them mainly in the Ukraine and Byelorussia. When they were eventually replaced by Soviet-built locomotives, many were transferred to railways in other Soviet bloc and central European countries.

The replacement of the Kreigsloks by newer designs was not always advantageous; the Class 42 that was used for passenger trains in Moldavia could haul 750 tons over the steeply graded main line, but the Soviet passenger engines sent to replace them could only manage 500 tons. In the flatlands of the Ukraine, the German engines were usually given trains of up to 2000 tons, but on occasion 4000-ton trains were tackled.

Engines used by Soviet Railways had to be re-gauged, and some were returned to standard gauge when sold to Polish and Bulgarian railways later. But in general, the locomotives that went to Russia remained the least changed. Smoke deflector plates, which were fitted to the Class elsewhere in Europe, were not fitted to the Russian engines.

For the post-war Austrian railways, the Kriegslok remained the standard heavy freight engine up to the end of steam. In France, on the other hand, all three designs (Classes 50, 52 and 42) remained in the background and had relatively short lives. In West Germany, the class survived almost to the end of steam. In the German Democratic Republic, the 50 and 52 classes outlasted the state itself. Here and there in eastern and central Europe, Kriegsloks can still be encountered at locomotive depots.

▲ After the war, the Austrian Kriegsloks became that country's standard heavy freight locomotive. This plate-framed example is shown working for a large Austrian private railway in the 1960s. Like other Austrian and East German units of the class, it has been fitted with a Giesl ejector and chimney.

Richard Wagner
Richard Wagner was responsible for the design of the Class 50, from which the Kriegslok classes were developed. As head of the DR design bureau Wagner had introduced a range of standard locomotives as well as the pair of streamlined 4-6-4 engines, Class 05, that proved capable of 124 mph. But the 01 and 03 Pacifics were probably his best-known designs. Wagner was a member of Britain's Royal Society and a holder of the Iron Cross, won in World War I. He retired in 1942, but was hauled out of retirement by the British in 1946 to oversee the running of the Frankfurt railway district.

Photographed at Izmir Basmane station, TCDD No 56517 was one of 53 Kriegsloks to
be supplied to Turkey in 1943–4. No 56517 was built by Maschinenbau und
Bahnbedarf in Berlin.

C38 class 4-6-2

NEW SOUTH WALES GOVERNMENT RAILWAYS

The C38s were the most successful locally designed and built express passenger locomotives in Australia. They incorporated many notable features and gave fast and reliable service. Three have survived into preservation.

The New South Wales Government Railways (NSWGR), built to the 4ft 8½in gauge – unlike the other states, which used either 5ft 3in or 3ft 6in – were more noted for elderly 4-6-0 and 2-8-0 steam engines on rural branches and main lines than for a steady influx of powerful modern locomotives.

Sections of the railway were heavily graded. On the north main line, for instance, the southbound climb from the Hawkesbury River was at 1 in 40 to 1 in 50 for five miles, while on the south line grades of 1 in 66 to 1 in 75 abounded, with one 17 mile section at 1 in 75 with short breaks; train loadings were such that a lot of double-heading was necessary on the severely graded sections.

The problem had been recognized soon after World War I. In 1921 and 1922, outline schemes had been prepared for 4-6-2s, one having three cylinders, but they were not proceeded with. From 1925, new large two-cylinder 4-6-0s (the C36 class) were constructed for working the heavy express traffic in the coastal belt and on the interstate south line to Victoria, and ultimately 75 engines of this class were built.

Inadequate power

The C36s were fine, capable engines with an excellent turn of speed, despite their 5ft 9in coupled wheels, but much double-heading was still necessary. There was even a later scheme to rebuild them as Pacifics, but it, too, came to nothing. Four years later came the D57 class 4-8-2s, 25

KEY FACTS

NSWGR C38 class 4-6-2
Nos 3801-3805 streamlined; 3806-3830 non-streamlined; 30 locomotives
Designer: Harold Young
Built: 1943-49. Clyde Engineering Co, Sydney and Eveleigh and Cardiff works
Service: Heavy express passenger trains from Sydney
Livery: Wartime – grey. 1947-48 – mid-green with lining. From 1950s – plain black with red lining
Performance: Max drawbar hp 2300 at 50mph. Max recorded speed 90mph
Withdrawn: 1961-73

▼The C38s were noted for their smooth riding characteristics. This was because the rotating masses only were balanced giving less hammer-blow on the track. On 24 October 1988, No 3801 waits for the signal before backing off Seymour shed. Currently, this is the only member of the class preserved in working order.

Bridge trouble
Throughout World War II, the Newcastle – Sydney service suffered from infuriating delays due to a structural fault in the Hawkesbury River bridge. Speed restrictions became more severe until finally a 5mph limit was imposed – providing the brakes were not used. This restriction led to express times being eased by as much as 14 minutes. A new bridge was constructed parallel with the old structure. On 24 June 1964, the new bridge was tested by two groups of three C38s thundering across it in parallel.

heavy three-cylinder freight engines with restricted route availability for heavy haul work. Otherwise, NSWGR went into World War II with almost all its engines of pre-1918 provenance.

But the inadequacy of the C36s for traffic needs would not go away, and a locomotive was needed which could work 450 tons unassisted over the south line. After investigating existing modern designs in Europe and North America for a suitable locomotive type, a Beyer-Garratt 4-6-4+4-6-4 based on the Algerian engines of 1936 was recommended because its lighter axleloads and spread of weight gave wide route availability. However, the Chief Commissioner would have none of it, so the Chief Mechanical Engineer was obliged to change tack.

In 1938, work started to design a two-cylinder 4-6-2. For various reasons the design work was prolonged, and an order for five engines, placed

▲The C38s powered the last steam hauled express trains in Australia. Their most famous trains were the Newcastle flyers between Sydney and Newcastle – a distance of 104 miles – which was often completed in 138 minutes. On 24 October 1988, No 3801 glides along the track at Mathiesons siding north of Wandong, with a Melbourne – Seymour excursion.

with Clyde Engineering Co, Sydney in December 1938 at least partly as an unemployment relief measure, was backed by little more than an outline specification.

It was to be four more years before the first engine came from the works – such were the supply difficulties brought about by the war. Even then, a considerable amount of material was manufactured in railway workshops to speed construction. But it was a splendid machine that eventually emerged from Clyde's erecting shop in January

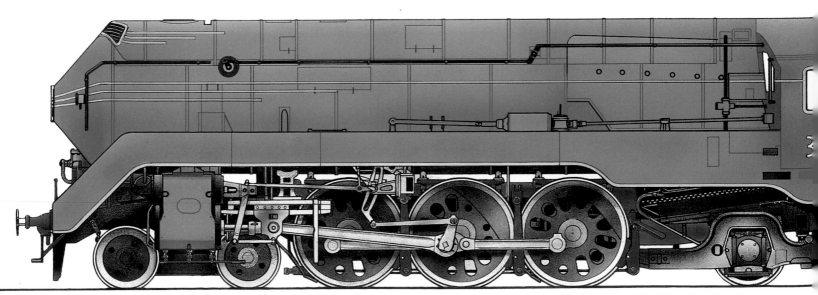

1943. Classed C38, numbered 3801 and painted in wartime grey, it was soon followed by four more.

Much of the design followed North American practice. Plate frames were shunned and a one-piece cast steel bed-frame, complete with cylinders, main air reservoir and all mounting brackets, was adopted. This was designed in detail by the General Steel Castings Corporation in the USA, the only firm producing such castings. The bed-frame weighed 18.7 tons and was reckoned to be four tons lighter than a built-up one – this weight saving was invested in the boiler. The bogie and trailing truck frames were also one piece castings from the same source.

The boiler, of nickel steel, worked at 245lb psi pressure – the highest figure on any Australian railway. It had a tapered barrel and wide Belpaire firebox. The steel inner firebox was rivetted, rather than welded, and contained no less than five arch tubes. A 36-element superheater was provided, with a multiple valve regulator in the header. The smokebox was fitted with baffle plates and mesh screens to be self-cleaning.

The coupled wheels were 5ft 9in diameter, and all axles ran in SKF roller bearings. The 21½in diameter cylinders were fed by 12in piston valves with 6½in travel and the whole steam circuit was generously proportioned to minimize pressure drop. A Franklin power reverser was provided. The bogie tender, weighing 83½ tons loaded, held 14 tons of coal and no less than 8100 gallons of water. A retractable tablet catcher, mounted below the footplate on the left-hand side, was operated from above. A five-chime whistle was, unusually, fixed horizontally to the side of the chimney.

Streamlined styling

An outstanding feature of the C38 was the streamlining and general styling which had overtones of the German Class 05 4-6-4. Grilles in the front of the styling casing admitted air which was deflected upwards behind the single chimney to prevent exhaust drifting to obscure the driver's view.

Hardly had No 3801 proved itself before orders were placed at the railway workshops at Eveleigh and Cardiff for 25 further engines of the class, each plant building alternate numbers. These locomotives were delivered between 1945 and 1949, and differed from the first five mainly in the absence of the skyline casing and conical smoke-

LOCO LIST

Between 1943 and 1949, 30 C38 class Pacifics were built. Nos 3801-3805 were streamlined and 3806-3830 were non-streamlined. None of the class was named.

Where to see them
Three engines escaped the torch. No 3801 is now preserved in running order for steam enthusiasts, while Nos 3820 and 3830 are kept as static exhibits.
● **3801** NSW Transport Museum, Thirlmere
● **3820** NSW Transport Museum
● **3830** Museum of Applied Arts & Sciences

◀ The liveries of the C38s were changed at least twice. The first five locomotives were given wartime plain grey, but in 1947-48 they were painted a medium green livery with horizontal yellow lines.
No 3805 was the first of the streamlined C38s to receive this livery and the locomotive shows off its lines soon after overhaul in May 1946.

High speed finale
The Class C38s were the fastest steam locomotives ever to run in Australia. Although the authorized speed limit on NSWGR was 70mph, some drivers coaxed their charges up to 90mph on occasion – outperforming many contemporary diesel locomotives. Towards the end of their working life many C38s were given a final fling on express passenger work and more than one bowed out with a last run of 70mph.

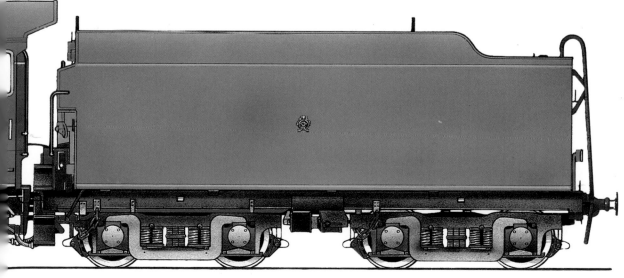

◀ Some railway historians have said that R A Riddles and E S Cox, who designed the BR Standard Britannia 4-6-2s, were influenced by the look of the C38 class. This may have originated from similarities in styling, but it seems more likely that any foreign influence in the Britannias sprang from E S Cox's visit to the USA in 1945.

Design specifications CLASS C38

2 cylinders: 21½in diameter x 26in stroke
Coupled wheels: 5ft 9in
Boiler diameter: 6ft 6⅛in
Grate area: 47sq ft
Boiler pressure: 245lb psi
Tractive effort: 36,200lb
Coal capacity: 14 tons
Water capacity: 8100 gallons
Length over buffers: 76ft 4⅝in
Weight in working order:
Engine: 111.7 tons
Tender: 83.5 tons

▼In 1988, NSWGR celebrated Australia's bicentennial by running a number of special steam hauled excursions using vintage motive power. On 22 October 1988, No 3801, on the 4ft 8½in track, passes Wandong station, while on the 5ft 3in lines Nos R761 and 639 double-head a train on its left. No K153 is seen in the distance.

box outer door.

All members of the class were initially allocated to Eveleigh shed, Sydney, whence they worked north to Newcastle, south to Albury on the Victoria border and west to Dubbo (assisted over the Blue Mountains). Nominally restricted initially to 70mph, this was more honoured in the breach, and at least one maximum of 90mph was recorded. The class could develop more than 2000hp and was light on coal.

Once in service, the authorities were soon to find out what a C38 could do. At first, working south, they ran the 399 miles to Albury without change – out one day and back the next. In each direction, coal was taken at the Demondrille coaling plant, 158 miles from Albury, without detaching the engine from the train. But on some workings it proved feasible to change engines at Cootamundra, giving the locomotives a daily out-and-home mileage of 530.

Smart look

Liveries on the class were changed at least twice. When new, Nos 3801-3805 wore wartime plain grey, but gained the medium green livery with horizontal yellow lines in 1947-48. The remaining

▲The C38s incorporated many notable features, particularly principles of North American practice employed at Alco. The boiler could produce enough steam to sustain very high cylinder horsepower – when working uphill, or very fast, full boiler pressure could be maintained without excessive firing.

engines carried this colour from new with red and straw lining. From the early 1950s, this changed to all-over black with red lining. A few reverted to green lining in later years.

The inauguration of electrification to Lithgow in 1957 displaced the C38s from the Dubbo route, though they returned to Lithgow later. Diesel traction began to erode their work on the south main line, although they lived on until 1964. Six of the class were transferred to Broadmeadow (Newcastle) in 1960 to continue the express work to Sydney, although in that year the wires reached Gosford, curtailing steam working to only 54 miles. This lasted until 1969, when electric working began throughout.

The general loss of work led to many C38s being put into store from 1963, and withdrawal, which had started in 1961, was completed with No 3813 in 1973.

Niagara class 4-8-4

NEW YORK CENTRAL RAILROAD

The Niagaras were the last word in US steam express passenger locomotives and were designed to move thousand-ton express trains at a hundred miles an hour. But the onset of dieselization meant that these mighty machines had no more than ten years of life.

The New York Central Railroad (NYC) Niagara 4-8-4s were, perhaps, the ultimate expression of the two-cylinder simple expansion steam locomotive capable of developing nearly 7000hp. In their brief heyday, they worked heavy express passenger trains between Harmon, a New York suburb, and Chicago 928 miles away.

Initially, the NYC headed north up the Hudson River Valley, with its considerable curvature, before swinging west at Albany, where it encountered the route's only severe gradients, before skirting the southern shore of Lake Erie. In contrast to the more mountainous Pennsylvania route, the NYC line was popularly known as the Water Level Route. Because of its undemanding gradients, six-coupled passenger locomotives of ever increasing size and performance were sufficient from 1903 until 1943.

By the early 1940s, even the latest 4-6-4s were becoming hard pressed on the most demanding duties and the need arose for eight-coupled wheels. Since 1916, the NYC had built up a huge fleet of 4-8-2 Mohawk-type fast freight and mixed traffic engines. Unlike the Pennsylvania Railroad, which was unusual in designing and building most of its own locomotives, the NYC always used private builders, in particular the American Locomotive Company (Alco) in Schenectady.

Design process

The NYC was closely involved in the design process and its prototypes were thoroughly road tested to an extent which was unusual in the USA. After studying the performance characteristics of the latest 4-6-4 and 4-8-2 designs, a provisional specification for a large passenger 4-8-4 was drawn up in mid-1943. This was done under the NYC motive power and rolling stock chief engineer, Paul W Kiefer, who was responsible for the highly successful Hudson 4-6-4s.

Because of World War II, the development of new locomotive designs was prohibited by the US War Production Board, but permission was given to NYC and Alco for a solitary prototype in April 1944. This was somewhat similar to the latest Union Pacific 4-8-4s, but had Baker, rather than Walschaerts, valve gear. Twenty-five production engines, Nos 6001-6025 were ordered in January 1945, to meet urgent traffic needs. The prototype, numbered 6000 in expectation of the locomotive developing 6000hp, was completed in March. It was essentially a standard engine, with the real groundwork done by the servicing and maintenance staff to achieve the high monthly mileages expected. The production engines were modified during construction in the light of

▼On 23 June 1950, Niagara No 6025, the last to be built, departs from La Salle Street station in Chicago with the New England States express bound for New York. Before the advent of air travel, there were 12 trains a day between the two cities. Often loaded to 15 cars, these trains would be whisked along the 928 mile journey in under 16 hours.

LOCO LIST

27 S1 4-8-4 Niagaras were built
including the prototype.
Another was fitted with poppet
valve gear which gave rise to
three sub-classes.
6000 S1a
6001-25 S1b
5500 S2a

Secrets of success
One of the key secrets to the
power of the Niagaras lay in
their excellent steam flow
circuit. This came about
following discussions
between Paul Lipetz, the
chief consulting engineer at
Alco, and the outstanding
French engineer André
Chapelon.

Lipetz was a Pole who
had been sent by Lenin to
the US as Technical
Representative of the USSR,
to learn about American
railroad technology. When
Lenin died, he was asked by
Stalin to return to Russia.
Lipetz wisely refused and
joined Alco instead.

▼The Niagara 4-8-4s had an
unusually smooth outline for a
US locomotive, with little
outside pipe work. There was
no steam dome at the top of
the boiler and the chimney was
7in tall. The 4-10-0 centipede
tenders had an 11ft rear
overhang in order to fit a 100ft
diameter turntable, and a coal
capacity of 41 tons, which was
consumed at the rate of four
tons per hour.

exhaustive tests carried out with the prototype.

Delivery of the NYC 4-8-4s, known as
Niagaras, began in October 1945. They were not
the largest American 4-8-4s, but a height restriction of 15ft $2^{3}/_{4}$in, with a boiler outside diameter of
8ft 4in, resulted in a chimney 7in tall. There was
no steam dome; the steam was collected through a
perforated pipe instead. The total wheelbase
included an excessive 11ft tender overhang in
order to fit existing 100ft diameter turntables.
Roller bearings were fitted to all axles and driving
rods to increase mileage, and to save weight, aluminium was used for running boards, cabs and
smoke deflector plates.

On test, No 6000, with its boiler pressure temporarily increased from 275 to 290lb psi, developed a peak of 6997hp – twice as much horse
power per ton as a 1907 NYC non-superheated
4-6-2. These tests also tried out two sets of coupled wheels, 6ft 3in and 6ft 7in diameter; the larger size, as used on the NYC 4-6-4s, was chosen.
Some modifications were also made to the firebox

▲On 30 May 1955, No 6016 stands at Englewood
depot, Chicago, shortly before withdrawal. Although
only in service for 10 years, the Niagaras hauled
more tons and ran more miles than engines which
had been in service far longer.

proportions, ashpan and trailing bogie truck in the
production engines.

It was calculated that a 4-8-4 could accelerate a
15-car 900-ton passenger train, on straight and
level track, from 0-60mph in $3^{1}/_{2}$ minutes, compared with five minutes by a J3a 4-6-4. The 4-8-4
was superbly designed with every modern feature,
including spring-loaded lateral motion control
devices on the coupled axles and Franklin automatic axlebox wedge adjustment to stop axlebox
knock – common on large two-cylinder locomotives. They incorporated the latest balancing techniques to minimize hammer blow on the track and
as a result they rode beautifully at high speeds.

Because no steam locomotive was allowed
inside the city limits of New York, the 4-8-4s took

over from third-rail electric traction 32 miles out and ran to Chicago. Water was picked up at speeds of 80mph from several sets of track pans (water troughs) – unusual for a US railroad. This meant that the Niagara tenders had more space for coal and only needed refuelling once every trip. Roughly mid-way, at Wayneport, their ashpans were cleaned and the coal supply was replenished from overhead chutes. The huge 4-10-0 centipede tenders had a record coal capacity of over 40 tons, which was normally consumed at the rate of at least four tons per hour. Such was the length of the mechanical stoker feed screws, that they sometimes broke, resulting in No 5500 being provided with a unique twin-screw arrangement.

NYC servicing procedures for steam were highly organized, achieving up to 16,000 miles per month with the J3a 4-6-4s. From new in May 1946 until March 1947, one of the Niagaras (No 6024) covered 227,000 miles, roughly equivalent to a quarter of a million miles per annum on express passenger and fast freight trains – a world record for steam traction.

Diesel challenge

On 1 April 1947, the Niagaras hauled the Twentieth Century Limited express to an accelerated 15½hr schedule, working from Harmon to Chicago without engine change. But all too soon they were to be challenged by the diesels introduced to overcome the effects of the 1947 coal strike. In addition, the original rivetted boiler shells, made from carbon/silicon steel to save weight, began to suffer from serious fatigue problems. Fusion-welded replacements in carbon steel solved the problem and were provided from late 1947 until 1950, by which time Alco decided that its future lay with diesel traction, in which General Motors was predominant, and had withdrawn from steam locomotive construction.

Although the NYC possessed state of the art steam power with its new 4-8-4s, Kiefer decided to conduct the most fair and exhaustive tests ever undertaken between steam and diesel traction. He compared six 4-8-4s in passenger service against twin-unit Co-Co diesel-electrics of 2000hp each, with separate freight tests between two four-unit

◄ The sheer power of a Niagara is demonstrated by No 6019 pulling the Advance Commodore Vanderbilt express. The sight of these 405-ton steam locomotives, hauling a 900-ton express train at up to 100mph, mile after mile, lasted 10 years. In its day it was an awe inspiring sight.

Where to see them
No Niagaras survive today, although a valiant attempt was made to preserve a J3 Hudson. In 1956, the president of the NYC, S J Pearlman, was approached by two members of the Smithsonian Institution seeking to buy a J3. Pearlman shared the prevailing American view that steam was out of date technology, and once the locomotives were withdrawn he had them scrapped.

Design specifications NIAGARA 4-8-4

PT-5 TENDER

CAB WIDTH 10'-2" (FRONT) 9'-10 7/8" (REAR)

ENGINE DESIGNED FOR 18°30'CURVE

WATER 18000 GALS
COAL 46 TONS

5400hp diesels and two L4 Mohawk 4-8-2s of similar maximum power. The 4-8-4s normally worked at an average of 4000hp, or two-thirds maximum capacity, but were capable of equalling the performance of a 6000hp three-unit diesel.

Comparisons showed that in terms of construction costs, the diesels were about half as much again as steam, and in terms of cost per rated horsepower, more than twice as much as a 4-8-4. In the steam/diesel tests, 4-8-4s averaged 24,000 miles a month compared with 27,000 for the two-unit 4000hp diesels. The diesels had a slightly greater availability for work (74%, compared with 69% for the Niagaras). Overall operating costs per mile for the two-unit 4000hp diesels were slightly lower at $1.11, against $1.22 for the Niagara steam locomotives, but were much higher at $1.48 for a three-unit 6000hp diesel. A significant proportion of this cost was fuel. While the overall drawbar thermal efficiency – the percentage of energy latent in the coal burned by the engine, channelled into pulling a train – was only 6% for the 4-8-4, compared with 22% for the diesel, the

▲The 4-8-4 S1 Niagara was the last US express steam passenger locomotive to be designed. These impressive machines could reach 100mph in 16 minutes with 912 tons from a dead stand – then sustain 102mph on level track. At 101sq ft, their fire grate area was the size of a small room.

cost of coal was a third of that for oil, but during the 1940s, railroad coal supplies were repeatedly jeopardized by miners' strikes.

Final fling
The Niagaras remained in service until replaced by diesel electrics following the NYC's policy decision of 1947. They spent their last years employed on fast freight duties. The legendary depot at Harmon closed to steam in the late summer of 1953, but NYC 4-8-4s could still be seen heading named passenger trains in Indiana and Ohio during 1954. The final active survivor, No 6015, was withdrawn in June 1956 and the era of the American express steam passenger train was nearly over.

TECHNICAL FILE

6001-25
2 cylinders: 25½in diameter, 32in stroke
Coupled wheels: 6ft 7in diameter
Grate area: 101sq ft
Boiler diameter: 8ft 4in maximum
Boiler pressure: 275lb psi
Tractive effort: 61,750lb
Coal capacity: 41 tons
Water capacity: 15,000 gallons
Length over couplers: 115ft 5½in
Weight in working order:
Engine: 214 tons
Tender: 190.7 tons

Special engine
A unique Niagara, No 5500, appeared in June 1946, equipped with Franklin poppet valve gear and a twin-screw mechanical stoker. Although it was constructed with a welded firebox, like the other members of the class, it soon needed a replacement barrel. The locomotive had some teething troubles in service. It was a non-standard locomotive and further work on poppet valves had been stopped. It was retired in 1951, after only five years' work, and cannibalized for spare parts.

Niagara No 6002 freshly outshopped from Beech Grove Works waits to leave
Englewood station with the all-Pullman Advance Commodore Vanderbilt in March 1946.
The train was named after a 19th-century president of the New York Central Railroad.

Niagara No 6000 passes Englewood station with the Mail train in October 1948.

242.A1 4-8-4

SOCIETE NATIONALE DES CHEMINS DE FER FRANCAIS

The most powerful European steam passenger loco ever built was the master work of the French designer André Chapelon. He packed the raw power of an American engine into a European sized frame to create a locomotive that astonished the railway world.

▼Powerful locomotives such as No 242.A1 were designed to sustain speed on steep gradients with minimal coal consumption. The high cost of coal was one of the quite specific factors that influenced French locomotive design. Other factors included the practice of allocating a locomotive to one driver, often for years at a time, thorough crew training – and even Napoleon III's decree that passenger trains could not exceed 120km/h (75mph) without permission.

It is difficult to exaggerate the importance of André Chapelon in the development of the 20th century steam locomotive. His design developments transformed French motive power and profoundly influenced the last generation of British locomotive engineers to work with steam. Even *Mallard*'s world record breaking performance of 1938 was due in part to a Chapelon development, the Kylchap exhaust system.

André Chapelon was born in 1892. After he had served in World War I he graduated from the Ecole Centrale technical university in Paris in 1921. He immediately joined the Paris, Lyon & Méditerranée Railway (PLM) but resigned in 1924 when the company ignored his suggestions for improvements to the designs of its locomotives. Chapelon then joined the engineering staff of a telephone company but was tempted back to steam by an offer from the Paris – Orléans Railway (PO) in 1925.

First steps

André Chapelon's first job for his new employer was to improve the performance of the fleet of four-cylinder compound 4-6-2s it used on its main lines to the Atlantic coast to haul its heaviest

▶ Because No 242.A1 carried a large boiler, Chapelon fitted a triple Kylchap exhaust and chimney to develop maximum draught for steam production. The term Kylchap is a combination of the names of the joint inventors – the Finnish engineer Kylala and Chapelon.

trains. For their size these engines were disappointing performers whose power output was limited by restricted steam flow and inadequate superheat.

Chapelon always paid great attention to the steam flow circuit in locomotives. He had studied the work of Kylala in Finland and Legein in

Belgium and developed the Kylala-Chapelon (Kylchap) system. This was applied successfully to several locomotive types, which improved steaming and reduced back pressure in the cylinders. But it was clear to Chapelon that a major rebuild of the 4-6-2s was necessary to achieve their full potential.

Chapelon's first completely rebuilt 4-6-2, No 3566, emerged from the Tours works of the PO in November 1929. It incorporated very large steam flow and exhaust passages, poppet valves actuated by oscillating cams from the existing Walschaerts valve gear, a double Kylchap blastpipe and chimney, and a thermic syphon in the firebox.

On its first trials No 3566 produced 3000hp in the cylinders where the previous superheated Pacifics could not better about 2200hp. At normal rates of working, the rebuilt 4-6-2 gave 35% more power and used 20% less coal than its contemporaries. The resulting sensation catapulted Chapelon to fame in the railway world but irritated the more conservative engineers, particularly those at the Office Central des Etudes du Matériel (OCEM).

Further rebuilds

The PO also sought to improve the running on its line to Toulouse which featured many long 1 in 100 gradients. These needed a more powerful engine, with greater adhesion, than any on their roster. Chapelon suggested that, rather than take the conventional step to build a 4-8-2, which had been done on other railways, a rebuild of their four-cylinder compound 4-6-2s as 4-8-0s would give the desired results.

As well as the features built into No 3566, the 4-8-0 required a new boiler with a very long narrow firebox – a foot longer than that in the GWR King. The grate sloped quite steeply at the front to make it easier to fire. The firebox contained a thermic syphon, and the boiler pressure was raised to 290lb per sq in. However, the frames from the original 4-6-2 were reused, although modified and greatly strengthened.

The first 4-8-0, No 4521, appeared in August 1932 and in the tests that followed it developed 3800 indicated horse power at 56mph and 4000ihp

▲The 4-8-4 was a rebuild of an earlier unsatisfactory machine. In the reconstruction, Chapelon made good use of the developments of other designers; he often said his key to success lay in building on their work.

at 70mph. Chapelon had produced a steam engine more powerful than the diesel-electric Deltic, which did not run on British rails until 1955.

Meanwhile the OCEM was asked by the Etat Railway to produce plans for a new 4-8-2. They felt that a simple expansion three-cylinder machine could be produced to equal the efficiency of Chapelon's rebuilt locomotives, while being less complicated, cheaper and more robust in critical areas such as the crank axle. The prototype, No 241.101, emerged in 1932 in a blaze of publicity.

Unfortunately this attempt to equal Chapelon's results was a failure. Not only did No 241.101 fail to outperform the Etat's own rebuilt Pacifics but it rode badly, causing damage to the track, and it

LOCO LIST

No 242.A1 was a rebuild of a simple three-cylinder machine of 1932, 4-8-2 No 242.101. Although other locomotives were planned – 4-8-4 heavy passenger, 4-6-4 high speed, 2-6-4 mixed traffic and 2-10-0 heavy freight – only No 242.A1 was completed. The locomotive was scrapped in 1961.

▲André Chapelon stands in front of his creation in 1946. He was the great great grandson of Englishman James Jackson, a Lancastrian steel founder who established the crucible melting process of steel making in St Etienne, France in 1814, near where No 242.A1 was built in 1946.

Compound locomotives

No 242.A1 was a three-cylinder compound locomotive, designed to use steam as efficiently as possible.

In the latter part of the 19th century many railway engineers tried to find ways to cut fuel costs in countries – like France – where coal was expensive. One solution to improve efficiency was to pass the steam through two sets of cylinders.

A compound locomotive passes the steam exhausted from one or more high pressure cylinders to the larger, low pressure ones, where expansion is completed.

The three-cylinder compound system used by No 242.A1 was based on that devised by Edouard Sauvage on a Nord Railway 2-6-0 in 1887. Because No 242.A1 was a prototype for testing, each set of cylinders had its own set of valve gear which was controlled independently by the driver.

was prone to derailment on sharp curves in depots. When, in 1939, its inside cylinder was fractured beyond repair, Chapelon, then with the recently nationalized SNCF, proposed the rebuilding of the locomotive as a three-cylinder compound. But this could not start until 1942 because of wartime conditions.

Improved design

Chapelon's first step was to strengthen the chassis of the disabled locomotive to permit a greatly increased power output. This increased the weight of the locomotive: the 4-8-2 was turned into a 4-8-4 by replacing the single axle trailing truck by a two-axle truck to spread the load.

The engine was converted to a three-cylinder compound using the system pioneered by Edouard Sauvage on a 2-6-0 for the Nord Railway in 1887 and later in the Smith system (as used by the Midland Railway in Britain). A single high pressure cylinder between the frames, driving the leading axle, exhausted into two outside low pressure cylinders driving the second axle. There was a reversion to piston valves, though with very large steam passages, although Chapelon preferred poppet valves which were much lighter.

As with all of Chapelon's rebuilds, care was taken to ensure unrestricted steam flow and the cross-sectional area of the steam and exhaust passages was greatly increased. Chapelon always said that he had learned the importance of this from Gaston du Bousquet of the Nord Railway, follow-

ing the early designs of Thomas Russell Crampton and the pre-World War I designs of George Churchward of the Great Western. Because of the large size of the boiler of the now re-numbered No 242.A1, Chapelon fitted a triple Kylchap exhaust and chimney to provide maximum draught for the 53.8sq ft grate which was fed by a mechanical stoker.

The last problem Chapelon had to tackle was the engine's poor riding. Drawing on the knowledge he gained on an earlier trip to the US, he modified the leading bogie to a design similar to that developed by the American Locomotive Company. This eliminated damage to the permanent way, and the engine rode very smoothly.

Outstanding success

Work on the locomotive was frequently interrupted by wartime problems and it was 18 May 1946 before No 242.A1 left the St Chamond works near St Etienne. It was immediately obvious that Chapelon had surpassed himself. When the transformed engine was put through its paces on the Vitry test bed, it developed 4000hp continuously at the tender drawbar, and more than 5000hp in the cylinders – the first time power on this scale had been recorded by a European steam locomotive. However, even this power was exceeded for short periods.

Test runs were made on ordinary service express trains strengthened with additional coaches and a dynamometer car and on these runs much time was recovered. On 19 September 1952 the

Design specifications No 242.A1

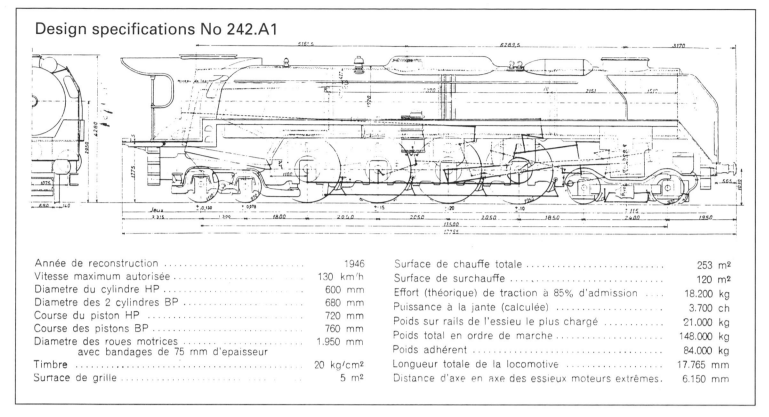

Année de reconstruction	1946	Surface de chauffe totale	253 m²
Vitesse maximum autorisée	130 km/h	Surface de surchauffe	120 m²
Diametre du cylindre HP	600 mm	Effort (théorique) de traction à 85% d'admission	18.200 kg
Diametre des 2 cylindres BP	680 mm	Puissance à la jante (calculée)	3.700 ch
Course du piston HP	720 mm	Poids sur rails de l'essieu le plus chargé	21.000 kg
Course des pistons BP	760 mm	Poids total en ordre de marche	148.000 kg
Diametre des roues motrices	1.950 mm	Poids adhérent	84.000 kg
avec bandages de 75 mm d'epaisseur		Longueur totale de la locomotive	17.765 mm
Timbre	20 kg/cm²	Distance d'axe en axe des essieux moteurs extrêmes.	6.150 mm
Surface de grille	5 m²		

▼In service No 242.A1 bettered the performance proposed for electric locomotives planned to run on the same line, which as a result were redesigned for increased sustained power ratings. This was a rare case of electric locomotive design being modified because of steam performance.

locomotive worked a 20-coach train of 810 tons from Paris to Le Mans, 211km (131 miles), at a net average speed of 116km/h (72mph). The net running time of 109 minutes was six minutes less than the fastest schedule over this section – normally with electric locomotive haulage and a lighter train. A group of visiting South American engineers, led by the eminent L D Porta, was very impressed. Chapelon's masterpiece was also very economical.

End of a legend

Unfortunately No 242.A1 had arrived too late. SNCF had decided that in the national interest it could no longer be dependent on expensive (and to some extent imported) coal. As far back as 1943 it was decided to electrify the Paris – Lyon main line. The 4-8-4 was transferred to Le Mans depot where the locomotive became the favourite of the local crews, who earned bonuses making up time lost on services from Paris to the Atlantic coast.

Steam locomotive construction ceased in 1952 after the French military authorities withdrew objections to the electrification of main lines from Paris to the north and east for which 100 three-cylinder compound 2-10-4s based on No 242.A1 had been ordered. These were cancelled and the unique 4-8-4 withdrawn from service.

The locomotive was put into store and remained at Le Mans depot until February 1961. Finally the locomotive was sent to St Brieuc and scrapped, despite appeals to the Ministry of Transport for its preservation and an offer of purchase from a Swiss locomotive enthusiast. However, the performance of No 242.A1 had persuaded the designers of PLM's new 2-D-2 electric locomotive to modify their proposals to produce a one hour rating of 4900hp instead of 3700hp.

▲A previous problem in three-cylinder compounds was to avoid a sharp pressure drop in the high pressure cylinder after the valves were opened to admit steam. Chapelon's solution was to use a very large high pressure steam chest around the cylinder which acted as a steam reservoir.

TECHNICAL FILE

Three cylinders: 1 high pressure 602 x 720mm (23²/₃ x 28¹/₃in) diameter; 2 low pressure 682 x 760mm (27 x 26⁴/₅in) diameter
Coupled wheels: 1950mm (6ft 4³/₄in) diameter
Boiler diameter: 1953mm (6ft 4⁷/₈in)
Grate area: 53⁴/₅ sq ft
Boiler pressure: 290lb psi
Tractive effort: 60,480lb
Coal capacity: 11¹/₂ tons
Water capacity: 7500 gallons
Length over buffers: (engine only) 17,767mm (58ft 3¹/₂in)
Total weight: 148 tonnes

Alco PA A1A-A1A

AMERICAN LOCOMOTIVE COMPANY

The Alco PAs have hauled passengers and freight for over 40 years. So popular have these diesels become in the folklore of American railroad enthusiasts, that the class has been accorded the status of honorary steam locomotive.

Railroad officials and mechanical engineers appreciate locomotives for how well they perform; railway enthusiasts cherish locomotives for how they sound and look. Among US diesel enthusiasts, a locomotive that has achieved fame of epic proportions – mostly on the strength of the physical proportions of its blunt, protruding nose – is the Alco-GE PA.

Whereas the Electro-Motive Division of General Motors (EMD) entered the railroad business without steam locomotive experience, the American Locomotive Company (Alco) was one of the big three steam builders. Seeing what the future held for steam, Alco made an early commitment to diesels. In partnership with the engine manufacturer Ingersol Rand and the electrical supplier General Electric (GE), Alco built their first standardized diesel locomotives between 1924-29. They acquired an engine company, McIntosh and Seymour, in 1929 and produced diesel shunters during the Depression of the 1930s.

In 1940, Alco introduced the DL-109, a streamlined needle-nose passenger unit styled by the noted designer Otto Kuhler. The DL-109 car body housed two separate diesel engines of just six cylinders each – EMD's competitive E units had two 12-cylinder engines. Seventy-four cab and four DL-110 booster units were sold by 1945, 60 of them to the New Haven Railroad.

◀ When introduced, the PAs were used on general passenger services. The eastern American giants, New York Central and Pennsylvania railroads, operated few PAs. On 17 August 1948, No 5759 of the Pennsylvania nestles amongst the infrastructure of the steam age.

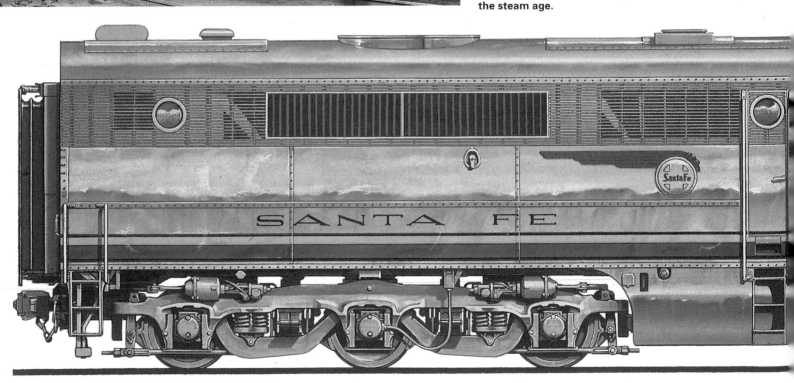

Alco engineers were also busy working on an improved turbocharged powerplant, the model 244. This superseded the earlier model 539 used in the DL-109, though this was installed in low-powered mixed traffic locomotives as late as 1957. In 1946, Alco produced the 12-cylinder 1500hp version in a high-powered mixed traffic locomotive, the RS-2, and in a Bo-Bo car body freight locomotive with a squared blunt nose, the FA-1. In the same year, a 16-cylinder 2000hp model was installed in a passenger locomotive, the PA-1, featuring A1A bogies and an elongated nose. Cabless booster units were designated PB-1. The electrical

▲The big, bold lines of an onrushing Alco PA were certainly an imposing sight, and offered a welcome change to the smoothly contoured lines of the E and F units, churned out by EMD of General Motors. With the locomotive painted in the famous Santa Fe warbonnet livery, a westbound Grand Canyon service calls at Streator station, Illinois.

▼Santa Fe No 51 was the first PA delivered and was an A-B-A trio of locomotives. The stylish gutter run-off strip over and behind the cab side windows was shortened on the later, more powerful, PA-3 model. The styling of the locomotive was the result of an inter-company contest and was won by a GE industrial designer called Ray Stevenson.

LOCO LIST

PA-1/PB-1: 170 cab and 40 booster units sold to US railroads
PA-2/PB-2: 28 cab and two booster units sold to US railroads
PA-3/PB-3: 49 cab and five booster units sold to US railroads; three cab units sold to Brazil
PA-4: Designation that DH gave to four ex-Santa Fe PA-1s it had rebuilt with Alco 261 V-12 2400hp engines by Morrison-Knudsen in 1975; locomotives later went to Mexico

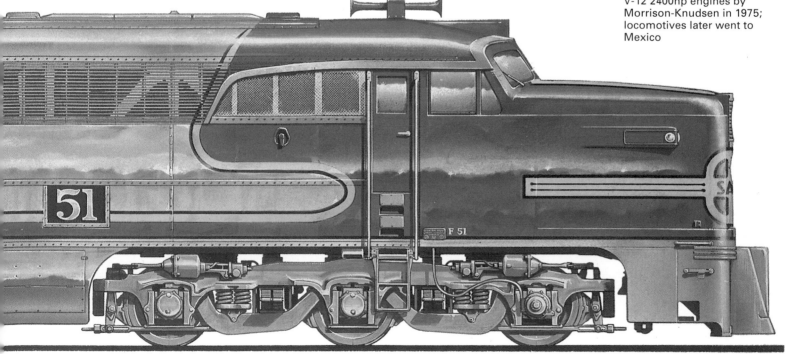

Where to see them
● **DH-16** – National
Railways of Mexico: stored
● **DH-17** – National
Railways of Mexico (former
DH-17, Santa Fe 60L):
operational
● **DH-18** – National
Railways of Mexico: stored
● **DH-19** – National
Railways of Mexico (former
DH-19, Santa Fe 54B, 66L):
displayed at National
Railway Museum, Puebla

Car body
When talking about
American diesel
locomotives, the term car
body is often mentioned.
This refers to the method of
construction involved. Car
body designs use the
outside casing as part of the
integral structure of the
locomotive. Nowadays, with
engines like the F40PH, the
underframes are much
heavier and the outside
shells act only as covers and
are termed shrouds or
cowls.

equipment, including the big Model 752 traction motors, were provided by GE.

Following World War II, the railroads stood in line to order diesels; there was enough business for all the manufacturers. The PAs offered a contrast in design and operating philosophy to the EMD E units. With two non-turbocharged diesel engines, an E unit still had considerable capability should one engine fail. Shop time to work on an E unit engine was costly, however, because in effect two engines were taken out of service. Achieving the same horsepower in a single engine, the PAs also had fewer component support parts, which theoretically meant less maintenance.

The first A and B units were formed into a 6000hp three-unit A-B-A demonstrator set (which Alco billed as its 75,000th locomotive). This was painted black and tested on the Lehigh Valley. A month later it was sold to the Santa Fe which ordered an additional 26 cab and 15 booster units, all decorated in the famous silver-red-yellow warbonnet livery – which is to this day considered the aesthetic epitome of the PA fleet's many colour schemes.

Secondary service
Santa Fe's Alcos were not entrusted with the crack Chicago to west coast trains, such as the Chief and Super Chief, which were pulled by Bo-Bo EMD F units. Instead, they worked the secondary main line trains and many of the shorter runs through Texas and California. The railroads of western America preferred four-axle locomotives on fast trains through the Rockies because of their better adhesion on steeply graded track.

▲The distinctive burbling sound of the Alco engine and the emission of clouds of black smoke during acceleration remained unchanged throughout the Alco PA series. The last widescale use of the PAs was in the Erie Lackawanna fleet of 14, which hauled goods trains throughout 1968. Two of these locomotives, units Nos 862 and 863, give a display of smoke for which the PAs were famous.

Southern Pacific owned the largest fleet which consisted of 53 cabs and 13 booster units. Rio Grande bought six units in 1947 for the California Zephyr, but in a few years they were demoted to lesser trains. Three railroads – the Lehigh Valley, Nickel Plate and New Haven – initially relied solely on PAs for passenger service; by the 1960s, most of the eastern railways that did purchase PAs employed them on freight work.

One of the most prestigious assignments given to a member of the class, was to haul the 1947-48 exhibition tour of the American Freedom Train. The locomotive was then sold to Gulf, Mobile & Ohio.

Although EMD's E7 outsold the PA series almost two-to-one, 16 US railroads and subsidiaries ordered the PA-1 and its updated versions. Three units went to Brazil, and countries such as Australia, Greece and Pakistan bought somewhat similar export models.

In 1950, Alco began producing the PA-2/PB-2, an externally similar locomotive with the 244 engine uprated to 2250hp. In the PA-3/PB-3 model of 1952, minor external changes accompanied internal improvements in the fuel injection, crankshaft and turbocharger. Remaining

Design specifications ALCO PA A1A-A1A

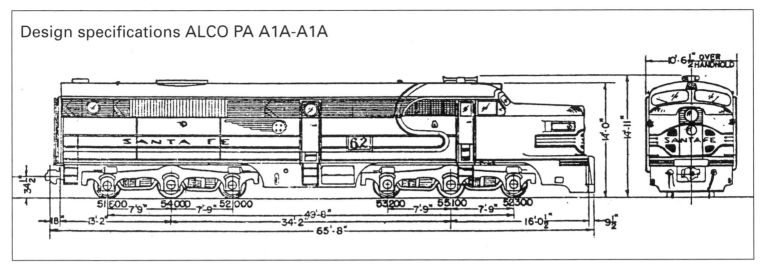

unchanged was the distinctive burbling sound of the Alco engine and the emission of black clouds of smoke during acceleration – caused by the time lag of the turbocharger as it speeded up to supply combustion air to the cylinders. From 1946-53, a total of 247 PA cabs and 47 PB booster units was built.

Uncertain future

Most PAs were retired during the 1960s. But in late 1967, a new Delaware & Hudson (DH) management bought four surplus Santa Fe PAs to spruce up a low-profile Albany, New York to Montreal, Quebec passenger service that had been operated with Alco mixed traffic locomotives. With the long nose painted in DH blue but retaining the Santa Fe stainless steel flanks, the four units began a cliff-hanging second life. DH passenger service ended with the creation of Amtrak in 1971; two PAs were leased to a tour operator

and two traded to GE. Then another new DH management took back the leased locomotives and reclaimed one from GE for company specials and enthusiasts' excursions.

In 1974, the state of New York offered to subsidize a New York – Montreal passenger service via the DH route; soon all four PAs were sent to Morrison-Knudsen at Boise, Idaho for rebuilding, including installation of new Alco 251 V-12 engines. In 1977, Amtrak turbotrains replaced the PAs, which were leased for Boston, Massachusetts commuter service in the following year. However, the quick acceleration and braking power demanded on suburban services were not suited to the PAs.

In 1978, the four PAs were sent to Mexico where they gradually suffered wrecks and mechanical failures. In 1989, one was surprisingly overhauled and placed in service, only to be moved to a museum in 1990.

▲With the GE traction motors in the long 21ft 11¹/₂in frames of the smooth riding bogies, the PAs were renowned for their excellent ride by the engine crews. Following their delivery from Alco, the Santa Fe Railroad gave their own PAs important internal improvements. This helped the electrical transmission and reliability.

TECHNICAL FILE

PA-1/PB-1
Wheel arrangement: A1A-A1A
Weight: 318,000lb
Length over couplers: 66ft 2in (A unit); 64ft (B unit)
Maximum speed: 80mph
Bogie wheel base: 15ft 6in
Wheel diameter: 40in
Diesel engine: One Alco 244 Vee 16-cylinder four cycle, turbocharged, rated 2000hp
Transmission: General Electric 5GT566C1 main generator; four General Electric traction motors
Tractive effort: 51,000lb
Fuel capacity: 1200 US gallons
Water capacity: 1800 US gallons for steam generator in PA-1

◄ The Southern Pacific Railroad owned the largest fleet of Alco PAs. It initially operated them on long distance services in the dazzling orange and red Daylight livery, but by the mid-1960s this colour scheme was phased out. On 11 November 1960, three different locomotives haul the Golden State Limited service through El Paso in Texas. The first unit is a PA3 coupled with an E7B and followed by two other E units.

The rounded contours of F unit No 35C hauling Santa Fe's westbound
Grand Canyon over Raton Pass provide a clear contrast to the more angular
profile of the later PA series.

Lima 2-8-4s

NICKEL PLATE ROAD

These 2-8-4s were the last main line steam locomotives to be built by a major American manufacturer. The type was progressively developed and undoubtedly the large wheeled version ranked among the most effective modern American steam locomotive designs of all.

KEY FACTS

NYC&StL Class S3 2-8-4
NYC&StL Nos 770-779
Designer: William Woodard
Built: 1949, Lima Locomotive Works, Lima, Ohio
Service: Express freight
Livery: Plain black with yellow lettering
Performance: On the Virginian Railroad, one 2-8-4 achieved 87mph on a downhill stretch. During dynamometer car tests, L&N M1 achieved a peak output of 4500 drawbar horsepower at 42mph.
Withdrawn: 1958, broken up 1961-63

Except when the American railroads came under direct government control during 1918-20, locomotive standardization was almost unknown during the steam era. However, between 1934 and 1949, the three major American locomotive builders, Alco, Baldwin and Lima, did produce 299 2-8-4s, with 5ft 9in coupled wheels and 90sq ft firegrates, to much the same design for seven different railroads. The first and last of these designs was for the New York Chicago & St Louis Railroad (NYC&StL), popularly known as the Nickel Plate Road (NKP).

Railroad empire

The NKP was one of a number of eastern railroads which were owned and administered by the two van Sweringen brothers, who had acquired it in 1916. By the 1920s, the railroad was facing tough competition from the giant Pennsylvania and New York Central systems, which had huge fleets of 4-8-2s with driving wheels of 6ft diameter. The NKP could only boast 2-8-0s and 2-8-2s, typical of that period.

The United States Railroad Administration (USRA) standard locomotives had been dominated by 4-6-2s, 2-8-2s and 2-10-2s, whose single-axle trailing trucks supported firegrates with sizes ranging from 67 to 88sq ft. The general philosophy of American railroads was to run heavier trains faster, with minimum maintenance costs.

In the early 1920s, designers at Lima, under the redoubtable Will Woodard, sought to enhance boiler capacity in order to sustain high horsepower at higher speeds. Lima's first essay in this direction was in 1922, with a large boilered 2-8-2 for the Michigan Central Railroad.

In February 1925, this design was eclipsed by a massive 2-8-4, with no less than 100sq ft of mechanically fired grate area in the huge firebox, which was supported by a large four-wheel trailing truck. Maximum cut-off was limited to 60% in forward gear to achieve greater expansion and more efficient use of steam when climbing gradients. Additional tractive effort was provided by a booster engine in the rear trailing truck.

Built as a demonstrator and labelled the Lima A1, this historic locomotive ran extensive trials on several railroads before being purchased by the Illinois Central Railroad (which eventually scrapped it in 1954). For the first time in the his-

▼In 1958, S2 No 766 arrives at Fort Wayne, Indiana, on its way to Calumet yard in Chicago, Illinois. It was not until the entry of America into World War II, with the consequent increase in railway traffic, that the 2-8-4 was brought to prominence. The War Production Board had forbidden the preparation of entirely new locomotive designs so existing designs continued to be built.

LOCO LIST

70 S series 2-8-4s were built for the NKP and completed in four batches from October 1934 to May 1949.
NKP Nos:
S 700-714
S1 715-729
S2 740-769
S3 770-779

Where to see them
Six NKP 2-8-4s were saved. Five S2s, Nos 755, 757, 759, 763 and 765 (renumbered 767) survive. Nos 759 and 765 have both worked special excursions. Of the final series, S3 No 779 is on display in a park in its native town of Lima.

Last out
The last main line steam locomotives to be completed by the major American manufacturers Alco and Lima were both 2-8-4s. Alco had completed its final steam locomotive in June 1948, leaving Baldwin to make the last commercial delivery of a steam locomotive (a compound 2-6-6-2 Mallet, for the C&O) to a major American railroad in September 1949. Despite the trend towards diesel traction, it is doubtful if anyone could have predicted that by 1959, only 10 years later, the last and most modern steam locomotives, built by these manufacturers – Lima works No 9830, Alco works No 75851 and Baldwin works No 74728 – would be awaiting the torch.

▲The S2 design was produced at Lima works from 1944 and was a refinement of two earlier classes. It included one-piece cast steel frame beds and roller bearings and set the pattern for the final series of 10 engines, designated Class S3. In 1956, S2 No 757 is seen in regular service at Calumet yard, Chicago, Illinois.

tory of locomotive design, theoretical boiler capacity exceeded cylinder demand at normal rates of working, making for greater efficiency and, therefore, fuel economy.

Into production
In early 1926, the first 25 production 2-8-4s were built for the Boston & Albany Railroad (B&A), whose lines ran through the Berkshire hills. Thereafter this wheel arrangement was generally known as the Berkshire. Although these engines perpetuated the 5ft 3in coupled wheel diameter of the pioneer A1, during 1927-29 the Erie Railroad took delivery of no fewer than 105 2-8-4s, from all three major builders, in which the driving wheel diameter was increased to 5ft 10in.

The Erie Railroad, like the NKP, was also owned by the van Sweringen brothers, who had the foresight to establish an overall Advisory Mechanical Committee (AMC). The AMC had produced the design specification for the huge C&O T1 class 2-10-4. Although essentially a larger version of the Erie 2-8-4s, the T1s incorporated two major improvements which became standard in future large American steam locomotives – a combustion chamber (an extension to the firebox) and a maximum cut-off to 80% (the limited cut-off of 60% had not proved successful).

Like the rest of the American railroad system, the NKP was badly hit by the Depression. In 1932,

▼Compared with its gigantic rivals in Schenectady, NY, and Philadelphia, PA, the Lima Locomotive works in Ohio was a relatively small concern. Nevertheless, it was by far the most innovative and it incorporated considerable refinement in its designs. The 2-8-4, 4-8-4 and the 2-10-4 were entirely new wheel arrangements and were part of the general philosophy of American railroads to run heavy trains at high speeds with minimal maintenance costs.

the domestic output of the three American locomotive builders fell to zero (compared to 1200 ordered only three years earlier). By July 1934, with the first green shoots of recovery, the NKP placed an order with Alco for 15 2-8-4s, which were delivered four months later. These locomotives were designated Class S and were a scaled down version of the Chesapeake & Ohio (C&O) 2-10-4 – with which they had a maximum interchangeability of components.

The original specification called for roller bearings throughout and a conical streamlined casing at the front end. But to keep costs down, these features were omitted. Numbered 700-714, the Class S 2-8-4s developed their peak drawbar horsepower at 40mph and normally hauled loads up to 4000 tons. However, the class had sufficient starting tractive effort to move a 10,000 ton coal train from cold when handed over to them by a C&O 2-10-4.

Further developments

In 1942, the Louisville & Nashville Railroad had received 14 2-8-4s from Baldwin. Classed M1, these engines were the ultimate in Super Power, being the first 2-8-4s to incorporate cast steel frame beds and roller bearings. Although dimensionally similar to the NKP engines, their piston stroke was reduced from 34 to 32in and boiler pressure increased from 245 to 265lb psi. Also, they sported Walschaerts, rather than Baker, valve gear.

During 1942-43, the NKP received a further 20 2-8-4s, Nos 715-729, Class S1, from Lima. These were substantially similar to the original 1934 design, but with separate cast frames and plain bearings. Rather more refinements, including one-

piece cast steel frame beds and roller bearings, were incorporated in Nos 740-769. These locomotives were designated as Class S2 and delivered in 1944.

As soon as World War II ended, diesel-electric locomotives began to make a rapid impact on American railroads. The NKP acquired its first main line diesels in late 1946. In June 1948, it made a detailed assessment of the relative operating costs of a steam 2-8-4 and the equivalent 4500hp diesel-electric units borrowed for fast freight service. Respective coal and oil fuel costs per gross ton mile were identical, and the diesel-electric showed no material advantage. Steam operation had long been developed to a high degree of locomotive utilization, with each of the 70 existing NKP 2-8-4s regularly averaging 7000-8000 miles per month in freight service.

NKP ordered 10 more 2-8-4s from Lima in July 1948, which proved to be their final steam order – although the company was still actively promoting

> ► The introduction in 1925 of the 2-8-4s by Lima began a new trend known as Lima Super Power. During initial trials, the locomotive's large firebox produced enough steam to make larger driving wheels more desirable; cruising speeds around 55mph were normal. On 3 January 1952, a westbound freight is hauled by S2 No 748 at Dunkirk, New York. The last revenue earning run by a NKP 2-8-4 was by S2 No 746 on 2 July 1958. However, five S2s survived into preservation.

NKP

The main route of the Nickel Plate Road ran for 523 miles from Buffalo, New York, to Chicago, via Fort Wayne, with major branches to St Louis, Peoria, Michigan and Toledo. The particularly fast single track Buffalo – Cleveland stretch ran along the southern shore of Lake Erie and largely duplicated the New York Central Water Level Route in this area. In American parlance, the NKP was described as a bridge carrier, as its prosperity depended on conveying freight from one railroad to another, principally across the states of Ohio and Indiana. Consequently, punctuality was essential.

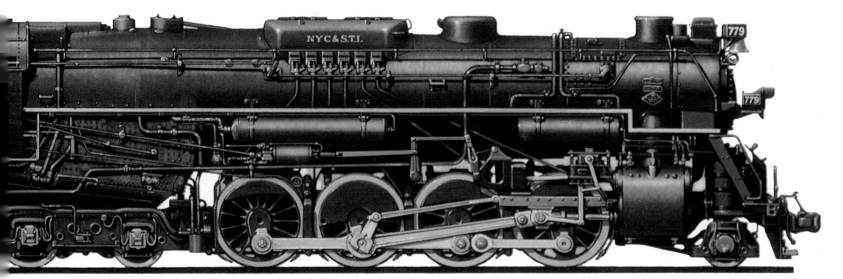

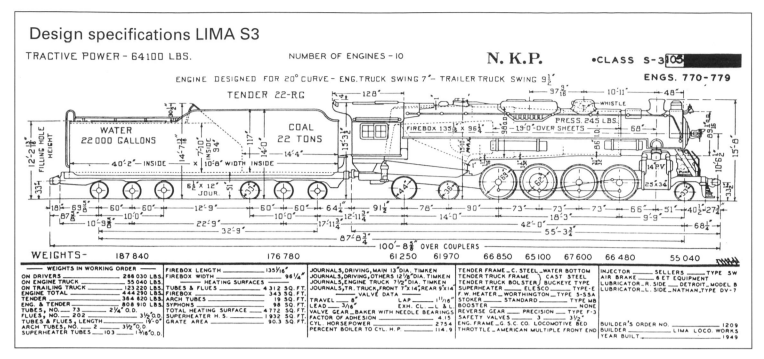

Design specifications LIMA S3

TRACTIVE POWER - 64100 LBS.   NUMBER OF ENGINES - 10   **N.K.P.**   •CLASS S-3 105   ENGS. 770-779

ENGINE DESIGNED FOR 20° CURVE - ENG.TRUCK SWING 7" - TRAILER TRUCK SWING 9½"

TENDER 22-RG   PRESS. 245 LBS.   WHISTLE

WATER 22 000 GALLONS   COAL 22 TONS   FIREBOX 135⅛ X 96¼   19'0" OVER SHEETS

40'2" INSIDE   10'8" WIDTH INSIDE

WEIGHTS-   187 840   176 780   61 250   61 970   66 850   65 100   67 600   66 480   55 040

100'-8½" OVER COUPLERS

WEIGHTS IN WORKING ORDER			
ON DRIVERS	288 030 LBS.	FIREBOX LENGTH	135 1/16"
ON ENGINE TRUCK	55 040 LBS.	FIREBOX WIDTH	96 1/4"
ON TRAILING TRUCK	123 220 LBS.	HEATING SURFACES	
ENGINE TOTAL	444 290 LBS.	TUBES & FLUES	4 312 SQ. FT.
TENDER	364 620 LBS.	FIREBOX	343 SQ. FT.
ENG. & TENDER	808 910 LBS.	ARCH TUBES	19 SQ. FT.
TUBES, NO. 73	2¼" O.D.	SYPHONS	98 SQ. FT.
TUBES, NO. 202	3½" O.D.	TOTAL HEATING SURFACE	4 772 SQ. FT.
TUBES & FLUES, LENGTH	19'-0"	SUPERHEATER H.S.	1 932 SQ. FT.
ARCH TUBES, NO. 2	3½" O.D.	GRATE AREA	90.3 SQ. FT.
SUPERHEATER TUBES 103	1 9/16" O.D.		

JOURNALS,DRIVING,MAIN 13"DIA. TIMKEN			
JOURNALS,DRIVING,OTHERS 12⅛"DIA. TIMKEN			
JOURNALS,ENGINE TRUCK 7½"DIA. TIMKEN			
JOURNALS,TR. TRUCK,FRONT 7"x14",REAR 9"x14"			
VALVE DATA			
TRAVEL 8"	LAP 1 11/16"		
LEAD 3/16"	EXH. CL. L & L		
VALVE GEAR BAKER WITH NEEDLE BEARINGS			
FACTOR OF ADHESION	4.15		
CYL. HORSEPOWER	2754		
PERCENT BOILER TO CYL. H.P.	114.9		

TENDER FRAME C. STEEL WATER BOTTOM		
TENDER TRUCK FRAME CAST STEEL		
TENDER TRUCK BOLSTER BUCKEYE TYPE		
SUPERHEATER ELESCO TYPE-E		
F. W. HEATER WORTHINGTON TYPE 5-SSA		
STOKER STANDARD TYPE MB		
BOOSTER NONE		
REVERSE GEAR PRECISION TYPE F-3		
SAFETY VALVES 3 3½"		
ENG. FRAME G.S.C. CO. LOCOMOTIVE BED		
THROTTLE AMERICAN MULTIPLE FRONT END		

INJECTOR SELLERS TYPE SW	
AIR BRAKE 6 ET EQUIPMENT	
LUBRICATOR-R. SIDE DETROIT-MODEL B	
LUBRICATOR-L. SIDE NATHAN TYPE DV-7	
BUILDER'S ORDER NO. 1209	
BUILDER LIMA LOCO. WORKS	
YEAR BUILT 1949	

▲Little is known of the 2-8-4s' tractive performance. One of the Louisville & Nashville Railroad Class M1s achieved 4500 drawbar horsepower at 42mph during dynamometer car tests. This was compared with 3130hp of the original Lima A1 prototype 2-8-4 of 1925 on the B&A. The improvement achieved over 25 years was partly due to increased boiler evaporation and combustion chamber fireboxes giving 40% more direct heating surface.

TECHNICAL FILE

Two cylinders: 25in x 34in
Coupled wheels: 5ft 9in diameter
Grate area: 90.3sq ft
Boiler pressure: 245lb psi
Tractive effort: 64,100lb
Coal capacity: 19½ tons (2240lb)
Water capacity: 18,400 gallons
Length over couplers: 100ft 8⁵/₈in
Weight in working order:
Engine: 198.3 tons
Tender: 161.6 tons

▶ After steam had finished in America, some locomotives were placed on display at parks and other public places. This stay of execution gave American preservationists a second chance and S2 No 765 was rescued by the Fort Wayne Railroad Historical Society, which moved it from park display and restored it to service in 1979. During the following year, the 2-8-4 awaits an excursion assignment at East Peoria, Illinois.

steam traction with a high-powered 4-8-6 design. Based on the earlier Class S2 and numbered 770-779, this batch was completed during April and May 1949 and classed S3.

The last locomotive to be constructed was despatched on Friday 13 May and went straight to the Chicago Railroad Fair for display, before entering regular traffic.

Full dieselization

In 1956, the NKP President announced the intention to achieve full dieselization on the railroad by 1962, but in the event this was achieved within two years. In 1958, a major industrial recession in the USA rendered many recently delivered diesel-electrics on other railroads temporarily surplus to requirements and, as with the Norfolk & Western Railroad further south, advantage was taken of this situation by the NKP to lease some of these and eliminate steam working.

The first 2-8-4 had been withdrawn in 1955, but most were still extremely active as late as 1957, working fast freights between Chicago and Buffalo, with maximum speeds of 70mph; several were in the process of being fitted with radio signalling equipment.

However, the procurement of spare parts was becoming a major problem, despite cannibalizing locomotives on other railroads which had been prematurely retired. Although three NKP 2-8-4s were outshopped from the Conneaut shops, following major overhaul in May 1958, these were hardly used as new diesel-electric deliveries resulted in the last revenue earning run by a NKP Class S2 No 746 on 2 July the same year.

A handful of engines remained in steam on standby for three weeks, and a substantial number was retained on the active list for a further two years to cover any sudden upsurge in traffic. Most were cut up during the early 1960s.

A precursor of the Nickel Plate Road 2-8-4s was the series built by Lima for the largely Michigan Pere Marquette, which was absorbed by the Chesapeake & Ohio in 1947. Built in 1941 No 1225 was put on display at Michigan State University in 1957. Twelve years later students began the long task of returning the locomotive to running order; in 1989 when No 1225 ran its first excursion out of Owosso.

Class Y6b 2-8-8-2

NORFOLK & WESTERN RAILWAY

The Y6bs were the world's most powerful low speed heavy freight steam locomotives. Although their echoes have receded into history, their haulage feats among the Allegheny Mountains of West Virginia have become legendary.

N&W Class Y6b 2-8-8-2
N&W Nos: 2171-2200
Designer: R G Henley
Built: N&W Roanoke workshops, Va 1948-52
Service: Heavy coal trains between Roanoke Va and Norfolk Va, and Roanoke Va and Williamson WVa
Livery: Plain black with yellow lettering
Performance: 5600 drawbar horsepower at 25mph
Withdrawn from service: 1959-60

▼The aim of the post-war N&W was to have a fleet of thoroughly modernized steam locomotives, including 100 2-8-8-2s. Efficient servicing methods meant that compared with three decades earlier, twice the traffic was worked by half the number of locomotives. At the Roanoke depot, a Y4, No 2081, undergoes maintenance.

At the beginning of the 1950s, when most other US railroads were actively dieselizing entire fleets of locomotives, not only was the Norfolk & Western Railroad (N&W) still 100% steam operated, but it was also building new steam locomotives to basic designs which dated back well over 30 years. The simple reason for this was coal.

The railroad transported 50 million tons of coal annually from the rich bituminous deposits in the Pocahontas region, where the states of Virginia (Va), West Virginia (WVa) and Kentucky meet. Traditionally, two thirds of this output was transported to the industrial Midwest, and one third went to Norfolk, on the Atlantic coast, for export.

The N&W's main line was 663 miles long, stretching from Norfolk, Virginia, to Colombus, Ohio. It was on the climbs, over the demanding 1 in 66 gradients of the Allegheny mountain range and on the numerous colliery branches in the deep Virginian valleys, that the 2-8-8-2 Mallet articulated compounds reigned for 40 years.

Continuous development

In 1918, the N&W built its prototype 2-8-8-2 compound Mallet, classified Y2, at its Roanoke workshops. This was an enlargement of the 190 highly successful Z1 class 2-6-6-2s, derived from a Chesapeake & Ohio Railroad (C&O) superheated design.

By the end of 1924, the N&W had a fleet of 111 Class Y2 and Y3 2-8-8-2s, built by their own workshops at Roanoke as well as by private builders, the Y3 being the United States Railway Administration (USRA) derivative of the N&W Y2. A further 10 of these locomotives, Class Y4, were added in 1927. These were given feedwater heaters to increase efficiency and power. Cast-steel side frames and cross tie units gave greater strength.

The N&W Mallets were provided with a simpling valve, enabling them to operate as four-cylinder simple expansion locomotives. At start-

▼The Y6bs were of the Mallet type, pioneered by the Swiss-born engineer of that name. The LP cylinders and driving wheels were mounted in a separate frame hinged from the main frame. This feature enabled large and powerful locomotives to have greater flexibility in negotiating curved tracks, of which the N&W had many.

NORFOLK AND WESTERN 2172

◄ In August 1952, Y6b No 2174
shows off its lines at
Hagerstown, WVa. The N&W
steam fleet included a larger
proportion of reliable, efficient
and modern locomotives than
any other railroad in the US. In
1955, this enabled the steam-
operated N&W to achieve a
higher productivity in gross
ton miles per freight train per
hour, than any other US
railroad.

An engineer's sigh
In 1953, just after his
appointment as General
Manager of Motive Power
and Equipment, Clarence
Pond, who later had to carry
through the new president's
dieselization programme,
said to a friend visiting
Roanoke as a Mallet roared
past 'When you hear that
engine's exhaust crack, with
the reverser notched up
right, you wonder what
anyone would want to
dieselize for.' With the
N&W's modern steam
power and maintenance
facilities contributing to the
highest profitability and
freight train productivity of
any comparable US
railroad, his question was
not hard to understand.

ing, the exhaust from the high pressure (HP) cylinders was taken directly to the blastpipe, instead of to the low pressure (LP) cylinders as normal. This eliminated back pressure on the HP pistons at starting and meant an increase in tractive effort.

During 1930-32, Roanoke built 30 Class Y5 engines. In these, the boiler pressure was increased from 240 to 300lb – a high figure for that time. By widening the firebox, the grate area was enlarged from 96 to 106sq ft. This increased the firebox heating surface and evaporative capacity of the locomotive. By enlarging the LP piston valves from 14 to 18in diameter and providing large bridge exhaust pipes from the LP cylinders to give freer exhaust, the steam flow was improved for higher power outputs at speed.

The Y5s set the basic pattern for the classic Y6 series, of which 35 were produced during 1936-40. This class had the added refinement of cast-steel frame beds with integral cylinders, roller bearings on all axles and a modified valve setting to

increase power. In 1942, N&W once again modified the design and 16 Y6a engines incorporated an improved type of mechanical stoker (an essential feature on locomotives burning up to 6 or 7 tons of coal per hour) and plain instead of roller bearings for the tender axles.

Last of the line
In 1948, just as the big three commercial US locomotive builders, Alco, Lima and Baldwin, were fulfilling their final domestic steam orders, Roanoke embarked on the construction of a further series of compound 2-8-8-2s. Ultimately, 30 were built, classified Y6b, and numbered 2171 to 2200.

Compared to the earlier Y6 engines, refinements included increased firebox heating surface and volume, the combustion chamber being extended by 4ft and the tube length correspondingly reduced. This resulted in better fuel combustion and increased evaporation. The blastpipe ori-

LOCO LIST

Ultimately, 30 Y6bs were built
and numbered 2171-2200. By
the time they were withdrawn,
all modifications had been
applied to all members of the
Y5, Y6 and Y6b classes which
were almost identical. The final
Y6b emerged in April 1952.

Design specifications CLASS Y6

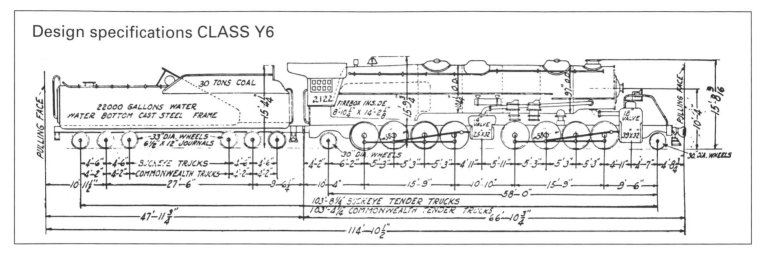

The N&W 2-8-8-2s were immensely powerful locomotives. In 1938, the French engineer André Chapelon travelled with Y6 No 2122 on dynamometer car tests. At one stage, 5500 drawbar hp was achieved at 19mph – the highest power ever developed by a steam locomotive at this slow speed. This result fully justified N&W's preference for compound drive for working over severe grades.

TECHNICAL FILE

Class Y6b
2 high pressure cylinders:
25in diameter x 32in stroke
2 low pressure cylinders:
39in diameter x 32in stroke
Coupled wheels: 4ft 10in diameter
Boiler diameter: 9ft 1in (max)
Grate area: 106.2sq ft
Boiler pressure: 300lb psi
Tractive effort:
Simple: 152,206lb
Compound: 126,838lb
Maximum service speed: 50mph
Coal capacity: 27 tons
Water capacity: 18,300 gallons
Length over couplers: 114ft 10½in
Weight in working order:
Engine: 260 tons (Nos 2171-2194); 273 tons (Nos 2195-2200)
Tender: 196 tons

▶The main work of the Y6bs was hauling heavy freight trains on the 340 miles from Williamson to Crewe Va, where they were ideally suited to both hauling and banking heavy freight trains over the demanding 1 in 66 gradients. They were also used on the numerous colliery branches. No 2172, the second Y6b to be built, powers a westbound freight train at Shaffers Crossing, Roanoke Va.

fices and chimney were enlarged to reduce power losses through exhaust back pressure. These factors combined to boost maximum drawbar horsepower of the original Y6s by 1000, achieving 5600 at 25mph.

The later Y6bs from new incorporated a booster device, whereby boiler steam at reduced pressure was mixed with exhaust steam from the HP cylinders. This increased considerably the tractive effort and power output of the LP engine unit and therefore the total locomotive power on heavy goods trains at slow speeds.

From 1953-55, the booster was retrospectively fitted to earlier Y6bs and Y6as, together with longer combustion chambers, improved valve setting and exhaust arrangements. Many of these

locomotives were provided with supplementary water tenders (known as canteens) in order to increase the length of runs possible between water stops.

The last six Y6bs incorporated 13 tons of lead ballast in the leading engine unit. This was in order to increase adhesive weight, minimizing any wheelslip tendency at higher power outputs and was applied to all 100 Y5, Y6 and Y6b engines.

With the building of the Y6bs, the N&W boasted 100 nearly uniform and very efficient 2-8-8-2s which, together with 43 simple expansion 2-6-6-4s mainly employed on the more easily graded routes and 14 remarkable streamlined 4-8-4s, worked the bulk of its main line traffic.

The N&W regarded itself as an integral part of

Where to see them
No Y6bs have been preserved but one, No 2200, was the last US main line steam locomotive to be built. Although the maximum service speed was 50mph, during a test run this locomotive was unofficially credited with achieving 70mph – despite its 4ft 10in driving wheels. However, no attempt appears to have been made to save the engine. This was possibly because an earlier Y6a, No 2156, fully modified to conform with the Y6bs, had already been presented to the National Museum of Transportation in St Louis in 1959.

the local coal industry, using part of its output and transporting the rest. Elsewhere in the US, the steam locomotive was rapidly vanishing under the withering onslaught of dieselization, despite which, the N&W consistently remained one of the most profitable railway enterprises in America.

Diesel arrival

Comparative tests in 1952, involving two brand new N&W steam locomotives – Y6b No 2197 and Class A 2-6-6-4 No 1239 – achieved a draw in operating cost and performance against a four-unit EMD diesel electric demonstrator with a nominal horsepower of 6000. This set had been specially uprated to 6800hp – a fact not advertised to N&W engineers.

Between 1949 and 1952, building costs of the Y6bs increased by some 18%. In late 1955, the N&W purchased some diesels for branch line service, retaining its modern steam power for trunk route operation. The following year witnessed the beginning of a profound change in traffic patterns, with more coal being shipped eastbound than westbound. Operating costs were forced up as banking engines were also required over the more severe eastbound grades. The N&W found that diesel units in multiple could handle heavier block train loads over these grades than steam could.

The well equipped workshops at Roanoke previously relied on a huge locomotive component supply industry, which rapidly perished or diversified following dieselization on other US railroads.

The N&W was then forced to manufacture its own air compressors, feedwater heaters and pumps, and other items in small batches at higher cost.

No new steam locomotives were built at Roanoke after 1953, with the completion of 45 0-8-0 switchers (shunting engines) of a thoroughly modernized USRA version of the 1919 design. This followed the purchase of 30 similar machines bought from the C&O in 1947.

In early 1958, on the retirement of the N&W President, Racehorse Smith, who supported the retention of coal-fired steam traction so long as it remained economically viable, the controlling Pennsylvania Railroad installed a new President, who promptly announced full dieselization for 1960. The next two years witnessed a massive purge of N&W modern (post-1935 and recently modernized) steam power, the rapidity of which was of questionable economic validity. Many locomotives were withdrawn for scrapping within a few months of receiving costly general overhauls.

At the dawn of 1960, only a handful of N&W 2-8-8-2s were still on the active list. Of these, Y6b No 2190 finally dropped its fire at Williamson, West Virginia on 6 May 1960.

No 2199 was still languishing in a Roanoke scrapyard 15 years later. During the energy crisis of the 1970s, André Chapelon proposed its rebuilding with high degree superheat, enlarged steam circuit and triple Kylchap exhaust. Unfortunately, the project was abandoned.

Spotless servicing
In the early 1950s, locomotive servicing on the N&W reached a peak that would appear fantastic to the workers on other steam powered railways around the world. The locomotives were serviced in the most highly developed depots built by any railway during the steam era. A complete servicing operation on a large Mallet could be completed in one hour. White-coated staff, working in a white-tiled workshop, applied soft grease and oil to lubrication points on the locomotives. The depot at Williamson, West Virginia, was a particularly outstanding example of efficiency.

N&W Y6 No 2132, seen here at Christiansburg, Virginia, was a predecessor of the later Y6b class. The Y6s had smaller firebox surfaces and volume, and smaller diameter blastpipe and chimney.

FL9 diesels

GENERAL MOTORS ELECTRO-MOTIVE DIVISION

The FL9s are the last of the streamlined cab style diesels, so characteristic of American railroads of the 1950s. With some of the class set to continue in service for a few years yet, this familiar outline will be around for some time to come.

KEY FACTS

EMD FL9 Bo-A1A
Numbers: 2000-59.
60 locomotives
Manufacturer: Electro-Motive Division
Built: 1956-60
Service: General freight and passenger service
Special features: Dual current capability
Livery: Many individual railroad variations

In America, railroading entered the 1950s with the transition from steam to diesel-electric well under way. The revolution was spearheaded by the streamlined cab style diesels produced by General Motors' Electro-Motive Division (EMD).

By the end of the decade steam would be all but eliminated from American railroads. The cab style configuration of the Bo-Bo FT, F2, F3, F7 and F9 freight diesels would be replaced by the functional form of the hood-style road-switcher (shunting engine). Yet the cab style diesel would end with a flourish, in the form of a remarkable combination diesel-electric and electric passenger locomotive – the FL9. In reduced numbers, this class is still performing valuable service in the 1990s.

F-series

From 1939, EMD grew in size through the building of the pioneering Class FT. Through successive years, exterior changes to the classic car body styling of the class were superficial, only the

expertise of railroad enthusiasts could tell the difference between models. After an initial major rebuild of the type 567 diesel engine, used in many of their designs, interior improvements were small and concentrated on upgrading the horse-power output and improving the electrical systems. These included the development of a new main generator in the F3s permitting an increase from 1350 to 1500hp, AC motors to drive the cooling fans and traction motor blowers (replacing belt drive), and redesigned dynamic brakes.

In 1949, refinements continued with the F7 model. The switches that changed high voltage from the generator to the traction motors were redesigned to extend their life and reduce maintenance. Automatic transition (which connected the diesel engine to the traction motors) was finally perfected and became standard. Originally, the driver had to match the ampere meter readings and use a lever to make the connection.

The Class F7 became the best selling of all F

▼The F7 was a refinement of the earlier FT and F3 models and became the best selling of all F units. A total of 2366 cab and 1483 booster F7 units were sold – more than double the sales of the F3 series. At the Raton Pass in New Mexico, F7 No 228C heads a six-unit lash up on a freight train.

units with sales of 2366 cab and 1483 booster units, more than double the 1111 cab and 696 booster sales of the F3. For passenger service, EMD produced twin engine Co-Co E units, but some railroads, especially those with mountain grades or tight curvatures, preferred Bo-Bo F-series units geared for passenger train speeds.

EMD responded to these demands by offering steam generators to provide steam for train heating in F as well as E units. The steam generator was an oil-fired boiler, using fuel oil from the locomotive's fuelling system, and water carried in a smaller tank hung under the locomotive.

Variations within members of the same class were common. Santa Fe placed the boiler in the cab units and carried the water in the booster units. In cold weather it could take almost as much fuel to make steam as pull the train. To provide more steam capacity, EMD brought out the FP7. This was an F7 modified for passenger service, with a car body lengthened by 4ft that suspended a 950 gallon water tank, and 376 of these locomotives were built.

Last orders
In 1954, the F9 replaced the F7, with the 567C engine upgraded to 835rpm from the 800rpm of the 567B engine, resulting in a boost to 1750hp. The F9, and its passenger companion FP9, also featured automatic wheel slip control and a sealed gear case. By this time railroads were fully aware of the capabilities of the newer hood-style road-switcher, as embodied in the GP7 introduced in 1949, and F9 sales were to suffer; only 254 F9s and 29 FP9s were built.

As F-unit orders decreased, the passenger oriented New York, New Haven & Hartford Railroad, known as the New Haven Railroad, was facing a particular problem. In 1907, the railroad had successfully electrified its main line from Woodlawn, New York, to New Haven, but heavy debt prevented extension of the electrification east to Boston, Massachusetts. West from Woodlawn, the New Haven Railroad entered Grand Central station over the electrified line of the New York

◄ New Haven Railroad's FL9 No 2026 runs under the wires in the New Haven Railroad's electrified territory between New Haven and Woodlawn, New York. Strict laws did not allow polluting rail traffic within the New York City limits, so EMD proposed a diesel locomotive that could also operate as a straight electric engine.

Central and into Pennsylvania station over the electrified line of the Long Island Railroad.

In the mid-1950s, the electric locomotives were showing their age, and worse, the New Haven Railroad feared its electricity generating plant would need replacement. An obvious solution would be to dieselize the electrified lines, which would also eliminate the awkward locomotive changes at New Haven, but non-polluting, electrified operation into New York City was still required.

Dual-voltage diesel

Since the current provided by the generator of a diesel locomotive is about the same – though fluctuating higher – as the 660V DC of the New York City third rail, EMD proposed a diesel locomotive that could also operate as a straight electric. Designated FL9 (L meaning lengthened) the car body was extended an additional 4ft beyond the 4ft stretch of an FP9. This housed a separate electrical cabinet, next to the regular cabinet, with equipment to regulate third rail current to the traction motors. The New Haven Railroad ordered 60 locomotives, the first two, Nos 2000-2001, arriving in October 1956 for testing.

EMD had suggested using third rail pick-up shoes, which were attached to both bogies via an oak wood beam mounted on the bogie frames. But the New Haven Railroad insisted that shoes placed on the rear bogie only would be adequate. But during testing, the incidence of flash-over occurring at point breaks in the third rail was considered enough of a problem to require shoes on the leading bogie. To provide space for this, the original passenger-style truck was replaced by a Flexicoil type, which has made the locomotives rough riding to this day.

During 1957, 28 additional FL9 units, Nos 2002-2029, arrived. The first 30 units had dynamic

► The principal task of the FL9 is running passenger services in and out of New York. After the New Haven Railroad finally went bankrupt in 1969, it was absorbed into the Penn Central Railroad. The new owners gave the FL9s new colour schemes, numbers and duties. No 5026 was one of four locomotives to be repainted in Penn Central colours.

▼The FL9 locomotives were a longer version of the earlier FP9 class, L meaning lengthened car body. This was extended an extra 4ft to house the electrical equipment and traction motors. With their electrical equipment becoming increasingly unreliable, the FL9s normally use their diesel engines only.

LOCO LIST

The two prototype FL9s appeared during 1956. In the following year, 28 additional FL9 units, Nos 2002-2029, arrived. These first 30 units had dynamic braking and retractable overhead power collectors. The second batch of units, Nos 2030-59, did not have dynamic brakes or the overhead power collector, but did feature the next diesel engine upgrade, the 567D1 rated at 1800hp. FL9 No 2059 was the last F unit built.

braking and a retractable overhead power collector (pantograph) for use in Grand Central station where there were interruptions in the third rail. Drivers seldom used these power collectors and they were later removed.

New Haven Railroad's worsening financial plight delayed delivery of the second 30 FL9s until June to November 1960. Reportedly, the railroad would have liked as many as 120. This second batch of units, Nos 2030-59, did not have dynamic brakes or the overhead power collector,

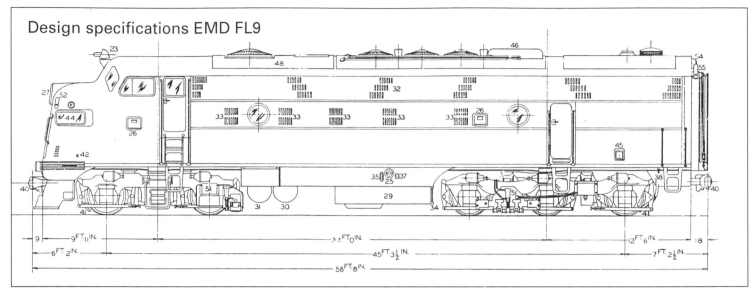

Design specifications EMD FL9

▲The FL9s were unusual locomotives. Not only could they operate using both diesel and electric traction, but they also had a Bo-A1A wheel arrangement. This was because a bridge at Park Avenue, New York had a severe weight restriction and required a modified three-axle rear bogie to distribute the locomotive's weight.

TECHNICAL FILE

Length: 58ft 8in
Distance between bogie centres: 34ft
Wheel diameter: 40in
Diesel engines: One 567C 16-cylinder 2-stroke rated 1750hp (first 30)
One 567D1 16-cylinder 2-stroke rated 1800hp (second 30)
Transmission: D57B traction motors, D22 generator, 3-phase alternator
Maximum speed: 90mph
Fuel capacity: 1200 gallons
Weight: 105.2 tons

Clearance problems
Station platforms along the New Haven Railroad presented clearance problems for the newly built FL9s. To overcome this an air valve, operated by the driver, raised the current collector shoes to a folded storage position or lowered them to make contact with the third rail. The shoes on the FL9 were able to take current from both the under-running contact rail of the New York Central and over-running rail of the Long Island railroads.

but did feature the next diesel engine upgrade, the 567D1, rated at 1800hp.

New Haven Railroad's slide into bankruptcy and absorption into Penn Central Railroad in 1969, began an involved series of new ownerships, colour schemes, renumberings and reassignments. In the early 1990s, Metro North, a government sponsored agency, operates over 30 units on the former New Haven and New York Central commuter lines out of Grand Central station to Danbury, Connecticut and Poughkeepsie, New York. Four other units, rebuilt in 1985, are owned by the Connecticut Department of Transportation.

Lack of maintenance of the engines' electrical equipment has made third rail operation highly unreliable, and locomotives normally operate in and out of Grand Central station under diesel power. The coaches are now electrically heated and air conditioned. In 1978-80, six Amtrak FL9s were rebuilt for the New York – Albany service. But in 1993, when the new General Electric diesels are delivered, they will be withdrawn.

▼An FL9 hauls an Albany-bound Amtrak train at Peekskill. In 1978-80, six Amtrak FL9s were rebuilt for the New York – Albany service. They face retirement when the new General Electric diesels are delivered in 1993.

Metro-North FL9 No 2042 works a commuter train north of Peekskill to New York City.

DDA40X Centennial

UNION PACIFIC

Union Pacific Class DDA40X
Do-Do Centennial
UP numbers: 6900-6946
Manufacturer: Electro-Motive Division of General Motors
Built: 1969-1971, LaGrange, Illinois
Introduced: Debut on the Union Pacific was pulling the Golden Spike Centennial Limited excursion train from Kansas City, Missouri to Salt Lake City, Utah, on 7-8 May 1969
Service: High-speed freight service over main lines
Special features: The world's largest and most powerful diesel locomotive
Livery: Body, armour yellow; top of hood, harbourmist grey; bogies, aluminium; lettering and striping, red Scotchlite

Hailed as the world's most powerful land vehicles, the Union Pacific's Centennials were the biggest diesels ever built. But like the Big Boys that went before them, they have passed into the history of the prairies they once roamed.

Perhaps more than any other US railroad, Union Pacific (UP) became synonymous with the vast western landscape it was chartered to conquer. Union Pacific's Centennial locomotives were as much a product of geography and history as they were of the erecting floor at General Motor's Electro-Motive Division (EMD).

On 10 May 1869, a golden spike ceremony was held at Promontory, Utah to commemorate the joining of the UP and Central Pacific – creating the country's first east-west transcontinental railroad.

This famous overland route became the major conduit of traffic moving between east and west. UP sought to move this traffic over the long distances with the biggest and best motive power available. In steam days, UP employed unique three-cylinder 4-12-2s capable of sustained speed and pulling power. They followed these with the first 4-6-6-4 Challengers and in 1941 introduced the famous 4-8-8-4 Big Boys, the world's largest steam locomotives.

Following World War II, the efficiencies of the diesel locomotive spelt the doom of the steam engine. There was only one problem: to equal the horsepower of steam locomotives, especially the powerful UP engines, the lower horsepower units – 1500-1750hp – of that day required a large diesel assembly or lash-up (the term applied by railroaders to a combination of individual diesel units operating together under the control of a

▼ **With a frame length of 98ft 5in (30m), the 6900s became the longest diesels on US railroads. The transverse passage in the centre of the locomotive marks the gap between the two huge 3300hp engines. A catwalk down the side of the recessed body – standard on US freight diesels – enabled the engineers to gain easy access to the engines for maintenance.**

LOCO LIST

Between 1968 and 1971 47 Centennials were built. All were powered by 3300hp engines, but Nos 6900-6902 ran with a higher rating through rpm for a while. As normal in US railroad practice none of the class was named.

▲Led by No 6905, a lash-up of three engines grinds past the grain elevators of Kimball County Grain Co-operative, Nebraska, with a westbound train. A lash-up was the joining together of two or more locomotives under the control of a single crew.

◄ Few exhibits can be as impressive as the huge bulk of Centennial diesel No 6946 at Portola Railroad Museum, California. The US railroads exploited their substantial loading gauge to the full, and at 16ft 4in (5m) tall the 6900s towered over most contemporary diesels.

single engine crew to form one locomotive – common in the US).

Development stages
Throughout the late 1950s and in the 1960s the US manufacturers continued to produce bigger and heavier diesel locomotives. In 1964-65 EMD built 45 5000hp locomotives with two engines in one car body for UP and SP. Based on this success, in 1968 UP commissioned EMD to build the DDA40X, using two of the new 645E3 3000hp engines introduced in 1966 in the GP/40.

The initial order for 25 DDA40Xs was amended to 47 locomotives early in 1969. The first loco-

Where to see them
All but one of the 12 preserved Centennials are based in the USA. Only one, No 6936, is operational.
- **6900** – Council Bluffs, Iowa
- **6901** – Pocatello, Idaho
- **6911** – Mexico City
- **6913** – Texas State Fairground, Dallas
- **6915** – Pomona, California
- **6916** – Ogden, Utah
- **6922** – North Platte, Nebraska
- **6930** – Union, Illinois
- **6936** – Cheyenne, Wyoming
- **6938** – North Little Rock, Arkansas
- **6944** – Kirkwood, Missouri
- **6946** – Portola, California

▲Centennial diesels were not often seen at the head of passenger trains as their massive power was needed for freight work. Here, Centennial No 6936 hauls an enthusiasts' special across the open western plains in October 1985. This locomotive was luckier than most other members of its class and is preserved at Cheyenne in operational condition.

engines were uprated to 3300hp (and even 3500hp on 6900-6902 for a time) by increasing the rpm from 900 to 950. EMD publicists touted the 6600hp locomotives as the world's most powerful land vehicles.

Into service

The Centennials went into service pulling the UP's fastest mail and freight trains. With the new Bailey classification (marshalling) yard and diesel servicing facility in place at North Platte, Nebraska, the domain of the 6900s was established as the main line west from North Platte to Sherman Hill and across Wyoming to Granger. Thereafter they either went north-west over the Blue Mountains to Portland, Oregon (1498 miles/2410km) or west to Ogden, Utah and south-west through the Utah and Nevada deserts to Los Angeles (1518 miles/2442km).

With long runs on high speed trains, the 6900s wracked up enormous mileages. Virtually every locomotive in the fleet (with the exception of two written off in accidents) attained more than three million miles (4,828,020km). Whereas UP's other diesels were shopped at 500,000 miles (804,670km) and one million miles (1,609,340km), UP shopped the Centennials at 600,000 miles (965,604km) (Class B overhaul – replacing major components and support systems) and 1,200,000 miles (1,931,208km) (Class C overhaul – complete overhaul, including rebuilding of engines and trucks and repainting). Most 6900s received at least two Class C overhauls in their

motive was rushed to completion to take part in the 1969 celebration of the golden spike centennial, and was therefore given the name Centennial and number series 6900.

The 98ft 5in (30m) frame was the longest ever placed under a diesel locomotive. The 6900s retained the recessed car body and catwalk configuration standard on US freight diesels, but displayed a full width nose that had been introduced on passenger cowl units for Santa Fe the year before. The sloping radiators and dynamic brake blister gave the roof line an angular, purposeful appearance. The four-axle (Do-Do) trucks were specially designed for the 6900s. With a height of 16ft 4in (5m), the 6900s were the tallest diesels yet built.

Internally, the two 16-cylinder 645E3 diesel

▼Locomotive No 6925 leads a westbound piggyback train over Sherman Hill – a location associated with the Big Boy steam locomotives. The 6900s were intended for use only on high speed trains and were rarely used on loaded coal or grain trains.

Speed limits

UP always enjoyed the reputation as one of the fastest US railroads. In the 1990s trains are limited to 70mph (112km). In the 1970s conditions were more liberal and the 6900s were allowed a top speed of 83mph (133km/h).

The manufacturer's warranty covered speeds only up to 83mph (133km/h). As a practical matter, UP set the overspeed governor for 88mph (141km/h) so the locomotives would not cut out if the train accelerated when going downhill.

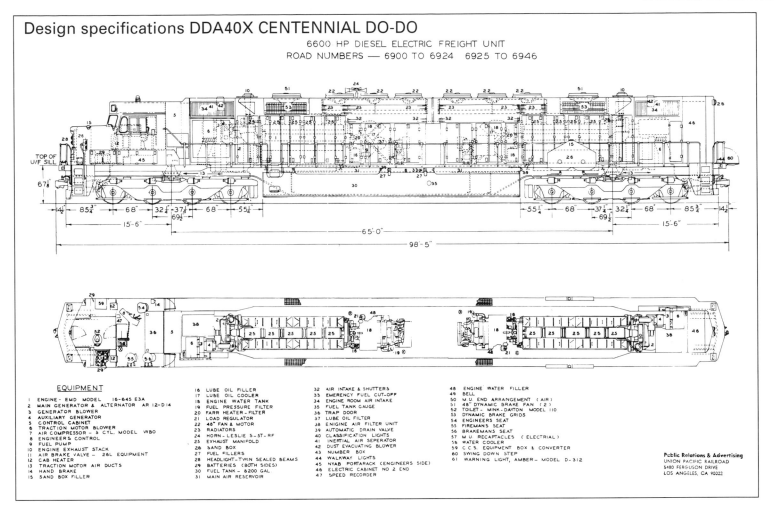

Design specifications DDA40X CENTENNIAL DO-DO
6600 HP DIESEL ELECTRIC FREIGHT UNIT
ROAD NUMBERS — 6900 TO 6924   6925 TO 6946

EQUIPMENT

1 ENGINE - EMD MODEL 16-645 E3A
2 MAIN GENERATOR & ALTERNATOR AR 12-D14
3 GENERATOR BLOWER
4 AUXILIARY GENERATOR
5 CONTROL CABINET
6 TRACTION MOTOR BLOWER
7 AIR COMPRESSOR - 3 CYL. MODEL WBO
8 ENGINEERS CONTROL
9 FUEL PUMP
10 ENGINE EXHAUST STACK
11 AIR BRAKE VALVE - 26L EQUIPMENT
12 CAB HEATER
13 TRACTION MOTOR AIR DUCTS
14 HAND BRAKE
15 SAND BOX FILLER
16 LUBE OIL FILLER
17 LUBE OIL COOLER
18 ENGINE WATER TANK
19 FUEL PRESSURE FILTER
20 FARR HEATER - FILTER
21 LOAD REGULATOR
22 48" FAN & MOTOR
23 RADIATORS
24 HORN - LESLIE 5-5T-RF
25 EXHAUST MANIFOLD
26 SAND BOX
27 FUEL FILLERS
28 HEADLIGHT - TWIN SEALED BEAMS
29 BATTERIES (BOTH SIDES)
30 FUEL TANK - 8200 GAL.
31 MAIN AIR RESERVOIR
32 AIR INTAKE & SHUTTERS
33 EMERGENCY FUEL CUT-OFF
34 ENGINE ROOM AIR INTAKE
35 FUEL TANK GAUGE
36 TRAP DOOR
37 LUBE OIL FILTER
38 ENIGINE AIR FILTER UNIT
39 AUTOMATIC DRAIN VALVE
40 CLASSIFICATION LIGHTS
41 INERTIAL AIR SEPERATOR
42 DUST EVACUATING BLOWER
43 NUMBER BOX
44 WALKWAY LIGHTS
45 NYAB PORTARACK (ENGINEERS SIDE)
46 ELECTRIC CABINET NO 2 END
47 SPEED RECORDER
48 ENGINE WATER FILLER
49 BELL
50 M.U. END ARRANGEMENT (AIR)
51 48" DYNAMIC BRAKE FAN (2)
52 TOILET - MINK-DAYTON MODEL 110
53 DYNAMIC BRAKE GRIDS
54 ENGINEERS SEAT
55 FIREMANS SEAT
56 BRAKEMANS SEAT
57 M.U. RECAPTACLES (ELECTRICAL)
58 WATER COOLER
59 C.C.S. EQUIPMENT BOX & CONVERTER
60 SWING DOWN STEP
61 WARNING LIGHT, AMBER - MODEL D-312

Public Relations & Advertising
UNION PACIFIC RAILROAD
5480 FERGUSON DRIVE
LOS ANGELES, CA 90022

▲Each Centennial locomotive contained two 16-cylinder 3300hp 645E3 diesel engines. When the Centennials were first launched the manufacturers promoted these 6600hp monsters as the world's most powerful land vehicles.

lifetimes. The locomotives normally exceeded 20,000 miles (32,186km) per month in service across prairies, over mountain grades and through blazing hot deserts many times on the same trip.

Power combinations
When introduced, a common power package was two 6900s operated back to back to eliminate turning at terminals. In 1972 EMD started production of the SD40-2 locomotive, an improved SD40 with modular electronic components (a feature first proven on the DDA40X) and high adhesion trucks. UP became a frequent buyer. The railroad specified that certain SD40-2 locomotives be geared to match the DDA40Xs to pull high speed freights.

During this period UP tried to maintain five horsepower per ton, carefully limiting fastest hotshot train lengths to 35-45 cars and assembling power packages to match. A common lash-up was two DDA40Xs spliced by one high speed SD40-2 in the middle. Lash-ups were designed not only for flat land speed but also to get the trains over the mountain districts without helpers.

In 1979 the Centennials – one, two and even three to a train – practically dominated the merchandise schedules across Oregon's Blue Mountains. Then, within a year, most were in storage, victims of a continued influx of new SD40-2s and a major recession which reduced traffic. As of April 1981 the entire fleet (along with hundreds of standard units) was in storage, with dim prospects for the future. However, traffic levels dramatically improved over the next two years and suddenly the 6900s were recalled from desert storage lines.

Many of the 6900s pressed into service had spent four years in storage; most had run over a million miles since their previous Class C overhaul. Size was a disadvantage as well as an advantage. No other railroad would accept the 6900s, which had a negative impact on the power pooling and run-through freight operations common in the US. Most critically, in a time of rising fuel costs, diesel technology had passed them by. New diesels, such as the SD50, offered fuel efficient engines delivering higher horsepower in single units.

The end of an era
By April 1985 only a handful of 6900s were in service, and in May the era of big power on the UP came to an end. The DDA40X became the motive power symbol of the railroad, much as had the Big Boys in steam days; they even appeared on billboards together, promoting the railway's image. And just as a total of eight Big Boys was preserved for posterity, 12 Centennials were saved from the scrapyard.

TECHNICAL FILE

Length: 98ft 5in (30,000mm)
Distance between bogie centres: 65ft (20,000mm)
Bogie wheelbase: 105¼in (2673mm)
Wheel diameter: 40in (1010mm)
Diesel engines: Two 645E3 16 cylinders 2-stroke each rated 3300hp at 950rpm
Transmission: AR-12 main generator and D-14 alternator, 8 D-77X traction motors
Continuous tractive effort: 72,300lb at 30mph
Maximum speed: 83mph (133km/h)
Fuel capacity: 8200 gals
Weight (loaded): 545,432lb

DDA40X No 6912 heads a freight over Sherman Hill, Wyoming. This class of locomotive was the diesel equivalent of the articulated locomotives that they superseded over the Rocky Mountains.

Train à Grande Vitesse

SOCIÉTÉ NATIONALE DES CHEMINS DE FER FRANCAIS

The rail world speed record holder, a sleek silver and blue train, is changing the way people travel in France. Its revolutionary motor, air suspension and on-board computer system are innovations which are influencing railways the world over.

On 18 May 1990, a train with a long stream-lined nose and tail, in an eye-catching livery of silver and blue, flashed through the vineyards south-west of Paris at 515.3km/h (320.2mph), a new world speed record for trains. The record breaker was a shortened and slightly modified version of the *Train à Grande Vitesse Atlantique* (TGV-A) fleet.

Setting this remarkable record was the latest stage in the revolution which has overtaken French Railways (SNCF) since World War II. SNCF embarked on the transformation of its network only after a comprehensive examination of new equipment and technology – a carefully considered approach that has served them well.

Experimenting with electricity

The old main line of the Paris-Lyon-Mediterranée Railway, which is now the Sud-Est (south-east) region of SNCF, was overworked for many years. Paris, Lyon, Marseille, Grenoble, Nice and Toulon were all served by it, and 40% of all French people lived within its catchment area.

To increase capacity, most of the 518km (322 miles) of line between Paris and Lyon were expanded from two to four tracks before 1939. After the war this route was electrified using a 1500V DC system, which was extended by 1961 to include the line to Marseille.

During trials designed to test wheel/rail stress, SNCF began to experiment with powerful electric locomotives. One train reached 243km/h (151mph) early in 1954. Further tests undertaken the following year on the line south of Bordeaux, which is also electrified on the 1500V DC system, culminated in a new world speed record of 331km/h (205mph).

▼TGV Atlantique is the flagship service of French railways and a source of national pride. The aerodynamic design was developed by the French Aerotechnical Institute and GEC Alsthom. Their research led to improvements which helped to reduce drag by 10%.

KEY FACTS

Train à Grande Vitesse – TGV
SNCF Nos: 23001-23100, 24001-24105, 33001-33009, 923001-923002. 216 sets
Manufacturer: GEC Alsthom
Built: 1976-1980, 1985-1989
Introduced: Sud-Est service 1981; Atlantique service 1989
Livery: Sud-Est – orange, grey, white; Atlantique – silver-grey, blue, white; Postal – yellow, grey, white
Best performance: 18 May 1990 – 515.3km/h (320.2mph) – world record
Special features: The motors in TGV Atlantique are the first to work from an AC power source.

216 power units were built for the SNCF in the years between 1980 and 1991.

TGV Sud-Est
23001-23100 dual voltage units
33001-33009 triple voltage units
TGV Atlantique
24001-24105 dual voltage units
TGV Postal
923001-923002 dual voltage units

Where to see them
● **TGV Atlantique** units depart for Bordeaux and Brest, Qimper and Le Croisic more than a dozen times a day from the Gare Montparnasse, Paris.
● **TGV Sud-Est** trains leave Paris Gare de Lyon for Lyon regularly.
● **TGV Postal** trains leave Paris-Charolais for Lyon and the northbound service leaves Lyon for Paris twice a day.

▼Although TGV Atlantique power cars are superficially similar to the units on the Lyon service, their motors are almost 40% more powerful than the earlier Sud-Est design. The improvement allows the SNCF to include two extra coaches in each set. They also cost 15% less per passenger to manufacture than the earlier version.

◀ The gradients on the line to Lyon are exceptionally severe, with some as steep as 1 in 28.6. But the TGV was designed to cope with such inclines and the loss of speed during the climb is normally limited to 50km/h (31mph). Going over the hills avoided the considerable expense of excavating tunnels which made the construction much cheaper.

But these tests revealed problems with collection of the current from overhead cables at high speed with DC motors. Instead, SNCF turned to gas turbine power cars. Only after the oil crisis of 1973 quadrupled the price of fuel were the experiments resumed using electric power. This time a cheaper and more efficient system using 25,000V AC was chosen. Converting the old power supply was too expensive, therefore SNCF turned its attention to a new purpose built line to the south which would relieve the pressure on the existing system.

The new train takes shape

A fresh start gave SNCF the opportunity to design trains and track together. High speed passenger stock with ample power spread over a number of axles could climb steeper gradients than more traditional locomotive and carriage combinations. This allowed the engineers to plan a more direct alignment and lop 87km (54 miles) off the old route between Paris and Lyon. Because an extension into the city would have been so expensive, the new *Ligne à Grande Vitesse* started at a junction in Lieusaint, 29km (18 miles) from the Gare de Lyon terminus.

This compromise meant that the engineers had to incorporate motors that could use both the old and the new power systems. Gradually, technical difficulties were overcome. DC motors were connected to the power supply through transformers. As extensions were planned to Lausanne and Berne, the power units on those routes would also have to cope with the Swiss standard of 15,000V AC. SNCF ordered 92 dual voltage and eight triple

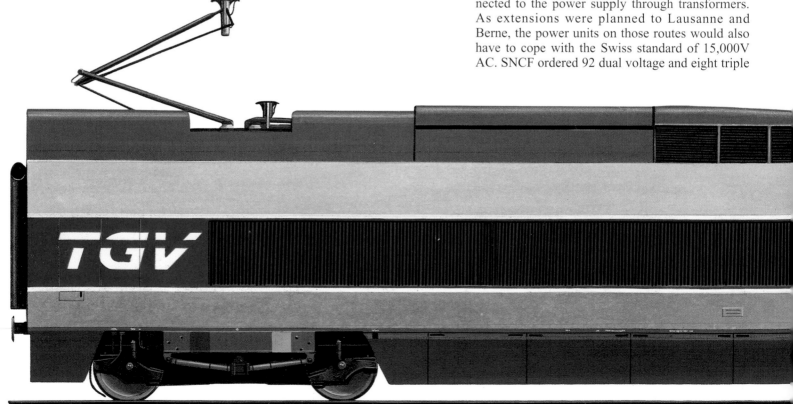

voltage train sets and two sets for postal traffic.

Each of the passenger sets consists of eight coaches permanently connected between two power cars. To save weight, adjacent coaches are connected by a common bogie. Both power cars have four power axles plus a connected power bogie in the adjacent passenger car, which together can exert up to 8650hp when using the 25,000V AC system. The power output is reduced to 4160hp on the 1500V DC system and 3750hp on the Swiss 15,000V AC system.

Winning back passengers
The first TGV units entered service on the Sud-Est region of the SNCF network in 1981, building up to a full timetable in 1983. After a running-in period, 270km/h (168mph) operation began in 1984. At the same time, the existing line south of Lyon was upgraded for 200km/h (124mph) operation,

▲TGV passenger services are attracting traffic back from the airlines by providing fast journey times between city centres. SNCF believe that a maximum journey time of three hours to a major city is the key to success. French railways have drawn public attention to the new services by designing distinctive liveries for each one.

which brought Marseille within five hours' travelling time of Paris.

These improvements greatly increased the popularity of the service; the number of passengers using the TGV rose from just six million in 1982 to 14.7 million in 1985. Many of these people were won back off the airlines – by the end of 1984 the service was carrying 56% of all passengers between Paris and Lyon.

These results encouraged the French government to authorize the construction of a new line,

Computer control
The TGV Atlantique has a network of computers and microprocessors which do everything from overseeing the driver to switching on the air-conditioning. The data network Tornad sends information from sensors in the equipment to the main computer in the cab. It checks all the equipment automatically before each journey and provides technical analysis on a display console on the driver's desk while the train is on the move.

Design specifications TGV ATLANTIQUE

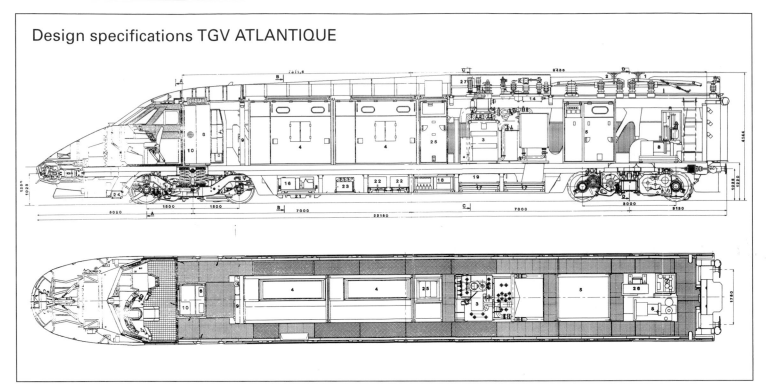

the TGV Atlantique, to the south-west in May 1984. Trains would start from a rebuilt Gare Montparnasse and join the purpose built track at Fontenay-aux-Roses 3km (2 miles) away. The line continued south-west for 124km (77 miles) to Courtalain Junction where it divided, one track turning west to Connerré to join the old line to Le Mans and the route to Brittany. The other spur extended to Monte, just beyond Tours, and connected with the line to Bordeaux.

The trains ordered for the line looked similar to the earlier Sud-Est units but a technical revolution in electric motor design made them more powerful. They could pull two extra passenger cars, which held 99 more people, and provide a faster, 300km/h (186mph) service.

The new three-phase synchronous AC motors developed 12,000hp and used state of the art electronics. Only eight motors were needed on each train rather than the 12 on the original units. Their record-breaking performance in May 1990 encouraged SNCF to replace the motors of the sets on the south-eastern route during the 1990s with the new design. The improved motors will also power the new double-decker TGV.

The TGV-A has two braking systems: rheostatic on the powered axles and disc brakes on the rest. The rheostatic brakes slow the train above 200km/h (124mph). Disc brakes are phased in as the speed drops below 200km/h (124mph).

The driver is advised when to apply the brakes by an electronic cab display; there are no lineside

▲The TGV Atlantique power car weighs only 67.8 tonnes because the exterior skin is made from light alloys while the chassis and body frame are special steel. As with the British Class 91, the motors are fixed to the body and connected to the bogie through a flexible drive.

signals. The display gives the driver continuous advice about current speed limits and information on the braking systems. It also monitors his performance, overriding him if safety is threatened.

The third *Ligne à Grande Vitesse* to the north is connecting Paris to the Channel Tunnel and Brussels. This is the first part of a European high speed network to be created by the start of the 21st century. To cope with the longer distances GEC Alsthom are developing third generation motors to give a standard 350km/h (217mph) service.

TECHNICAL FILE

TGV-A Power Car
Overall length: 22.15m (72ft 8in)
Maximum body width: 2.814m (9ft 3in)
Maximum height above rail: 4.1m (13ft 5in)
Weight: 67.8 tonnes
Number of powered axles: 4
Nominal diameter of wheels: 92cm (3ft)
Maximum axle load: 17 tonnes
Electrical supply: single-phase AC, 25kV, 50Hz
Motors: Eight synchronous three-phase
Continuous rating of motor: 11,000kW (1500hp)

▶French railways have built new maintenance depots which deal exclusively with TGV units. The facilities include jacks which can lift the superstructure of an entire train in one move. The on-board Tornad computer monitoring system automatically sends instructions on repairs to the depot in advance of the train's arrival.

Chapter 2
The World of Rail

Unusual railways

Hardly had steam locomotion burst upon the world before inventors and entrepreneurs were trying to improve or even replace the system. The permutations were endless and ingenious. Some succeeded, many failed – and a tiny number held true revolutionary potential.

One of the earliest challenges to the conventional steam railway concerned the locomotive itself. Detractors pointed out that this unwieldy monster, besides being dirty, noisy and obtrusive, had to carry its own supply of fuel and water – a non-fare-paying deadweight that affected both speed and cost. It would be much better, they argued, if a train could run off fixed power plants set at regular intervals along the track. But what would provide the propulsive force? The answer, literally, was nothing.

Vacuum-powered 'atmospheric railways' hit Britain in the 1840s. The principle was quite simple. Between the rails was laid a tube into which fitted a piston connected to the leading carriage. Meanwhile, pumping stations set every few miles along the track created a vacuum in the tube to suck along the piston and its attached carriages.

The system was quiet, quick, clean and comfortable. But above all, as railway companies were keen to note, it was cheap.

In the first flush of enthusiasm, a number of atmospheric lines were built, the pioneer being a commuter dash between Croydon and Forest Hill that incorporated – at Norwood – the world's first flyover. The most famous, however, was the South Devon Railway, covering a proposed 57 miles – 41 of them atmospheric – and constructed under the aegis of the uncrowned king of engineering himself – Isambard Kingdom Brunel.

Devon folk called it the 'Atmospheric Caper'. And even Brunel had to admit it was little else. The problem lay in the continuous valve, running the length of the tube, that maintained an airtight seal before and behind the piston. The countless hinged flaps which made up the valve were

▼A twin-boilered locomotive of the Lartigue Monorail waits to couple up to its train at the west Irish town of Ballybunion at the turn of the century. Opened in 1888, and running for 9¹/₂ miles between Ballybunion and Listowel, the line was an immediate success. But the divided construction of the rolling stock meant that passengers had to cross to and fro by special steps until the two halves of each coach were equally balanced.

Something in the air

For all the good intentions of atmospheric railways, their operation had a number of unpleasant side-effects. On the South Devon line three groovemen, employed to maintain the system's airtight valve, were run over by the silent trains – one, admittedly, having drunk too much and 'fallen asleep on the Tube while at work'.

And every morning when the pumping houses started up they ejected from their vents a shower of rats which had crept into the tube during the night – a phenomenon that intrigued one Victorian author so greatly that he recorded its outlandish details in a volume titled *Curiosities of Natural History*.

▶An artist's impression of 1909 shows passengers playing a game of billiards as their gyroscopic monorail car tilts to one side while taking a curve. Scientists who watched a practical demonstration of the system were duly impressed, and there were confident predictions that it would revolutionize railway engineering.

padded with treated leather, the best solution current technology could offer.

But it was woefully inadequate. Heat melted the sealing compound, while wind hardened it. Frost stiffened the leather, as did drought, and the piston's passage ripped it to shreds.

The system leaked like a colander. By 1848, when passengers had been whisked atmospherically for no more than a few months, Brunel conceded defeat. The plant and equipment were sold at a heavy loss, recouping less than eight per cent of the initial investment. (The Croydon – Forest Hill line had closed down eight months earlier.)

Only at Starcross, one of Brunel's 11 Italianate pumping stations, did the South Devon achieve a lasting place in society: it was turned into a chapel and is now a museum containing relics of Brunel's abortive venture.

Making fresh tracks

The next aspect to which improvers addressed themselves was the track. For one exciting moment in the 1840s it looked as if trains could be made to run on wooden rails. This was thanks to a process whereby timber was semi-petrified by being impregnated with oxide of iron and lime.

An experimental line 174yd long was laid down near Vauxhall Bridge in London and, after extensive tests equivalent to seven years' traffic at 12 trains a day, the wooden rails were found to be virtually unscathed. Unfortunately, however, this revolutionary advance was lost in the miasma of railway politics.

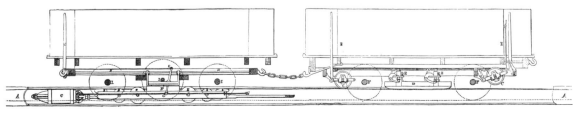

◀ ▲This vehicle (above), on display at the National Railway Museum in York, was used in 1861 by the Pneumatic Despatch Company for the underground transport of mailbags. Sixteen years earlier, the Croydon Atmospheric Railway had pioneered the use of vacuum power (left).

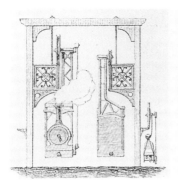

▲In 1880, a Mr Collett of Cardiff produced plans for an overhead railway in which the locomotive and coaches were suspended from wheels running on a rail above the train. Although Collett's scheme got no further than the design stage, it embodied a principle which became widely adopted.

The Never-Stop

A commuter system that intrigued the world was developed in Britain during the early 1920s. The Adkins-Lewis Varying Speed Continuous Transport System – or the Never-Stop, as it was known – was driven by a revolving continuous screw. The train engaged with the screw thread by means of rollers mounted between the running wheels.

At stations, the screw thread was fine, and the train crept along at 1 mph, but on the open line it widened to allow speeds of up to 36 mph. The Never-Stop was almost noiseless, thanks to rubber tyres that rolled over concrete tracks, and it required neither drivers, conductors nor signalmen. Millions were carried without mishap during the train's trial at the Wembley Exhibition in 1924 and '25, passengers stepping on and off as it slowed down at stations.

▶There have been various schemes for slipping and picking up coaches from a moving train. One proposal, made in 1902, was for a saddle car with wheels above as well as below. The idea was for those above to engage with rails on top of the train. On approaching the next station, the rails would be depressed and the saddle car let down again on to the track.

Still, the nonconformists persisted. If savings could not be made on the rails' composition, surely they could be made on their number? Monorails had much in their favour: they were easy to build; they allowed greater speeds over curves; they could be placed over rougher terrain; and, of course, one rail was half the price of two.

One of the fiercest advocates of the monorail was a Frenchman, C Lartigue, who developed a line comprising a single rail laid across a succession of A-shaped trestles. Astride this edifice, the rolling stock hung like saddle-bags, stabilized on either side by guide rails that ran halfway down the trestles.

Lartigue's system was not entirely unique. In 1869, the Director of Public Works in Syria had constructed a very similar line. Nor was its reputation entirely spotless: on one demonstration run, the French Minister of Agriculture was thrown into a ditch. But it nevertheless proved its worth when, on 1 March 1888, it became the United Kingdom's first and only public monorail.

The track ran 3ft above the ground for 9½ miles between the west Irish towns of Listowel and Ballybunion and at its peak carried more than 1400 passengers a day and some 10,000 tons of freight per year. In the railway's 36-year history there was only one accident, and that a minor one, and as late as 1915 its General Manager was claiming substantial profits. But by 1924 costs had risen, road transport had become widespread, and

the line was finally dismantled and sold for scrap.

One drawback to the Ballybunion line was its discomfort. In 1907, a passenger wrote that '...the motion reminds one of riding on a horse attached to a steam roundabout of the undulating type, working at full speed, only more so – very much more so, in fact'.

Perhaps this problem had been noted by Louis Brennan, an Irish torpedo expert, for in 1907 he exhibited a model, and in 1909 a lifesize example, of a silk-smooth, self-balancing monorail that adjusted itself by means of gyroscopes.

As the 40ft long monorail car slid out of its shed, it appeared to bystanders like 'some uncanny monster' that, 'on its single row of bogie wheels, moved steadily over serpentine curves, merely leaning to one side or the other to maintain its balance, and took the circle, and then the straight, with as much stability as if it had been supported on two sets of rails'.

Spinning top train

At either end of the locomotive – which could be driven by any power source – gyroscopes whirled at 3000 rpm, allowing the vehicle to be manipulated like a gigantic spinning top. So smoothly did it ride that the *Illustrated London News* heralded it under the headline, 'Billiards on a Slanting Table in a Train'.

Unlike Lartigue's version, which involved elaborate, raised drawbridge crossings, Brennan's

◀ Featured in the *Illustrated London News* in 1911, this 'new American train built on the Du Pont system' was 'specially constructed for passing through very narrow tunnels'. Unfortunately, no further details were given.

monorail was set at surface level and could even be adapted for inner-city trams. It was seemingly the perfect means of transport – an impression that was strengthened when in 1910 the Home Secretary Winston Churchill travelled on the monorail at the White City exhibition centre in London and even took a turn at the controls.

Like Lartigue, however, Brennan could not compete with the rapid developments in road travel. The train's power plant weighed so much that its top speed hovered around a mere 20 mph. And the gyroscopes' ball-bearings soon wore out, with potentially disastrous consequences. Before long, his invention had faded into obscurity.

Overhead railways

By that time, however, the question was no longer whether trains should travel over one or two rails. It was whether they should travel over them at all. Many now held that the rails should be supported on overhead gantries, with the train being slung underneath.

Overhead railways had several advantages, the main being their suitability for hilly or built-up areas, and the world's first had been completed as early as 1903, running over eight miles along the steep-sided valley of the River Wupper in Germany. The Schwebebahn, or 'swinging railway', as it became known, was a runaway success.

Construction costs were a sixth of those for an underground, and a third of those for a conventional track. And the safety record was admirable. In its first 50 years of use, some 80 million passengers were carried with only one fatality – and that was the passenger's own fault.

Although overhead lines never became widespread, they seized the public imagination as the way of the future. And no development was more futuristic than George Bennie's Railplane. With the end of World War I, Germany had found itself with a surplus of Zeppelin equipment, and engineers had tried to apply the redundant machinery to rail travel.

A number of remarkable, if terrifying, propellor-driven locomotives were successfully produced. But it was only when Bennie applied the idea to an overhead system similar to the Schwebebahn that it began to be taken seriously.

The Bennie Railplane consisted of a lightweight vehicle to each end of which was fixed an airscrew propeller driven either by a diesel engine or electric motor. The Railplane was suspended from a single rail set in an overhead lattice of girders.

Below, stability was maintained by a slender guide rail. The system, so Bennie claimed, could achieve speeds of up to 200 mph. It was safe, too, thanks to a revolutionary device that automatically stopped the vehicle if it ran through a red light.

In 1930, an experimental 426ft long track was erected over a disused spur of the London & North Eastern Railway at Milngavie, near Glasgow. So promising were the runs over this line that a series of elaborate schemes were mooted, the most ambitious being a London – Paris link that would take just 2½ hours – including a cross-Channel seaplane flight.

But it seems that the cost of the scheme was more than investors could stand, and the Bennie Railplane hung forlornly outside Milngavie until the test track was demolished and sold in 1956.

Bennie, Brennan and Brunel are among the famous failures. But there were a multitude of others, less well-known, who tried to produce an alternative to the conventional steam railway. Ideas ranged from sail-propelled trolleys to trains sliding over water-lubricated tracks. The man who finally brought it off was Dr Werner von Siemens, who at an exhibition in Berlin in 1879 laid down the world's first electric railway.

▼ Looking like machines from a futuristic fantasy by H G Wells, these bizarre vehicles sprang from the imagination of an American inventor in the early 1900s, who thought he had found a way of enabling trains to pass each other on a single-track railroad.

**This bizarre monorail was demonstrated by Louis Brennan at Gillingham in Kent, England, in 1909. The
40-foot long car was balanced on the single rail by the action of gyroscopes that revolved at 3000rpm.
When the gyroscopes were stationary struts projected from the side of the car to hold it upright.**

The Canadian Pacific Railway

**To most Canadians, the idea of building a
railway across the 3000 miles of wilderness that
lay between the Atlantic and the Pacific was a mere pipe
dream. It took the Canadian Pacific Railway just
five years to make the dream reality.**

The trouble with Canada, one of its prime ministers observed, is that it has too much geography. The builders of the Canadian Pacific Railway (CPR) would have agreed wholeheartedly. Spanning the North American continent between Montreal and Vancouver, the CPR runs almost 3000 miles over some of the wildest country on earth. When completed in 1885, it was hailed as a landmark in human endeavour.

The idea of a trans-Canadian railway had been mooted as early as 1849, but it was not until 1857 that an Imperial Commission despatched Captain John Palliser, an officer in the Waterford Artillery Militia, to survey a possible route through the interior.

When he returned, four years later, it was with disheartening news. While admitting the possibility of railway construction, he warned that, 'The knowledge of this country as a whole would never lead me to advocate a line of communication from Canada across the continent to the Pacific.' And there, for a while, the matter rested.

The price of a railway

But politics soon intervened. In 1867, Canada became a self-governing dominion within the British Empire, and its first prime minister, John Macdonald, looked forward to the emergence of a powerful Canadian nation, including British Columbia in the west. There was, however, a snag. The British Columbians were not yet under Canadian rule, and their price for joining the new dominion was the construction of a transcontinental railway.

As things stood, their only access to the east coast was by boat around Cape Horn, by rail across the United States, or overland by a cumbersome combination of steamboat, stage coach, dogsled and canoe.

Under the agreement signed between Canada and British Columbia in July 1871, the dominion committed itself to begin work on the railway in two years and complete it within 10 years. A tall, bearded Scot, Sandford Fleming, was appointed chief engineer of the Pacific Railway Survey. To him fell the task of finding the most practical and

18617

▶The railway builders advance through the Lower Fraser Valley, working at a speed that astonished onlookers. 'Round me,' wrote the British novelist Morley Roberts, 'I saw the primeval forest torn down, cut and hewed and hacked...The brute power of man's organized civilization had fought with Nature and had for the time being vanquished her.'

A-4302

◀ A half-built bridge rears over the waters of the Winnipeg River. Hundreds of such spans appeared in the course of the CPR's construction, and so skilful did the bridge-building crews become that on several occasions trains ran in the late afternoon over timbers which had been part of the virgin forest at daybreak.

Rogers Pass

One of the most troublesome sections on the CPR was the 4300ft high Rogers Pass through the Selkirk Mountains. Here, conditions could be appalling, with avalanches of over a million tons thundering down the hillside at speeds of 60 miles per hour.

For a distance of five miles the track had to be protected by ingeniously designed sheds that diverted the snow away from the line. Frequently, however, these failed, and in winter snow ploughs and repair gangs were on constant standby to clear the line.

Nor was maintenance any easier in summer. Fire patrols monitored the wooden barriers day and night, lest they burn down in the tinder dry conditions. By 1916, Rogers Pass had become too much of a problem, and it was bypassed with the five mile long Connaught Tunnel.

economical route through a daunting barrier of swamps, grasslands and mountain ranges.

His diary detailed the terrifying obstacles he encountered. Of one precipitous traverse he wrote, 'I do not think I can ever forget that terrible walk...We are from five to eight hundred feet high on a path of from ten to fifteen inches wide and at some points almost obliterated, with slopes above and below us so steep that a stone would roll into the torrent in the abyss below.'

Nor were matters much better on the flat: 'We have many fallen trees to climb over, and it is no small matter to struggle over trees ten feet and upwards in diameter. We have rocks to ascend and descend; we have a marsh to cross in which we sink often to the middle. For half a mile we have waded, I will not say picked, our way to the opposite side, through a channel filled with stagnant water, having an odour long to be remembered...Rain continues falling incessantly.'

Railway route agreed

Fleming covered little new ground – at least two others had already tramped in Palliser's wake – but what he did cover he covered thoroughly. And in 1872 his efforts bore fruit with the acceptance of his proposed route along the north shore of Lake Superior, up the Saskatchewan Valley and through the Rocky Mountains at Yellow Head Pass.

From then on, however, the project stagnated. The original agreement had been to complete the railway by 1881. But by 1879, thanks to a combination of inefficiency, corruption and economic recession, only 713 miles of track were in place. The British Columbians were outraged and threatened secession.

As the dominion dithered, a new construction syndicate stepped forward. The Canadian Pacific Railroad Company, as it later dubbed itself, undertook to complete the track by 1891 in return for $25 million, 25 million acres of land 'fairly fit for settlement' and a guarantee that there would be no competing railways for 20 years.

Into the swamps

The plan was for gangs to battle from east and west to beat the schedule. The eastern team, under a veteran US railroader, William Van Horne, set off on 2 May 1881. First, it had to contend with the muskegs, the limitless swamps of Southern Ontario. Ton after ton of infill was poured into their depths, but still the rails sank under the weight of the work's engines. The problem was eventually solved by bedding the rails on 40ft sleepers.

Next the labourers had to blast their way along the rocky north shore of Lake Superior, working just a few feet above the waterline to carve a passage beneath towering cliffs.

Multiple threats

The landscape was not the only difficulty the construction teams had to face. Near-Arctic weather conditions often halted work. Bears were a frequent threat. And on one occasion, troops had to be called in to deal with displaced and angry Indians. Poor food and primitive living conditions led to a steady southward seepage of workers seeking employment on US lines.

▼Subjected to extreme danger and back-breaking hardship, and paid only meagre wages, the men who built the CPR found their main consolation in alcohol. Although prohibition was in effect all along the line, the whisky peddlers always managed to find a hiding place for their supplies – two favourites were the boilers of disabled locomotives and the bellies of dead packhorses.

A-4316

▶Winter snow blankets a CPR construction camp on the north shore of Lake Superior. Conditions in such camps were primitive, with between 60 and 80 workers crammed into one airless and insanitary shack. Baths and plumbing were unknown, and the men slept in double-decker bunks on mattresses of hay.

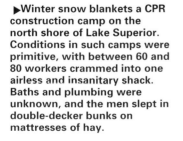

Life was no easier for the 7000-strong western workforce, consisting mainly of Chinese and led by another American, Charles Onderdonk, which had begun advancing in May 1880 through the rugged terrain of British Columbia. Along one stretch almost 600 men were killed by avalanches and epidemics – an average of four men for every mile of track laid.

So difficult was it to bring supplies overland that a specially constructed steam boat was employed to navigate the uncharted waters of the Fraser River.

The westerners could, however, take consolation from the fact that it was Van Horne's crews which had actually to break through the massive barrier of the Rockies.

Conquering the prairie

The easterners, meanwhile, were doing well. By August 1883, Van Horne's contingent of 7,600 men and 1,700 teams of horses had crossed a thousand miles of undulating prairie to reach Calgary. Contemporary accounts marvelled at their methodical advance through empty terrain where both food and materials had to be transported hundreds of miles to the railhead.

'The bridgemen proceeded in advance along the waste; in a few hours the timber was sawn and arranged; in a few hours more the piles were driven, and in six-and-thirty hours, and less at times, a...bridge was erected where no bridge had ever been before!'

Track laying triumph

Behind the bridgemen came the track layers. 'Moving along slowly, but with admirable precision, it was beautiful to watch them gradually coming near, everything moving like clockwork – each man in his place, knowing exactly his work, and doing it at the right time and in the right way. Onward they come, pass on, and leave the won-

A-4303

dering spectator behind while he is still engrossed by the wonderful sight.'

By November 1883, the tracks had begun to climb the Rocky Mountains themselves. As one writer later described it, '...every mile of tunnel and track was sealed with the blood of men...There are bridges that hang in the air – mere spider webs of iron...There are places where the masonry is plastered, so to speak, against the solid rock of the mountains. There are ledges midway between heaven and earth, and elevations where the whirling trains plunge headlong into clouds.'

Way through the Rockies

Eventually, the railway penetrated the Rockies, though not at Yellow Head Pass, as suggested by Fleming, but by a shorter route further south. At more than 5,300ft, Kicking Horse Pass – so named after a painful incident during Palliser's journey – was the highest point in the entire railway. It was also a nightmare for the men who had to work on its dizzy inclines.

Unable to use heavy drills on the slopes, they had to punch out all the blasting holes by hand. Even so, they managed to move a million and a

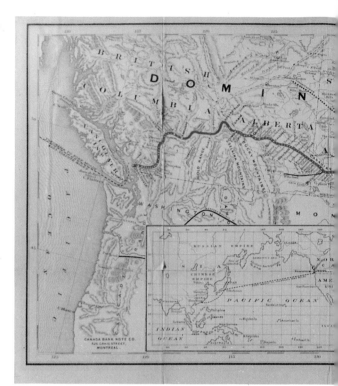

▼To whites, the narrow canyon of the Fraser River was known as 'Hell's Gate'. To the Chinese railway coolies who laboured on its massive flanks it was known as 'The Slaughter Pen' – a grim acknowledgement of the large number of lives it claimed.

483

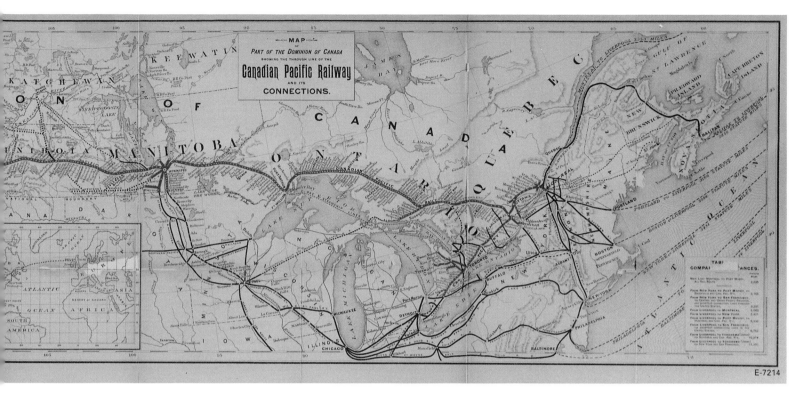

E-7214

▲An early map of the CPR shows the epic scope of the railway builders' achievement. According to one eyewitness of the line's construction, 'It was Magic – like the mirage on the prairies, changing the face of the whole country.'

half cubic yards of earth and rock during 1884.

But the ordeal was far from over. For beyond the Rockies lay the equally formidable Selkirk Range, where gangs slogged their way through the 4,300ft high Rogers Pass, a desolate spot bedevilled by deep snows in winter and forest fires in summer.

At length, Van Horne's men met those of Onderdonk in Eagle Pass in the Gold Mountains, where the final spike was driven in on 7 November 1885 – six years ahead of schedule. One of those who attended the short ceremony was Sandford Fleming. 'It seemed,' he later recalled, 'as if the act now performed had worked a spell on all present. Each one appeared absorbed in his own reflections.' The silence was broken by a cheer, 'and it was no ordinary cheer. The subdued enthusiasm, the pent-up feelings of men familiar with hard work, now found vent.'

After more cheering and congratulations, the whistle of the locomotive that had brought the official party from the west sounded for the start of the return journey. At the same time, the conductor yelled, 'All aboard for the Pacific!'

A-4411

The Big Hill

Locomotive drivers soon learned to hate the Big Hill, as the 7½ mile section of track leading west from Kicking Horse Pass, through the Rocky Mountains, was called. With a gradient of 1 in 22, it was the steepest ever encountered on a main line. A standard freight train needed four locomotives to make the ascent.

On the way down, drivers had to creep along at six miles per hour, halting every two miles to inspect the brakes for signs of wear. The risk of a runaway was ever present, and special trap sidings were constructed in case of such an eventuality.

Not until 1909 was this perilous slope made redundant, when engineers re-routed the line through two spiral tunnels with a lesser gradient.

◄ Workmen line one of the newly carved rock cuttings along the north shore of Lake Superior. So hard was the rock in this area that it had to be blasted with dynamite – a process fraught with danger. On one occasion, a man tried to tamp a cartridge with a crowbar, and was blown to bits.

Port Arthur at the head of Lake Superior was reached by rail from Winnipeg and came to be served by the Canadian National and Canadian Pacific railroads. In conditions that have long posed severe difficulties to the country's railroad operators, a steam locomotive gets under way.

The Trans-Siberian Railway

The Trans-Siberian Railway runs from Moscow to Vladivostok – a distance of more than 9600km (6000 miles). But building it was a herculean task – it was dogged by both war and revolution – and it took a quarter of a century for the world's longest continuous railway to reach completion.

Siberia had many advantages: limitless space, fertile soil, bountiful wildlife, staggering natural resources – everything, in fact, to commend it to the Russian Tsars who, from the 16th century, undertook a steady annexation of the region. But there was one major drawback: the place was well-nigh impassable. In winter, it was a frozen desert, in summer a waterlogged morass. Rivers and lakes were a constant impediment, as was the taiga, the vast tracts of swampy eastern pine forest which were home to legions of mosquitoes and the ferocious Manchurian tiger.

If Russians wanted to voyage from west to east of their vast empire, they had to go via a rudimentary trail known as the Great Siberian Post Road. So inaccessible was Siberia that, after much deliberation, the tsars could find no use for it other than as a huge, natural prison camp.

Yet the area had undeniable potential. And in the mid-19th century, an American, Perry McDonough Collins, put forward the first proposal for a trans-Siberian railway. In December 1856 he set out from St Petersburg along his suggested route to the River Amur. The following July, having travelled 9600km (6000 miles), he reached the Pacific port of Nicolayevsk, from where he wrote an enthusiastic report trumpeting the strategic and commercial advantages of a railway.

The government prevaricated. Russia did not have the technical capability. It would be too difficult. It would be too expensive. Besides, it would upset landowners in the west, who might be ruined by cheap imports of eastern wheat. Months later, after Collins had given up hope and returned to the United States, he received a note from Russian officials saying his plan was premature. There were other ideas, some more fanciful than practicable – one Englishman suggested a horse tramway; a Russian proposed a 3000km (1800 mile) wooden tunnel – but all were dismissed until

▼ A train crosses one of the newly completed bridges on the Trans-Siberian Railway. The terrain through which the line had to pass was scattered with lakes and rivers, and bridges were built in abundance. But some of these were so flimsy that wagons had to be rolled over them one by one, as they could not bear the weight of a train.

▲ A trackside signpost gives an indication of the awesome distances traversed by the Trans-Siberian Railway. Isolated in a wilderness of seemingly limitless pine forest, those struggling to build the line had to rely on supplies brought in from the outside. In some cases, these were landed at the Siberian port of Vladivostok and shipped to the construction sites by river.

the late 1880s, when the exigencies of trade and defence gave the opening up of Siberia fresh urgency.

The new Tsar, Alexander III, wrote that 'up to the present the Government has done scarcely anything to meet the demands of this rich but forsaken country. It is time, it is high time!' In 1891, he formed the Siberian Railway Commission (SRC), appointing his son and heir, Nicholas, to oversee the project. It was the Russian Finance Minister, Sergius Witte, however, who took charge of the day-to-day planning and construction.

Witte divided the route into six main sections: the West Siberian; the Central Siberian; the Ussuri; the Circumbaikal; the Transbaikal; and the Amur. Construction of the Far Eastern section began on 19 May 1891, when Nicholas dug the first turf at the Pacific port of Vladivostok. Building of the West Siberian line was started two months later just outside Chelyabinsk. To raise extra money for the project, Tsar Alexander prompted his ministers to form a state liquor monopoly. This did little to reduce vodka consumption, but it did raise an impressive $12 million per year. Yet even this unceasing source of finance could not hide the difficulties which the

SRC had to overcome.

On the West Siberian, heavy frosts limited construction to only four months of the year. In some places there was such a shortage of materials that supplies had to be carried from distances of up to 800km (500 miles). The same problem applied to skilled labour, which was imported from as far afield as Italy, Turkey and Persia.

The Ussuri line was bedevilled not only by the landscape – near-impenetrable taiga – but by a workforce comprising Russian soldiery, Chinese coolies and Siberian convicts. The coolies refused to turn out if it was raining or if a Manchurian tiger was rumoured to be in the area; the soldiers refused to work next to criminals; and the criminals were so industrious that the murder rate along the construction sites averaged almost 10 a week. At the same time, men succumbed to malaria, horses to Siberian anthrax and the tracks to devastating floods.

Arctic Circle supplies

The Central Siberian was constricted by a working window of only three months in the year, during which the iron-hard ground melted into a glutinous quagmire. Rivers abounded: along one 80km (50 mile) stretch it was necessary to erect more than 80 bridges. In addition, there were overwhelming logistical problems: supplies had to be sent from the west by sea, either round the Cape of Good Hope or, in the case of a cargo of rails from England, above the Arctic Circle.

An Englishman, James Young Simpson, observed some of the rail gangs going about their business. 'In the heat of the midday sun,' he wrote later, 'it was assuredly hard work, and one was not surprised to see the somewhat deliberate fashion in which any task was carried through. The great majority of the labourers were toiling in white (or what had once been white) cotton shirts and pantaloons, barefoot, bareheaded. Some of their tools and implements were primitive – e.g. the wheelless barrow shoved along a plank.'

▲ For many Russians, the Trans-Siberian Railway was a potent symbol of their country's greatness. Opinion in the West tended to be sceptical, however, and one British newspaper dismissed the project as 'Rusty streaks of iron through the vastness of nothing to the extremities of nowhere.'

▼ Three construction workers stand with a small handcart on the latest of one of the Trans-Siberian's many river bridges. Foreign observers were surprised by the crudity of the tools and implements used for building the line, noting the absence of equipment such as excavators and tip-wagons.

Throughout its length, Simpson noted, the line was accompanied on either side by excavations of varying size, from which the soil was taken for its construction. Where the ditches were broad, they filled with water, and became 'the spacious nurseries of myriads of mosquitoes and other objectionable forms of insect life'.

As if working conditions were not trying enough, the surveyors everywhere were both incompetent and corrupt. They planned lines on frozen railbeds that were doomed to sink in the summer thaw. They built curves so tight that a train travelling at only 16km/h (10mph) would be derailed. They charged exorbitant fees for routing the line through a town.

The merchants of Tomsk, convinced that the surveyors could not ignore a city of such size and importance, refused to go along with the extortion – only to find the city duly bypassed by the railway. The authorities in St Petersburg did not discover the omission until the Trans-Siberian was completed, necessitating the construction of a special – and costly – loop line.

Conniving contractors

The contractors were no better. Paid by the kilometre, they happily slapped down tracks of the lowest quality on the flimsiest foundations. Rails were half the standard weight and thickness. Sleepers were of uncured wood that warped and cracked with the coming of spring. Bridges were impossibly rickety. Cuttings were so narrow that they scraped the sides of coaches. One contractor built an embankment of snow instead of earth, so that the thaw caused the track to subside by 1.2m (4ft) throughout the length of his section.

All these faults, along with those of the surveyors, necessitated expensive rebuilding. And yet, somehow, the lines came in on, or even ahead of, schedule. The West Siberian was completed in 1896, the Ussuri in 1897 and the Central Siberian in 1899 – the latter, a year ahead of the deadline.

Graveyard run

In the Russian Civil War that followed the Bolshevik Revolution of 1917, the Trans-Siberian Railway (TSR) was a much fought over prize. The stations were crucial strategic points and many of them were the scene of prolonged bloodshed. At Irkutsk station, the commander of the anti-Bolshevik White Russians, Admiral Alexander Kolchak, was captured while travelling in a six-train convoy with a large horde of looted treasure to Vladivostok. He was shot. Further east, the Cossack warlord, Grigory Semyanov, and his men rode in armoured trains, murdering and robbing as they went. Those in particular danger were stationmasters and their staffs, who were executed for alleged Red sympathies.

In 1919, with the Whites on the verge of defeat, the TSR became clogged with refugees trying to make their escape. Famine and typhus added to the horrors of the bitter winter, and it was said that every station became a graveyard.

Key

West Siberian line (1400km/900 miles)
Central Siberian line (1800km/1000 miles)
Ussuri line (750km/500 miles)
Amur line (1900km/1200 miles)
Transbaikal line (1100km/700 miles)
Circumbaikal Loop (250km/160 miles)
Chinese Eastern Railway (1200km/750 miles)
existing line

SCANDINAVIA

RUSSIA

Great Siberian Plain

Ural Mountains

MOSCOW

PERM

EKATERINBERG (SVERDLOVSK)

CHELYABINSK

OMSK

Ob River

NOVONIKOLAYEVSK (NOVOSIBIRSK)

Angara River

KRASNOYARSK

IRKUTSK

VERKHNEUDINSK (ULAN-UDE)

Lake Baikal

PORT BAIKAL

MYSOVSK (BABUSHKIN)

Yablonovyy Mountains

CHITA

SRETENSK

Amur River

KHABAROVSK

MANCHURIA

VLADIVOSTOK

KHAZAKHSTAN

MONGOLIA

►Workers lay track on the Central Siberian section of the railway. There was no mechanical equipment and the construction was carried on by a vast army of labourers, including many foreigners. They slept in mud huts during the winter and tents in summer, and suffered from a constant lack of food and medical facilities.

Steaming on thin ice

In February 1904, Russia found itself at war with Japan. Men and munitions poured eastwards – and stopped at Lake Baikal. The Circumbaikal Loop had yet to be completed and the two ferries which would otherwise have made the crossing were trapped in 1.5m (5ft) of ice. So a line was hastily laid across the frozen lake, using extra-long sleepers to spread the load. But the test locomotive steamed over a section which had been weakened by warm underwater springs and plunged down to the lake bed, opening up a massive crack in the ice more than 20km (12 miles) long.

Thereafter the trains were dismantled and dragged piece by piece to the opposite shore, the army marching in their wake. Seventeen hours and 40km (25 miles) later, the convoy reassembled and the Russians continued to the war – which they lost.

Work had started, meanwhile, on the Transbaikal section, where the railway gangs faced the iron-hard foe of permafrost.

Ordinary tools, such as pick axes, were useless in such conditions; the only way to advance the line was with dynamite, or by thawing the ground with fires. But nothing could be done to tame Siberia's tempestuous weather. At one point, in the Yablonovyy Mountains, the railway was wiped out by a colossal wall of water some four metres (13ft) high. Hundreds of villages and tens of thousands of cattle were lost along the Ingoda, Onon, Shilka and Amur rivers.

However, in January 1900 the Transbaikal section was completed. At the same time, the line from Irkutsk to the western shore of the vast, freshwater Lake Baikal was opened. By now work

had also begun on the Circumbaikal Loop, which was to run round the southern shore of the lake – the depth made a bridge impossible – and over some of the most mountainous terrain on the route. For five years, between 1899 and 1904, labourers struggled against almost impossible odds, building 33 tunnels and more than 200 bridges to take the line – often along cliffs that fell sheer into the water – over its 250km (160 mile) course.

Until the Loop was finished, trains crossed Lake Baikal by means of a ferry, the *Baikal*. Built by Armstrong Whitworth & Co of Newcastle, it was shipped in 7000 sections to St Petersburg, from whence it was taken by barge, sled and train to the shores of Lake Baikal. Here it was reassembled under the supervision of British engineers, going into regular service in April 1900. Not only could the 4000 ton vessel carry an entire express train, but it also had deck space for 650 third class passengers and cabins for 150 first or second class passengers. In addition, it boasted a number of grandiose facilities, including a chapel, which soon became popular for local marriages.

A smaller ship, the *Angara*, also built by Armstrong Whitworth, was ordered as an ice-breaker. Alas, it was not always equal to the task. In the winter, when the lake was covered by 1.5m (5ft) of ice, it was the *Baikal*, unloaded, which had to clear a way for the *Angara*. Sometimes, both vessels became icebound, in which case passengers were bundled into huge baskets and transport-

◄ An estimated 15 million sleepers were used in the construction of the Trans-Siberian Railway. But the contractors, with their concern for profits rather than safety, were unscrupulous in their use of inferior materials, so that it was not unusual for sleepers to be made of green, uncured logs that warped and cracked with the coming of spring.

ed to the opposite shore on horse-drawn sleighs. At one point, there was a relay service of 2000 sleighs skittering across the frozen expanse.

One of those who crossed the lake before completion of the Transbaikal Loop was an American travel writer, Michael Myers Shoemaker. 'If inclined to suicide,' he wrote, 'I should avoid that passage of Baikal as I would Niagara, for like that cataract, the death cold waters of that awful channel fascinate and are intolerable.'

The Amur line, meanwhile, had been set aside in favour of a more direct and less expensive route. Taking advantage of the largely bankrupt Chinese government, Witte negotiated a deal which allowed him to link the Transbaikal and Ussuri sections with a line driven through Chinese Manchuria. The Chinese Eastern Railway (CER), as it was called, was as nightmarish to build as any other stretch of the Trans-Siberian. Asiatic cholera and bubonic plague decimated the workforce of more than 200,000 coolies, and an army of 5000 Russian railway police was required to keep at bay the local *Hunghutze* (Redbeard) bandits.

Nevertheless, by 1900 the CER was almost complete. It was now, however, that China was swept up in the Boxer Rebellion. Fervent Chinese nationalists, with the passive support of the Peking government, attacked all things foreign, massacring hundreds of Chinese Christians and Western missionaries, and destroying and looting vast amounts of property.

The rebellion was eventually crushed by a combination of Western, Japanese and Russian forces. However, by the time order was restored along the CER in 1901, only about one third of the completed 1280km (800 miles) remained in working order. Yet, miraculously, a regular service was running from Moscow to Vladivostok only two years later. It seemed that the dream of a Trans-Siberian Railway had at last been realized.

Litany of woe

But any sense of jubilation was short-lived. In 1904, Russia became involved in a brief, but disastrous, war with Japan. With Manchuria now under the influence of the Japanese, and part of the CER actually controlled by them, the SRC set to work again. The Amur line was resurrected and replanned along a wide northern loop. For eight years from 1908, a work force of 80,000 underwent the usual litany of woe – taiga, permafrost, mosquitoes, accidents, disease – until, in 1916, the 1900km (1200 mile) line was finished.

Tsar Nicholas II – as he had become – could now travel uninterrupted from his capital, St Petersburg, to the port of Vladivostok, where he had turned the first sod of the Trans-Siberian Railway a quarter of a century earlier. But he never made the journey. Following the Russian Revolution of 1917, he and his family were shot by the Bolsheviks. What the Russian press had hailed as 'the fairest jewel in the crown of the Tsars' now belonged to their Soviet successors.

Fallen among thieves
The engineers who travelled from Newcastle to Lake Baikal to supervise the reassembly of the British-built train ferry, the *Baikal*, were in for a gloomy time. An English MP, Sir Henry Norman, who visited them in 1900, described the village in which they were living as 'a nest of crime and robbery', where every civilized person carried a revolver.

The whole population, lamented Norman, was ex-convict or worse. 'The boss of the labourers on the Baikal was in Siberia for outraging a child; the man who conducted me...was a murderer from the Caucasus; a short time before my visit another murderer employed on the ship had tried to repeat his crime, and had been consigned to the chain gangs again; the very day I was there the police were looking for a man supposed to have obtained work in the yard, who was wanted for killing eight people...'

▼ Although the stations on the Trans-Siberian were officially divided into five categories according to size and amenity, all stations of any importance, even those in categories III and IV, soon began burgeoning into towns. The station shown here is believed to be a category III type.

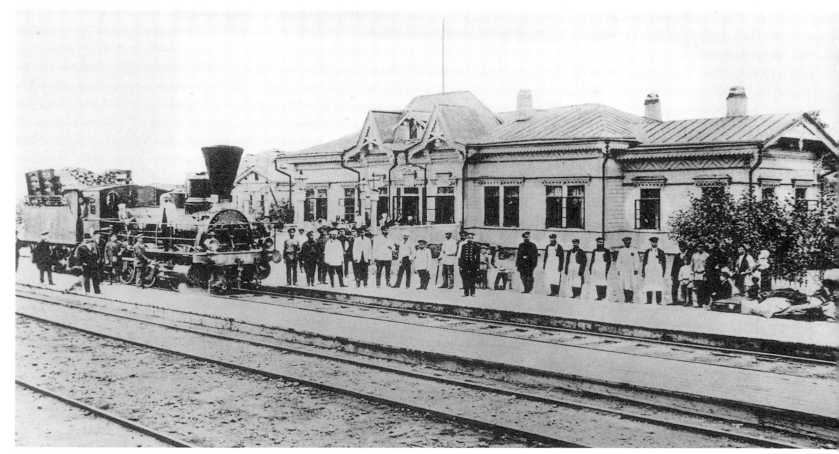

The immense distances of the Trans-Siberian, coupled with the relatively short time that early steam locomotives could operate without servicing, meant that locomotive depots had to be provided at regular intervals.

Until the railway along the southern shore of Lake Baikal was completed in 1904, the largest freshwater lake in Asia had to be crossed by train ferry. This was the larger of two vessels, the *Baikal*, which weighed 4000 tons and was capable of breaking through ice 3 feet thick.

The Royal Scot in America

In 1927, the new Royal Scot class of locomotive began to ply the West Coast route to Scotland. The event was a great publicity coup for the London Midland & Scottish Railway. But a few years later came an even greater triumph - the spectacular Royal Scot tour of North America.

On 1 May 1933, the citizens of Montreal watched the unlikely spectacle of a British train steaming out of Windsor station. As the gleaming 4-6-0 locomotive and its eight coaches raced through towns and woodland on the way to Toronto, thousands turned out at wayside stations along the route to cheer them on.

At times, so great were the crowds that the driver had to slow down to 15mph to avoid running them over. Such was the start of The Royal Scot's historic tour of North America – a six-month Odyssey that took it from the Atlantic to the Pacific and back again.

The venture had been mooted three years earlier during a visit to America by the chairman of the London Midland & Scottish Railway (LMS), Sir Josiah Stamp. The LMS had been invited to exhibit a locomotive of its new Royal Scot class at the forthcoming World Fair, or Century of Progress Exposition, in Chicago, and Stamp had suggested combining this with a tour by a complete train. Never before had such an event taken place, and Stamp's proposal aroused tremendous enthusiasm on both sides of the Atlantic. In March 1933, however, on the eve of the train's departure from England, the United States was gripped by a financial crisis which paralyzed the nation's banking system. It was decided, nevertheless, to go ahead with the trip, and on 5 April the locomotive and its

eight coaches were loaded on board the Canadian Pacific steamship *Beaverdale* at London's Tilbury Docks. On 21 April, the train was unloaded at Montreal and re-assembled at the Angus shops of the Canadian Pacific Railroad.

As far as the crowds were concerned, the locomotive they had turned out to cheer was the first of the Royal Scot class, No 6100 *Royal Scot* itself. In fact, the LMS, believing that a newer locomotive would be more reliable, had provided a substitute. The real *Royal Scot* had exchanged its famous name and number with locomotive No 6152 *The King's Dragoon Guardsman*, and this was the engine that won the admiration of the Canadians and Americans. (The renumbering remained permanent and the original 6100 retained its less illustrious identity until it was withdrawn from service in 1962 and scrapped.) On 4 May, when the new *Royal Scot* and its coaches crossed from Canada into the United States, some 10,000 people waited at midnight in pouring rain at Niagara Falls to watch the event. For Driver William Gilbertson and Fireman John Jackson, it was

◄ Bearing the title of the famous train from which it takes its name, *Royal Scot* waits at Montreal at the start of its epic 1933 tour of North America. *Royal Scot* has also been fitted with a headlamp and bell – compulsory fixtures for main line locomotives in Canada and the United States.

▲The world's largest floating crane, *London Mammoth*, hauls *Royal Scot*'s chassis on board the steamship *Beaverdale* at Tilbury in April 1933. The locomotive was stowed in *Beaverdale*'s hold in three sections, while the eight coaches were firmly secured on deck, four forward and four aft.

Iron Horse Britannia

Royal Scot was not the first British locomotive to visit the United States. In 1927, the Great Western Railway (GWR) had been invited to supply an engine for the Fair of the Iron Horse, the centenary celebrations of the Baltimore & Ohio Railroad.

The GWR offered the first of its latest and biggest locomotive class, a Cathedral 4-6-0, which was due to be unveiled later that year. However, as it became clear that the locomotive was being regarded as a representative of Britain rather than just the GWR, it was decided to change the name of the class to King. Thus it was the locomotive *King George V* that appeared at the Iron Horse Fair.

Accompanied by an enthusiastic female admirer decked out as Britannia, it was given the honour of leading the Fair's daily procession. As a finale, it made a run of 272 miles.

a foretaste of what was to follow.

Bagpipe welcome

Wherever the train stopped, it was besieged by admirers. At New York City, where it was greeted by the skirl of bagpipes, more than 80,000 visitors walked through the coaches and inspected the locomotive.

Even at stations where *Royal Scot* was not scheduled to stop, large crowds gathered. At Huntingdon in Pennsylvania, for example, there were more than 400 people standing on the platform at two o'clock in the morning, just to see the train speed past. Eventually, after three weeks of solid if unspectacular running, the train arrived in the Fair Grounds at Chicago at 5.56am on 25 May – four minutes ahead of its scheduled time.

The Exposition opened the next day and The Royal Scot proved a major attraction from the start. Queues built up from first opening each morning and were still there when the Exposition closed down for the night. For those whose roots lay in England or Scotland, the train was a tangible reminder of home. The engine itself had been built by the North British Locomotive Co in

Glasgow and families drove hundreds of miles to 'touch a piece of Scotland'. Many were seen to leave the display site with tears in their eyes.

It was not just English and Scottish immigrants who clamoured to see the train. Native-born Americans, who would normally have been dismissive of anything made outside the USA, were fascinated by this 'British engine, small and trim'. As one American newspaper put it, 'The American train gives the impression of having been built on square lines, whereas The Royal Scot is rounded wherever possible, giving an impression of ease and grace that is missing from the American product.'

Launching a new tour

The total number of visitors to the train during its five month stay in Chicago was officially given as 2,074,348. The original plan had been for The Royal Scot to take a more or less direct route back to Montreal, with exhibitions at some of the intermediate stations. But requests for further visits flooded in from all over North America and it was decided that the train should embark on a post-Exposition tour covering a further 8,560 miles.

The send-off on this further excursion was a

▼Visitors cram into Montreal's Windsor station to inspect the famous LMS express train before the start of its tour. According to one report, 'thousands left their beds early in the morning to view the spectacle of an English train rushing over Canadian soil'.

▲Having arrived in Montreal, *Royal Scot* and its coaches were reassembled at the workshops of the Canadian Pacific Railway. During the trial run that followed, the train reached a speed of 75mph. Thousands turned out to watch the event, setting a pattern that was to persist throughout the tour.

riot of flag-waving and cheering. Chicago's schoolchildren had been given the day off and the side of the tracks was thronged with well-wishers up to the outskirts of the city. Accompanied for the first 40 miles of its journey by the famous Burlington Flyer, the British express was accorded a cacophonous salute of factory sirens, car horns and blasts from other locomotives.

Admiration unbounded

Every stop was packed with well-wishers. At Indianapolis station, thousands had to be turned away because the concourse was overcrowded; at Louisville, even though special trams were laid on to serve the crowds, the police had difficulty in keeping order; at San Francisco, the train was followed by admirers, riding on every kind of vehicle, and yelling 'Good old England!'

Many people wanted souvenirs, and at Bloomington half a mile of coins were laid on the track to be crushed by the mighty wheels of *Royal Scot*, thereby becoming highly sought-after collectors' items. Not surprisingly, there were thefts of small items from the train itself; 500 lightbulbs and countless antimacassars disappeared, and hundreds of autographs were written on the walls and ceiling of the coaches.

It was on the sections of track furthest from the big cities that *Royal Scot* impressed professional railroaders. They were sceptical about the ability of the locomotive – tiny in comparison with some of the local behemoths – to pull its full load up the steep gradients of the mountains which cross the continent from north to south.

They were proved wrong as *Royal Scot* managed the notorious Horseshoe Bend on the Pennsylvania Railroad and the 1 in 40 gradient on the Canadian Pacific main line over the Rockies without the aid of a second engine, something the local engines were unable to match. The professionals were also impressed by the smoothness of *Royal Scot*'s running and its economical coal consumption.

The train re-entered Montreal's Windsor station on 11 November, Armistice Day, and Driver Gilbertson's first action on stepping down from the cab was to lay a wreath from LMS railwaymen on the war memorial to the men of the Canadian Pacific Railway. Two weeks later, *Royal Scot* and its coaches were reloaded aboard the *Beaverdale*, which then sailed down the icy St Lawrence on the first stage of the long journey home.

On arrival at Tilbury Docks, the train was taken to Crewe works, where it received an overhaul before being reassigned to more normal duties. It had covered 11,743 miles under its own steam, without the engine or carriages needing a single replacement part (except for new fittings to replace those taken by souvenir hunters).

It had been visited by 3,021,601 people and seen by many millions more. *The Times* wrote that the trip had 'blazed a trail of friendship which it will be hard to efface'. The Royal Scot's triumph had aroused much excitement in Britain, and the train was dispatched on a promotional tour of the LMS network.

No 6100 continued to pull main line trains and heavy freight until it was withdrawn from service in 1965.

▲During its five month stay at the World Fair in Chicago, The Royal Scot, seen on display next to an illustrious American express, The Burlington Flyer, attracted over two million visitors. So enthusiastic was the public response that the British train extended its post-Fair tour by more than 8000 miles.

◄ Although much smaller than North American locomotives, *Royal Scot*, seen here steaming through the Canadian Rockies, impressed local railroad professionals with its power and endurance. At the end of six months, and having faced every kind of weather, Driver William Gilbertson was able to boast that 'We took a whole truckful of spare parts and we haven't used one.'

Railways and the cinema

Film-makers were quick to realize the box-office appeal of the railway, and countless trains, stations and locomotives have been committed to celluloid. The end of steam in the 1960s was a problem, but producers then began turning to the preservationists.

It may come as a surprise for many people to realize that the first railway film was made around a century ago. In July 1895, the two French inventors, Auguste and Louis Lumière, were on holiday and decided to test out their new cinematograph for an 'action' scene. So they filmed the arrival of a train from Marseilles at La Ciotat, featuring an excellent three-quarter view of a Bourbonnais class 2-4-2 locomotive and a highly polished line of little four wheel carriages, followed by a bustling platform scene.

The Lumières exhibited their 15 minute film in Paris on 28 December 1895, as part of the world's first public cinema show. When the scene of the train steaming into the station was shown, a man sitting out of sight of the audience released a series of loud hisses from a compressed air cylinder. So realistic was the effect that people in the front rows leapt back lest they be mown down by the oncoming engine.

Two months later, the film came to London, appearing first at the Regent Street Polytechnic and then transferring to the Empire Music Hall in Leicester Square. Among those watching was a photographer from Hove, George Albert Smith, who was so impressed that, on returning home, he got a local engineer, Alfred Darling, to build him a camera and projector. In May 1896, Smith went to Hove station on the London, Brighton & South Coast Railway and filmed the arrival of the London Express, headed by a Gladstone class locomotive.

Opposition from the Alhambra

That same month, another film-making enthusiast, Robert Paul of Muswell Hill in London, using equipment he had evolved from Edison gear, went to a site alongside the Great Northern Railway at Wood Green and filmed trains coming up from King's Cross, including old Stirling singles and a North London Railway tank with a local going to New Barnet. This was later shown at the Alhambra Music Hall, also in Leicester Square, in direct opposition to the Lumière show.

It was not long before film-makers began featuring the railway in works of celluloid fiction. One of the pioneers was George Albert Smith, whose *Kiss in the Tunnel*, made in 1900, was among the first of the story films. The main influence, however, came from the US, with Edwin S Porter's 1903 production, *The Great Train Robbery*. Shot in and around Paterson, New Jersey, and using typical American 4-4-0 locomotives of the day, this simple tale of crime on the iron road ushered in a whole new film genre – the railway melodrama.

The following decade saw hundreds of such films, not least in Britain, where audiences thrilled to productions such as *When the Devil Drives* (1907). Made by Robert Paul for Charles Urban, this included rare shots of the Dreadnought 2-2-2-2s bought by the London & North Western Railway.

The public's appetite for story films was whetted by the inclusion of a new and irresistible ingredient – the train crash. Again, the recipe was first tried in America, where the Vitagraph Company staged a collision between two old 4-4-0s for its film *The Wreck* (1914).

The first British film to include a crash was *The Wrecker* (1929). Based on a play by Arnold Ridley (better known today for his playing of Private Godfrey in the television comedy series *Dad's Army*), and produced by Michael Balcon, it made considerable use of scenes shot on the Southern Railway (SR).

▼ The British comedy *Oh! Mr Porter*, made in 1937, starred Will Hay as the incompetent stationmaster of a dilapidated and supposedly haunted railway station on the borders of Northern Ireland and the Irish Free State. In fact, the film was shot mainly on the abandoned Basingstoke – Alton branch line of the Southern Railway and the locomotive and carriages were former London & South Western Railway stock.

▲ Michael Redgrave, seen here armed with a revolver, made a suitably intrepid hero in Alfred Hitchcock's 1938 thriller, *The Lady Vanishes*, set on a train travelling to the Balkans. No director was more adept than Hitchcock at capturing the drama and excitement of a train journey.

In the spectacular climax, a Stirling 4-4-0, heading a set of eight wheel coaches, charges down a 1 in 40 embankment into a Foden steam lorry loaded with cement and explosives. The crash, staged at Spain's Crossing near Herriard on the abandoned Basingstoke – Alton line, still provokes gasps of astonishment. (Unfortunately, such realism was achieved at a high price – the destruction of the first bogie vehicles built by the South Eastern & Chatham Railway.)

As Balcon was completing his film in 1929, a new cinematic wonder arrived – the Talkies. *The Wrecker* was issued in a half-sound version and another railway film then being made at Elstree Studios was hastily converted to sound. It may, indeed, have been the first British Talkie, just pipping Alfred Hitchcock's *Blackmail* to the post. Directed by Castleton Knight, it was called *The Flying Scotsman* and featured a young and unknown Welsh actor, Raymond Milland, who was to find fame and fortune in Hollywood as plain Ray Milland.

But the real star of the film was the unbilled London & North Eastern Railway (LNER)

Gresley Pacific No 4472 *Flying Scotsman*, whose exclusive use Knight was given for six weeks. He made the most of this advantage, deploying his skills as a newsreel director to overcome the deficiencies of a ludicrous script. He placed a camera on every available foothold of the engine, as well as building a special camera platform on one side.

However, no account had been taken of the fact that the locomotive might roll about at speed, with the result that half the platform was cut clean away in Ponsbourne Tunnel, leaving Knight and his cameraman clinging on for dear life.

There is excellent coverage of the run from King's Cross to Edinburgh, but the detailed action involving the stunt shots, the switching of points and the race through the countryside was staged on the Hertford Loop between Crews Hill, Cuffley and Bayford. Audiences were duly enthralled, though the scene of the villain uncoupling the locomotive from its carriages, which are then left to go racing on in pursuit of the engine, provoked a pained response from Sir Nigel Gresley.

Gresley objected to the implication that the LNER had not yet adopted the vacuum brake and demanded a special title pointing out that 'Dramatic licence has been taken in this film with the normal safety equipment of the LNER'.

Channel ferry crash

In 1932, two years after *The Flying Scotsman* appeared, Alfred Hitchcock included some good

night shots of a Gresley Pacific on the run from Liverpool to Harwich in his film *Number Seventeen*. The final sequence shows a chase between a runaway goods train and a Green Line motor coach, climaxing with a crash into a Channel ferry. This was filmed with the help of a vast 0 gauge layout built at the once thriving Elstree Studios.

Over the next two decades, Hitchcock was to make a string of screen thrillers with a railway background, including such classics as *The Thirty Nine Steps* (1935), *The Lady Vanishes* (1938) and *Strangers on a Train* (1951).

A contemporary of Hitchcock's who also found inspiration in the railway, albeit of a rather different kind, was the French director Jean Renoir. In 1938, Renoir's *La Bête Humaine* (*The Human Condition*) exploded on to the screen. Based on a novel by Emile Zola, the story of an engine driver who murders for love is underlined by the railway background. For the final sequence, in which the driver, on the footplate of the Paris express, confesses to his fireman, the camera was mounted in front of the engine and the sound, instead of being dubbed in later, was recorded as the film's action unfolded.

The effect is stunning, with the torment of the driver's mind reflected, as one critic put it, by the recurring spectacle of 'trains tearing and screaming through the sunny countryside, trains burrowing through tunnels towards pinpricks of light with a muffled but redoubled roar, trains clanking and wheezing in the temporary repose of the junction'.

The celebration of various railway centenaries

▲ One of the most popular films with British audiences was the comedy thriller *The Ghost Train*, produced in a silent version in 1925 and remade twice as a Talkie, in 1931 and 1941. In the 1931 version, not very convincing models were used to show a train plunging into a river from a swing-bridge.

in the 1920s and '30s led to a spate of commemorative films. First off the mark was Britain, with an LNER film of the Darlington centenary celebrations of 1925, which featured a parade made up in part of the best preserved steam locomotives in the world at that time, including Stockton & Darlington No 1 *Locomotion*.

In Germany, which celebrated its railway centenary in 1935, Willy Zielke produced an extraordinary film, *Der Stahltier* (*The Iron Horse*), which includes a superb replica of William Hedley's *Puffing Billy* (known in the film as *Puffen Wilhelm*) and an even better full-scale reconstruction of the opening of the Liverpool & Manchester Railway in 1830, complete with *Rocket*. There was also full credit given to the French for the first steam road locomotive.

It was only after providing this historical background that the film went on to show the opening of the first German railway in 1835 between Nuremberg and Fürth. The sequence included an accurate replica of the first German steam locomotive, *Adler* (*Eagle*), though it was made clear that the engine was built in England by Stephenson and driven by an Englishman, 'Mr Vilson' (William Wilson of Newcastle).

The first to see the film after it had been completed was Dr Goebbels, the Nazi Minister of Propaganda, who was outraged that it paid full credit to the real pioneers of steam railways and was not just a paean of praise to German industry and invention. Furthermore, Goebbels considered that it was shot in an extravagant *avant-garde* style not appropriate to the new German Reich.

Zielke was promptly whisked off to an asylum

◀ A flag-draped 0-6-0 pulls into Oakworth station on the Keighley & Worth Valley Railway during the filming of *The Railway Children* in 1970. Some members of the film crew had been apprehensive about working with preservationists, but were delighted to discover how professional they were.

▶ It was a railway station that provided the unlikely setting for the classic 1947 weepie, *Brief Encounter*, which starred Trevor Howard and Celia Johnson as a middle aged couple torn between love and duty. Although most of the film was made in the studio, some sequences were shot at an appropriately sombre Carnforth station.

Spot the difference

Some film-makers showed scant concern for the realities of railway operation. In the 1941 version of the British comedy thriller, *The Ghost Train*, the express leaves Paddington hauled by a King, arrives at Teignmouth headed by a Castle, slows for a curve pulled by a bullet-nosed, streamlined King and comes to a halt with a Saint.

Even Alfred Hitchcock was not immune to error. In his 1935 film, *The Thirty Nine Steps*, the hero leaves King's Cross bound for Edinburgh on a London & North Eastern Railway train hauled by a Gresley Pacific. However, a later shot shows a Great Western Railway train bursting out of Box Tunnel near Bath, headed by a King. Hitchcock commented 'There is something more important than logic; it is imagination.'

for the insane. He came out briefly to shoot scenes for Leni Riefenstahl's famous film of the 1936 Berlin Olympics, but was then returned to his cell. As a result, he survived the war (which is more than Goebbels did) and lived for many years afterwards. Goebbels had ordered the film to be destroyed, but a single copy survived, and this was smuggled to France and looked after during the war by the French Resistance.

The popularity of railway films continued well into the post-war years, with audiences enjoying such offerings as *The Titfield Thunderbolt* (1952), *The Train* (1964), *Von Ryan's Express* (1965) and *Murder on the Orient Express* (1974).

In *The Titfield Thunderbolt*, produced by Michael Balcon, a country line is saved by the villagers it serves. The writer of the screenplay, T E B Clarke, got his inspiration on a visit to the Talyllyn Railway (TR) in North Wales. Clarke was amazed to find that the TR was 'a private line run through the summer months by railway enthusiasts from all parts of the country...Thus was born the idea of *The Titfield Thunderbolt*: the idea of a village with sufficient love of its little branch-line railway to buy it up and run it with an amateur staff when it came to suffer the fate of so many pleasant but uneconomic lines in these materialistic times.'

Life after steam

As main line steam came to an end, film-makers looked increasingly to railways such as the TR. In Britain, a major-turning point was reached in 1970 with the making of *The Railway Children*, based on the novel by E Nesbit. Steam had come to an end on BR two years before, so the film was made entirely on the Keighley & Worth Valley Railway (KWVR) in West Yorkshire, which was especially suitable, since Nesbit's book was set in the countryside around that area.

The film was a great success, generating an enormous amount of goodwill, not only for the KWVR in particular, but for preserved railways in general. Today, these lines are in regular demand by film and TV companies, which realize that nothing is more evocative of years gone by than the sight and sound of a steam train.

◀ The real star of *The Titfield Thunderbolt* (1952) was *Lion*, built by Todd, Kitson & Laird of Leeds in 1838 for the Liverpool & Manchester Railway. *Lion's* owners, the Liverpool Engineering Society, were reluctant at first to loan the engine, but agreed on seeing the script.

One of the greatest films made about railways was Cecil B De Mille's 1939 classic *Union Pacific*, which starred Barbara Stanwyck and Joel McCrea. Telling the story of the railroad's construction in the tradition of John Ford's *The Iron Horse* (1924), the film used four steam locomotives, including this 4-4-0 Baldwin of 1875 which was named *Inyo*.

The armoured train

**Clad in armour plate and bristling with guns, the
train took on the aspect of a formidable fighting machine.
But appearances were deceptive, and although this new military
monster would play an important role on battlefields from
America to Africa, it was to prove highly vulnerable to simple
acts of sabotage.**

The art of winning, according to an American
Civil War general, consisted of 'getting there
fastest with the mostest', so it is appropriate that
this was the conflict that saw the first effective use
of armoured trains. In an era of poor roads and
horse traction, the rail-mounted gun was, indeed,
the fastest way of getting heavy weaponry into
position. The Confederates were the first to try this,
mounting a 32-pounder on a railway flatcar, encasing it in iron plates, and sending it off to fight in
the Battle of Savage Station in 1862.

The Federals imitated the idea but, instead of
single guns, placed an entire battery on rails.
Before the end of the war they were operating what
is regarded as the first authentic armoured train,
which they used for reconnaissance and defence on
the Baltimore & Ohio Railroad. This was not simply an assembly of rail-mounted guns, but consisted of six vehicles with their own permanently
attached locomotive, and with provision for
infantry as well as artillery.

But the train came to an untimely end when its
locomotive boiler was hit by a Confederate shell.
In later wars efforts were made to provide quite
thick armour for the locomotive, but this was limited by the weight that the track could bear.
Sometimes a fairly small locomotive had to be
used simply to permit the use of heavy armour.

However, armoured trains were always vulnerable, for not only could they be immobilized by an
unlucky shot, but an enterprising and mobile
enemy could achieve the same effect by simply
wrecking the track before and behind the train.

This meant that the armoured train could
not normally be used in attack, where it could
so easily be cut off. But it could play a posi-

▼In 1940, as invasion
threatened, a number of
armoured trains were
assembled to help defend the
British coast. Even the narrow
gauge Romney, Hythe &
Dymchurch Railway in Kent
acquired its own miniature
Molloch. Made up of an
armoured 4-8-2 coupled
between two gun-wagons, the
train was kept constantly at
the ready, with steam-up 24
hours a day.

tive role in defence, acting as a fast reinforcement for threatened sectors of the front.

Unfortunately, such considerations had little impact on military thinking in Britain. With the outbreak of the Boer War in 1899, the British fought a campaign over huge distances and made great use of rail transport. However, having failed to study the lessons of previous wars, the army command regarded the armoured train as a form of cavalry, to be sent out on offensive thrusts. So, though local foresight had ensured the construction of 10 armoured trains before hostilities began, one of these was destroyed on the very first day of the war.

Even this loss failed to change the British tactics. In the months that followed several trains were damaged while making narrow escapes, and another was actually captured by the Boers. Among those on board was a young war correspondent, Winston Churchill.

In his book, *London to Ladysmith via Pretoria*, Churchill described the train as consisting of an engine and tender (situated, as usual, in the centre, which was the safest place for a train designed to run in either direction), ahead of which was a car with armoured, loopholed sides, and containing a platoon of infantry. At the front there was a car transporting a naval gun. Behind the engine came

two more infantry vehicles, which also accommodated a breakdown crew and, finally, there was a vehicle carrying repair materials and tools.

As the train rounded a long curve, it ran into a Boer ambush based on the top of a nearby hill. 'The long brown rattling serpent with the rifles bristling from its spotted sides,' wrote Churchill, 'crawled closer to the rocky hillock on which the scattered black figures of the enemy showed clearly. Suddenly three wheeled things appeared on the crest, and within a second a bright flash of light... The Boers had opened fire on us... The train leapt forward, ran the gauntlet of the guns, which now filled the air with explosions, swung round the curve of the hill, ran down a steep gradient, and dashed into a huge stone which awaited it at a convenient spot.'

Although the vehicles in front of the locomotive were wrecked, the engine itself and the vehicles behind it were still intact. Under Churchill's direction, volunteers cleared the line of debris, and with the forceful young journalist by his side on the footplate, the driver put on full steam and reversed down the line.

But they had gone only a short distance when they noticed that the undamaged cars had been left behind. Somehow they had become uncoupled in the crash. Churchill and the driver then steamed back in the hope of rescuing their stranded comrades – only to fall into the hands of the enemy. Churchill later became a national hero by escaping from a Boer prison camp.

Adopting new tactics

Eventually, the British commanders in South Africa adopted more sensible tactics. Armoured trains were to be used mainly for patrol and escort,

▲Members of a British-based Polish unit man an armoured train at North Berwick in February 1941. The possibility of an armoured train had first been raised in 1859 by the English locomotive engineer, William Bridges Adams. But it was the Americans, caught in the turmoil of civil war, who gave practical expression to the idea.

Aiding the enemy
In the early days of the Boer War, the British armoured trains were commanded by army officers rather than civilians – an arrangement that sometimes led to unfortunate consequences.

According to the head of the British Army's Department of Military Railways, Major Percy Girouard, 'Armoured trains were constantly rushing out against orders of the Traffic department, sometimes without a line clear message, and this caused serious delays to traffic.

'In fact, instead of assisting traffic by preventing the enemy from interrupting it, they caused more interruption than the enemy themselves.'

◀ During the chaos of the Russian Civil War a Czech national army, formed in Russia to fight the Austrians, captured much of the Trans Siberian Railway and used armoured trains to patrol it. Here, under camouflage, Czech machine gunners take up their positions.

▶ Unloading from trucks hauled by an armoured locomotive, British troops pile up earth for field works in northern France during the winter of 1916. Many locomotives were destroyed in the intensive artillery bombardments and both sides were forced to improvise, putting together strange looking hybrids such as the one seen here.

and their offensive role was confined to cutting off enemy retreats when it was safe to do so.

But there could still be complications. There was one celebrated occasion when the main line was blocked for hours after a local commander decided to allocate an armoured train to escort a herd of cattle making an on-the-hoof move parallel to the railway. For the most part, however, the armoured trains justified themselves, albeit fairly unspectacularly, in the later stages of the war.

With the start of World War I, armoured trains were used in the African campaigns and occasionally on the European fronts. But it was in Russia, in the civil war that followed the 1917 Revolution, that they came into their own again. The French and British troops based in Archangel and Murmansk, part of an international force that had been mobilized to crush the new Bolshevik regime, assembled several of these trains to patrol their own vital rail lines, while in the main campaigns between the Bolsheviks and their Russian opponents both sides used armoured trains. The war was fought with considerable savagery, with some prisoners being thrown, alive, into the fireboxes of the locomotives.

It was again in Russia, with its vast expanses, scarce roads and severe weather, that armoured trains were most widely used in World War II. Although a great deal of improvisation was involved, a largely standard formation was devel-

▼The armoured train of Italian dictator Benito Mussolini, its anti-aircraft guns at the ready, halts by a bombed-out country station. In World War II, though still used for the rapid deployment of firepower, armoured trains began to lose their potency in face of the new military factor of overwhelming air attack.

Klim Voroshilov and driven by a woman, took part in the defence of Rostov, Moscow and Stalingrad before being sent to support the attacking Red Army.

The Germans tried to obstruct the Russian trains by tearing up the track during retreat – a tactic which the Russians countered by fitting the trains with longer range guns. They also equipped some trains with rocket launchers.

Trains of the invaders

Armoured trains were also used by the Germans in these campaigns, some built in Germany itself and some captured from the Russians. One vehicle which the invaders brought with them was their standard eight-wheeled armoured car, the Sd Kfz 231, which had been designed to run on road or rail.

The Germans also deployed armoured trains in France, where by 1944 the Maquis guerrillas were posing a serious threat. They had engineered many derailments, and the Germans used the trains to escort particularly important rail traffic.

In Britain during the early months of the war armoured trains were regarded as a vital line of defence against an expected German invasion. Forty were built at Ashford works, with firepower provided by a Hotchkiss gun and a light machine-gun. The LNER supplied for them small tank locomotives that were camouflaged and fitted with armoured cabs, and they were then deployed on coastal lines in the south and east of the country.

Even the 15in (381mm) gauge Romney, Hythe & Dymchurch Railway, on the south coast, had an armoured train operated by an expatriate Polish brigade. One explanation for the railway's inclusion is that the War Office official charged with deciding which coastal lines should have armoured trains put the Romney, Hythe & Dymchurch on his list, not realizing that it was merely a tourist attraction.

▼A German armoured train rests on a railway embankment near Helsinki, a reminder of Finland's involvement in the fighting between Nazi Germany and the Soviet Union. It was Russia, with its bad roads and vast distances, that became the main arena for armoured trains in World War II.

oped. The Russian trains usually consisted of an armoured locomotive, flanked at each end by a truck with anti-aircraft guns and then a roofed vehicle with two field guns and four heavy machine-guns. There were also four service cars – two at each end – which carried rails, sleepers, fire extinguishers, lifting jacks and other materials.

Such trains were used intensively against the German forces besieging Odessa and Sevastopol, destroying aircraft and tanks and breaking up infantry formations. Sometimes they operated in pairs, one covering the other. Many of them had a short life, but others moved from front to front and survived to take part in the great Russian counter offensives later in the war. One of these, named

This heavily armoured train was named *Soviet Armenia* and was paid for by
means of funds collected in the US in support of the Soviet war effort.
The date is January 1943.

The rather crudely contrived No 2 Armoured Train in South Africa, which was
manned by British troops during the Boer War. It was on a train similar to this that
Winston Churchill narrowly escaped death before being captured.

Chapter 3
Towards the Future

The quest for speed

Today's long distance railways are striving to win back travellers from the motorways and airlines. Speed is the key and, in a special trial, even the magic 300mph barrier has been broken.

At 10.06 on 18 May 1990, TGV No 325 flashed over the viaduct across the River Loir at 515.3 km/h (320.2mph), creating a new world speed record – its fourth in six months. Although the five vehicle train had been specially prepared for these trials, it was adapted from a standard blue and silver set, similar to those already running commercially at 300km/h (186mph) on the TGV-Atlantique.

This was the second of the French purpose-built high speed lines to be constructed, with the rolling stock designed to enable the trains to run at 300km/h (186mph) from the outset. The service set a new world record, beating that previously held on their TGV Paris – Sud-Est line.

The idea of a new purpose-built high speed line south-eastwards out of Paris started in the mid 1960s when the SNCF set out to develop a train which could achieve at least 260km/h (162mph). Initially gas-turbine propulsion was proposed, but oil crises ruled this out.

The familiar grey and orange electric sets appeared at the end of the 1970s, two of them setting up world speed records of 371km/h (230.5mph) and 380km/h (236.1mph) in February 1981. The commercial success which followed the

▼ **The record breaking run by the French TGV No 325 was the culmination of over six month's preparation. The specially prepared Atlantique set consisted of just three coaches and the usual two power cars. Its 515.3km/h (320.2mph) run through Vendôme on the Paris-Bordeaux line was the train's fourth world record in six months.**

new services was to place France in a commanding world position with high speed rail transport.

The world's first

It was the Japanese National Railways (JNR) which successfully opened the world's first dedicated high speed line, the Tokaido, running between Tokyo and Osaka.

The now famous Bullet trains were introduced in October 1965, setting a new world record by averaging 163km/h (101mph). Traffic boomed and the 30 trains a day in each direction quickly rose to 44 and then 51. By 1991 the total over this stretch reached 130. The original route has been extended westwards to Hakata, 733 miles (1180km) from the capital.

To increase speed the Series 300 Bullet trains have a much lower profile than previous designs. When fully loaded they are 25% lighter than the Series 100, use aluminium alloy instead of steel, have no bolsters and lighter seats. In addition to reducing the drag, their lightweight construction reduces the power required, which in turn reduces

▲ An example of the tilting Pendolino Class ETR450 built by FIAT stands behind one of the prototype ETR500 sets. The steep climbs on many of Italy's long distance routes particularly demand high speed trains. Direct lines were first built in the 1920s but the first of the new generation of lines, connecting Rome and Florence, was fully opened in May 1992.

Speed technology

Higher speeds of tomorrow are the result of advances in technology in the fields of traction, suspension and current collection. Advances in braking and signalling also play their part. Designers of trains built specifically for high speeds face the same aerodynamic challenges as those confronting aircraft designers – the design techniques and technology used are also similar. For example, computer aided design gives a three dimensional image, and air flow imaging aids streamlining.

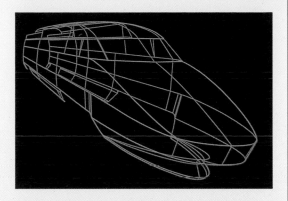

▼ An air flow visualization over the TGV – at high speed, efficient streamlining is critical as the higher the speed, the greater the energy needed to overcome wind resistance.

▲ By presenting a three dimensional image on screen, computers allow designers to test their designs fully. Changes can then be made before costly prototypes are built.

Noise reduction

The pioneering work by the Japanese National Railways threw up problems of noise. As well as lineside acoustic treatments – such as the construction of noise prevention walls – the design of the trains was modified. This included noise reducing covers for the pantographs these created a considerable amount of noise from electric sparks and wind as they drew current from the overhead wire.

British main lines since 1976, and established the world's fastest diesel hauled services.

In July 1984 BR were authorized to electrify the East Coast main line, the financial case being based on the lower maintenance costs. Initially, six-axle 125mph (201km/h) locomotives were planned to haul modified Mark 3 coaches, but this was exchanged to provide four-axle Class 91 locomotives and Mark 4 coaches, each rake being capable of running at 140mph (225km/h).

The £400 million project was completed in June 1991, but before BR can reap the full benefits of the new speed capabilities, automatic train protection (ATP) will need to be installed. Although BR use the simpler automatic warning system (AWS), a full cab signalling system is usual on trains travelling at over 125mph (200km/h), coupled with equipment to prevent the train over-running a danger signal.

▲ Two examples of Japanese motive power are the Series 300 (left) and 100 Bullet trains. Employing light alloys, the newer Series 300 model is 50km/h (31mph) faster than its predecessor at 270km/h (168mph) and over 200 tonnes lighter. Carriages can be made compact and lightweight by using asynchronous motors which allow a simpler method of construction. The next generation of Central Japan Railway's Shinkansen trains is the 300X, which reached 354.1km/h (221.3mph) in September 1995.

▶ The German InterCity Experimental was given a thorough testing over five years in everyday conditions before entering commercial service. On some sections of ICE routes the trains travel at 250km/h (155mph), but are permitted to touch 280km/h (174mph) in restricted areas when making up time. By the end of the 1990s the railway will be able to offer a service twice as fast as cars and half as fast as aircraft over comparable routes.

the level of noise.

These sets are running at speeds up to 270km/h (168mph) on the Tokaido Line, while the older design is already reaching 275km/h (171mph) in the depths of a tunnel on the Joetsu Line. In the evening peak there are no less than nine departures an hour from Tokyo to Osaka, but the most impressive statistic about the whole of the Shinkansen is that there has not been a single passenger fatality in over 25 years of operation.

UK speed revolution

In Britain in 1973 the prototype High Speed Train (HST) set a world record of 143.2mph (230.5km/h) for diesel rail traction. From the HST developed the fleet of InterCity 125 sets. These trains have revolutionized rail travel on many

Service upgrade

On the already electrified West Coast route a modest upgrading of track and motive power enabled maximum speeds to be lifted to 110mph (177km/h), with the result that BR now operates more trains at over 100mph (160km/h) than any other country except Japan. With the completion of the East Coast electrification, BR went out to tender for the InterCity 250 trains, which are expected to reach 155mph (250km/h) on parts of the upgraded system.

For services from London through the Channel Tunnel to Paris and Brussels, a jointly owned fleet has been constructed. These inter-capitals super trains are capable of taking power supplies from the Belgian, French and BR Southern Region electric systems. The performance of these trains is severely limited in the UK until the high speed line across Kent is built, by 2002 if all goes well.

Tomorrow's trains

Increases in commercial line speeds demand continual development in new designs for the future. These prototypes, the British Rail InterCity 250 train for the West Coast main line, which awaits funding, and the first ICE-2 trains for Deutsche Bundesbahn, are just two. The French have built their TGV-Nord, linking Paris with the Channel Tunnel, for 320 km/h (199mph) running. Although faster than any line in the world, its speed is still some way short of the record of TGV No 325. But one off records are achieved decades before such speeds are common in commercial services.

Britain's APT

The UK attempt to resolve the problem of increasing speeds over sharply curved track without constructing purpose-built high speed lines led to the development of the Advanced Passenger Train. Design features included self steering bogies, water turbine operated brakes and tilting coaches. But, because of technical problems, only one complete public run between London and Glasgow was made in the first week. Adverse publicity and a goverment refusal to finance the project further led to indefinite postponement of a series production version.

Speed worldwide

A derivative of the InterCity 125, the XPT has been in operation in Australia since 1981. The XPT represents the first export of the 100-plus-mph (160km/h) rail technology anywhere in the world. This success has prompted proposals for a railway of more than 200mph (322km/h) linking Sydney and Melbourne via Canberra.

In South Korea, a contest for the contracts to build a high speed line between Seoul and Pusan was won by a consortium led by GEC Alsthom. Completion is due in 2002.

In Canada the so-called Light Rapid & Comfortable (LRC) trains are still heavyweights by European high speed standards, and their availablility outside the maintenance depot has been extremely low. Maximum speeds are limited by having to share the tracks with heavy freight trains and by the numerous open level crossings.

There have been may proposals for dedicated high speed lines in various parts of the United States, but none has yet materialized – the automobile still reigns supreme. The American railroad construction industry is now virtually confined to designing freight diesels, and the passenger trains in the heavily populated North East Corridor between New York and Washington are worked by electic locomotives of Swedish design. Sweden's tilting X-2000 train sets are also being considered for use by Amtrak.

For the high speed Neubaustrecke in Germany, a totally new train was designed, the ICE (InterCity Express, although the initials originally stood for InterCity Experimental). Benefiting from much goverment funded wheel-on-rail research, the short experimental train achieved some very high speeds, including a new world record of 406.84km/h (252.8mph) in 1988, eclipsing the French achievements for just over a year.

The commercial ICE sets consist of up to 13 coaches between a pair of 6435hp power cars, with each set costing about £15 million. From June 1991 they were introduced on a new InterCity route from Hamburg and Munich via Frankfurt. A further high speed line is planned between Cologne and Frankfurt for 1998, a year after the opening of a line from Hanover to Berlin.

Italy and Spain

Italy's curvaceous lines were not initially designed for high speeds. For high speed running, FIAT developed the Pendolino tilting train and this is now running at 250km/h (155mph) on some sections of the Direttissima line. The tilting principle is also being adopted elsewhere, and FIAT have received orders from Germany as well as from other countries.

In Spain the fastest existing service is worked by the Talgos. Of an unusual design, these trains consist of a number of quite short coaches with wheels at one end only, the other end being supported by the next vehicle. The latest version is equipped to tilt, but still achieves a maximum of only 160km/h (100mph).

To improve its links with the European community, Spain has undertaken an ambitious plan to upgrade its railways. One idea was to convert the whole network to standard gauge from the Iberian five feet six inches. This proved too costly, but the new high speed lines are standard gauge, the first of these, between Madrid and Seville, being opened in 1992. Its TAV train sets are based on the French TGVs, although the cab signalling on the 300km/h (186mph) line is derived from the German LZB system. Ultimately, it is intended to link these high speed lines with those in France as well as extending them through Portugal to Lisbon.

A modified version of the Swedish X2000 train was trialed by Amtrak in 1993.
Its tilting capabilities would be particularly useful on the sinuous line between
New Haven and Boston.

High speed networks

In the west and Japan new high speed rail networks are taking shape. Using a combination of upgraded existing lines and purpose-built new ones, Europe is set to be linked by trains travelling at speeds of up to 350km/h. Britain will be one of the last Western European countries to join the high speed club.

Speed pays; if it didn't, railways would not have relentlessly pursued faster maximum and average speeds. Inevitably it has been the fastest speeds that have captured the imagination of the public, ever since *Rocket* reached 29mph (46km/h) at the Rainhill Trials in 1829.

For a century the slow pace of technological development permitted only small increases: it took 110 years to raise the maximum speed to 133mph (212km/h), but only another 51 to break the 300mph barrier, when in May 1990 TGV No 325 reached 515km/h (320.2mph) to establish a new world record.

But it is the average speed that is of greater interest to the railway manager, for high average speeds attract passengers. The rivalry of the railway companies between the world wars was as much over the honour of running the fastest train

as achieving a new record for the locomotive.

The pioneer

A lot of nonsense was written by early critics of the railways. Amongst the silliest comments was an opinion on the value of the proposed London & Birmingham Railway: 'It is not one traveller out of a thousand to whom an arrival in Birmingham or London three hours sooner would be of the slightest consequence.'

Any doubts that may have existed over the ability of high speed trains to make a handsome commercial return through increased traffic were dispelled by the remarkable success of the first dedicated high speed line. In October 1965 bullet trains began a service over the Tokyo – Osaka Shinkansen (new line); within a year the number of passengers doubled, requiring an increase in the

▼The TGV Atlantique route entailed the construction of 282km (176 miles) of new line. The route heads from Paris to Courtalain where the line forks, the northern arm reaching west towards Brest and Brittany and the other continuing south-west towards Bordeaux. When inaugurated in September 1989, the service over the line to Brittany became the fastest scheduled service in the world, the 201km (126 miles) between Paris Montparnasse and Le Mans being covered at an average speed of 219.9km/h (137.4mph).

▶ The famous designer of fast cars, Pininfarina, was responsible for the external and internal styling of the Italian ETR500 train sets for dedicated use over the Alta Velocita (AV) high speed network. The non-tilting sets have a top speed of 300 km/h (187 mph).

number of daily trains in each direction from the initial 30 to 44. By 1991 the one-way figure had reached 139.

Aspects of the Japanese experience highlight some of the dilemmas that surround the operation of high speed lines. Without recourse to tilting trains, a railway has to be specifically designed with high speeds in mind and whether or not tilting technology is employed, high speed trains need to be segregated from stopping or freight trains when the disparity between their speeds becomes too great.

Another point has even become an issue for the Japanese Shinkansen: in March 1992 the third generation of bullet trains entered service on the Tokyo – Osaka line, initially operating two trains a day each way. Capable of 270km/h (168mph), the new trains' faster acceleration and higher speed, both through curves and in absolute terms, means that the older trains are having to be modified to prevent them obstructing the progress of the new arrivals.

Spread of Shinkansens

So successful has the first Shinkansen service been that Central Japan Railway is expecting to run out of line capacity between Tokyo and Osaka and is already planning a new line between the two cities, the Chuo Shinkansen, which will take a different route to serve other cities. The fourth generation trains are being designed to run at speeds in normal service of 350km/h (218mph).

The ability of bullet trains to attract passengers from the airlines encouraged the construction of further lines. The Osaka line was extended for 164km (102.5 miles) to Okayama and subsequently on to Hakata, a further 398km (249 miles). Plans exist to complete the Shinkansen network from Kagoshima at the south of Kyushu island to Sapporo on Hokkaido, and lines off the central route to Komatsu and Nigata.

TGV network

Second in the field of high speed lines was SNCF

◀ The lounge coach for meetings on the TGV Atlantique exemplifies the new facilities provided on high speed trains. The TGV-A includes a nursery, telephones and family rooms, and the new generation of double deck TGVs will have two areas set aside for teenagers.

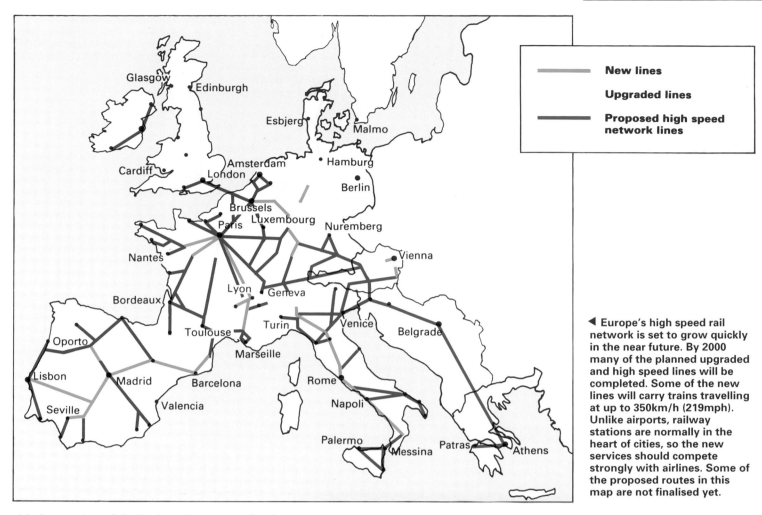

◀ Europe's high speed rail network is set to grow quickly in the near future. By 2000 many of the planned upgraded and high speed lines will be completed. Some of the new lines will carry trains travelling at up to 350km/h (219mph). Unlike airports, railway stations are normally in the heart of cities, so the new services should compete strongly with airlines. Some of the proposed routes in this map are not finalised yet.

with the opening of the Paris to Lyon route for the Train à Grande Vitesse (TGV) in September 1981. Within three years, from 1982 to 1985, the annual number of passengers increased from just under 6 million to 14.7 million. So profitable has the line been that the loans taken out to finance construction will have been repaid within 11 years.

A second line, the TGV Atlantique, serving the west and south-west, opened in September 1989, and the TGV Nord was fully opened in May 1994. It links the Channel Tunnel with Paris, with a major interchange at Lille en route.

By the year 2010, SNCF plans to have 4700km (2937 miles) of dedicated high speed line open for trains running at up to 350km/h (218mph).

ICE trains

Germany first introduced its high speed ICE (InterCity Express) trains on two new lines between Hannover – Würzburg and Mannheim – Stuttgart. The ICE's trailers feature sealed interiors to counteract the changes in air pressure caused by the many tunnels on the two routes. Though the new lines are cleared for 280km/h running, trains normally travel at 250km/h.

▶ One of the GEC-Alsthom AVE's (Alta Velocida Espanola) crosses a viaduct on the standard gauge high speed line between Madrid and Seville. Fears that the line might not flourish commercially after Expo 92 proved groundless; in fact, the frequency of services had to be increased to meet demand.

◀ The impossibility of extending the platforms used by TGVs has compelled SNCF to develop a doubledeck train to increase capacity. An order was placed in early 1991 for 100 doubledeck train sets, which will provide the same seating capacity as 148 singledeck trains. One of the first to be delivered is seen here on test. They are intended for the TGV Nord and Sud-Est.

A European network

The success of France and Japan in developing high speed lines has encouraged plans for a European high speed network. Germany, Italy and Spain have already joined France in operating services over dedicated high speed routes, bringing the total to over 2,000km (1,250 miles). Some of these lines have been built with national considerations in mind. Now governments and railway administrations are being urged to think internationally.

In January 1989 the Community of European Railways published proposals for a 30,000km (18,750 mile) high speed network. A third of this would be new lines built for speeds of 250-350km/h (156-219mph) and half would be good for 200km/h (125mph). A working party under EC Transport Ministers has been working to turn these plans into reality.

In this they were encouraged by the EC Transport Commissioner, Karel van Miert, and by the growing acceptance amongst progressive governments that railways offer the best solution to some of the transport and environmental problems confronting Europe. The EC's target of stabilizing emissions of carbon dioxide at 1990 levels by the year 2000 is only one of a range of factors that highlight the futility of road building to meet growing transport demands. Equally the limited capacity of the air traffic corridors, coupled with the longer distances over which rail is competitive with aircraft as train speeds increase, gives railways a growing window of opportunity for journeys up to 1000km (625 miles).

Technical hurdles

Apart from the obvious difficulty of funding such major investments, the principal obstacle to the development of international high speed links is technical. Some countries, like Italy and Sweden, have opted for tilting trains that do not require as straight a track alignment as the non-tilting French TGVs or German ICEs. Spain has both tilting and

High speed comfort
Speed is not the only inducement to travellers to forsake the airlines or roads for the train: the facilities and standard of comfort provided by SNCF and DB for their high speed passengers are impressive. Both have buffet-restaurant cars. The TGV Atlantique has a nursery, small family rooms, public telephones and liquid crystal screens to provide information about the journey. The ICE has six audio channels on headphones at every seat, access to an on-board information system through a wall-mounted keyboard, video screens in the back of some seats and card telephones. A conference room with electric typewriter, copier and fax machine is also available.

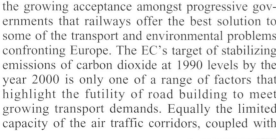
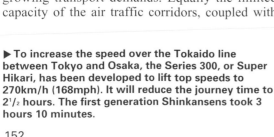

▶ To increase the speed over the Tokaido line between Tokyo and Osaka, the Series 300, or Super Hikari, has been developed to lift top speeds to 270km/h (168mph). It will reduce the journey time to 2½ hours. The first generation Shinkansens took 3 hours 10 minutes.

non-tilting high speed trains, on different gauges.

Similarly, the signalling, control and electrical feed systems are seldom compatible. These difficulties can be overcome – at a cost. For example, the Channel Tunnel Eurostars pick up power from three very different systems. Working parties have been set up to look into the opportunities for harmonizing some of the differences.

Prospects for Britain

The Channel Tunnel is the first major investment in an international link that is supposed to be part of a high speed network. The French built TGV Nord in readiness for the opening of the Channel Tunnel in 1994, but it took the UK government until 1996 just to choose the consortium to build the link through Kent; trains tear across northern France at 300km/h (186mph) on TGV Nord, but then have to compete with commuter trains for paths up to Waterloo over lines that permit only half the French speed.

British Rail's plans for a high speed line through Kent were worked out to government guidelines; they represented years of planning and expenditure of £140 million. In October 1991 the proposals for a southerly route through Kent were rejected by the government, which said that a link would not be needed until 2005. British Rail had forecast that it would be turning away 4 million passengers a year if the new high speed link was not in operation by 1998.

The government expressed a preference for a more easterly route, now slimmed down to two rather than four tracks, thereby dealing a blow to prospects for fast freight transits from the Channel to London. The planning time lost means that it is very unlikely that the link will be in operation by the year 2002; however, at a Commons Transport Committee inquiry, every witness rejected the government's claim that the link would not be needed before 2005.

The President of SNCF, Jacques Fournier, predicted that the contrast between the progress of trains through the two countries would be so marked that Britain would be quickly shamed into joining Europe's high speed network. He overestimated a government's capacity for shame.

High speed in the US
The most promising high speed proposal, for a triangle of lines between Dallas/Fort Worth, San Antonio and Houston, bit the dust in 1995 as a result of opposition from farmers and airlines.

It now looks as though the country's first foray into high speed running will be over the existing North East corridor between Boston-New York-Washington, rather than over specially built new lines. Following trials with the Swedish X2000 and Germany's ICE, a Request for Proposals was issued in late 1995 for 26 trains capable of 240km/h (150mph).

▼The inauguration of the first InterCity Express (ICE) services over the Hamburg-Frankfurt-Munich route in June 1991 was the culmination of almost 20 years planning. Running at speeds of up to 250km/h (156mph), the 13-coach sets cut an hour off the journey between Hamburg and Munich.

Tilting trains

In most of Europe, tilting trains are seen as the best way to increase speeds without building new lines. Britain may still be licking its wounds after the APT fiasco, but on the Continent there's a strong leaning towards new tilting technology.

There are two ways a railway can increase speeds dramatically: it can either re-lay its track to eliminate the sharper curves, or build tilting trains. Trains that are able to tilt allow an increase in speed of up to 30% through curves with about the same comfort level as conventional trains.

The problem with conventional rail travel is that when speeds are high and curves sharp, powerful centrifugal forces can be uncomfortable for passengers. Within limits, these forces can be moderated by raising the outer rail of a curve to a higher level than the inner – this is called cant or super elevation.

However, with canted track every train is tilted to the same angle, regardless of its speed. This means a slow train may be over-compensated while a fast train could suffer cant deficiency. On all but the gentlest curves, high speed trains that share a route with other trains can run at top speed only with a cant deficiency that is very uncomfort-

able. The lateral forces that are registered are strong enough to throw a standing passenger. The tilting train is designed to solve this problem.

A new slant

Much trial and error over two decades has finally made the tilting train a practicable proposition. BR's Advanced Passenger Train (APT), although finally abandoned, made its own contribution to an understanding of the problems involved. BR had in mind the winding West Coast main line north of Preston, but even on straighter routes the APT could have cut journey times by raising the speed limits through curves. The lifting of speed restrictions and the consequent reduction of constant braking and acceleration mean tilting trains achieve energy savings of 10% or more.

Twisting, sinuous rail routes, with cities close enough to make intercity travel a paying proposition, are ideal for tilting train operations. It is no accident that Spain and Italy are in the forefront of

▲Sweden's X2000, built by ABB Traction, is capable of speeds of up to 210km/h (130mph). The active tilt system features radial steering bogies that ease both track and wheel wear. An initial order for 20 trains was placed in the mid-1980s and further orders followed in 1993 and 1995.

◄Europe's first truly successful tilting train was the Italian ETR401. The prototype Pendolino tilting train is seen here descending from Brennero towards Colle Isarco, on its way home from running trials in western Germany in 1987. ETR401 must have acquitted itself well, because trains based on the more recent ETR450 design are now on order for Germany.

ger-carrying trailers, with a driving cab at each end. Because the power cars were central, passengers could not pass down the full length of the train. It was a lightweight aluminium design, and its passenger vehicles weighed one-third less than conventional cars. Because of the high speeds envisaged, an entirely new hydrokinetic (water turbine) brake system was used.

Problems with the brakes, poor riding of the articulated bogies and gearbox difficulties made up a large proportion of the defects that plagued the service trials. These were eventually corrected, but at a cost in time and enthusiasm which con-

The Pendolino

Italy's Pendolino, built by car giant Fiat, can tilt up to nine degrees with the aid of high level jacks acting in the vehicle roof. A cross beam rests on the secondary coil suspension; the body is supported on the cross beam via hydraulic jacks. The train is adjusted to tilt at a maximum of three degrees a second – too fast a tilt disorientates passengers.

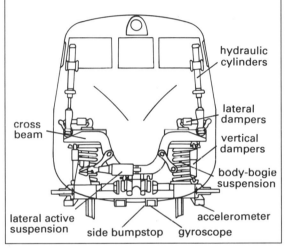

this technology. In Italy several cities are already served by ETR450 Pendolino trains. Mountainous Spain, which for decades has been using its lightweight Talgo trains, has now accelerated services by designing them with a tilting mechanism. Japan and Sweden, both with twisting lines, have sought the same solution.

There are two ways of providing tilt: passive and active. In passive tilting, as favoured by Spanish Railways, coach bodies are suspended so that they are free to react to the forces acting on them over a curve, and these forces impose a natural tilt. Such a tilt is less than that attainable by active tilting, but for most purposes is enough. In active tilt, as favoured by the British, Italians and others, the coach bodies are tilted by mechanical jacks. This provides more tilt but imposes higher complexity and cost.

APT – the tilting test bed

The APT project, jointly financed by BR and the government, began in 1967 and resulted in the prototype gas turbine train (APT-E), followed by a 14-car prototype design (APT-P). After an inaugural public run in 1981, APT-P struggled through a series of problems until the project was finally abandoned in 1985.

The APT was not merely a tilting train but an entirely new concept that included several fundamental innovations – one reason for its downfall was that there were too many novelties for one design. The APT consisted of two power cars sandwiched between two six-car rakes of passen-

▼APT was not the only tilting train to suffer lean times. In all 31 power cars of Canada's LRC were built by Bombardier in the early 1980s. Intended for an upgraded route between Montreal and Quebec, the line was never improved. By 1991 only eight of the original 20 power cars were in service.

▼British Rail's APT (main picture) might have been a white elephant, but it was an elegant one. On a bright July day in 1982, APT 370007 eats the gradient at Shap on a rare revenue earning service – the 16.00 Euston to Glasgow. Sadly the APT suffered from a surfeit of innovation. Its brakes and wheel design were, ironically, at first more troublesome than the revolutionary tilt mechanism.

From the cab of the APT (inset) the dramatic tilt effect of the train is apparent. Full tilt compensation was found to disorientate passengers when they looked out of the windows.

tributed to the APT's demise. As with most new technology, further teething troubles were experienced – the tilting mechanism sometimes jammed or failed, for instance – but many of these faults were also slowly put right.

However, even when it operated well the tilt presented virtually insurmountable problems, partly because it was not realized that there was no perfect solution. The difficulty was partly in timing and partly in the amount of tilt required.

Tilting the APT coach bodies by means of jacks, and suspending the bodies so that they could be tilted, presented few problems. But it was important that the tilt should not be jerky and should precisely match the curvature and speed.

A train might straddle straight and curved track, or curved track and the gentle transitional curve leading into it, so at a given moment some cars might be tilted and some untilted. At first BR had sensors on each coach which could feel the lateral tug and actuate the jacks. But this meant that the tilt operated too late. An interim solution was to place the sensor for one coach on the vehicle immediately ahead, but finally transponders were favoured. These transponders – radio beacons permanently fixed on the track at key points – can transmit information to processors on a passing train.

BR engineers assumed that the ideal amount of tilt would fully compensate for the lateral forces acting on a seated passenger, though standing or walking passengers with their different centres of gravity were less comfortable. Technically, the most serious obstacle to this goal was that when fully tilted the coach bodies might project beyond the loading gauge – this was why the APT body sides were noticeably curved. BR's new Mark 4 coach features sloping sides in case it is ever adapted for tilt technology – which at the moment seems very unlikely.

BR at first paid little heed to passenger complaints of nausea on both experimental and public service runs. Rather late in the day, it was realized that 100% tilt compensation was a mistake. With full compensation, a passenger who was reading or talking had no inner awareness that his or her body was no longer vertical and was moving in an arc. A glance out of the window would suddenly inflict a perspective quite incompatible with the inner feelings; this disorientation could lead to sickness.

The Italian job

The Italians took the disorientation problem more seriously when the Fiat experimental ETR401 Pendolino went into service in July 1976. They listened to passengers and discovered that backward facing seats were part of the problem, so in later designs the seats were rotatable. This expensive change was acceptable as the Italian tilting trains (unlike the British) were first class only.

Too fast a tilt was also found to disconcert passengers. The five degrees per second registered by the Pendolino prototype when maximum tilt was gained was far too fast. Around three degrees per second proved more comfortable and was all that was required for most curves at the Pendolino's normal speeds.

One way of achieving slower tilting of the passenger compartment is to have a smaller degree of tilt, and since passengers are uncomfortable with 100% compensation of cant deficiency (70% seems to be the most comfortable), quite small degrees can be acceptable. With Spain's passive Talgo Pendular trains, only four degrees can be obtained in any case. The Pendolino was designed for nine degrees, which may be one of the causes of the *mal-de-tilt* experienced by some of its passengers. When the Pendolino was tried in Germany, 70% compensation was the aim and this needed no more than a maximum seven degree tilt angle. This tilt permitted curving speeds to be increased by 20% over the normal limit.

Different designs present different solutions. Like the APT, the Swedish X2000 (originally the X2) tilts by means of hydraulic jacks acting on the car floor. The Fiat preference is for the jacks applying pressure to the roof.

Passive tilts are not entirely self regulating. On

▼The experimental 1973 APT-E was originally powered by gas turbine. This revolutionary train was designed from the start to tilt at up to nine degrees. After the 1973 fuel crisis the production APTs were powered by electricity.

Sweden's X2000

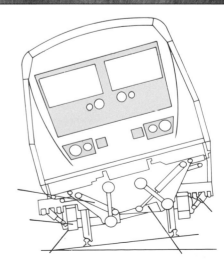

The APT's tilt system has been vindicated to an extent as the new Swedish X2000 has adopted a tilting bolster with underfloor-mounted angled hydraulic jacks similar to the ATP design. The active hydraulic system gives a maximum rotating angle of 6.6° and a maximum tilt speed of 4° per second. The system is controlled by accelerometers and allows an increase in curving speed of up to 30%.

Tilting services

Regular tilting train services already exist in several parts of Europe. The Spanish Talgo Pendular trains circulate not only internally but also penetrate France as far as Paris. In Italy the ETR450 trains link Rome with several cities. The Swedish X2000 design has been introduced on numerous services and the S220 Pendolino operates in Finland.

Outside Europe, in Japan tilting trains have been running since 1973. The Series 381 EMUs operate on the tortuous Nagoya – Nagano line; a more modern tilting unit has recently been introduced. Amtrak has tested the X2000 in the US Northeast Corridor service. The Swedish system is also being studied in Australia.

▼The Spanish Talgo Pendular, introduced in 1980, uses a passive tilt mechanism with coach bodies suspended so they tilt naturally in bends – this gives a 20% faster service over existing routes. The Pendular is hauled by a Series 354 locomotive constructed for the Talgo Pendular in 1983.

the Talgo Pendular, to prevent the coach bodies swinging from side to side on straight track, the pneumatic suspension has to be locked. Locking and unlocking can, however, be automated by the use of transponders at the beginning and end of curves.

Keeping the pantograph level while the train tilts is another problem. On the APT there was a tilt compensation linkage, but Fiat prefers to anchor the pantograph to the only other non-tilting part of the train, the bogie. With Talgo Pendular there is no problem because these trains are hauled by non-tilting locomotives.

The way ahead

The Japanese built 150 tilting trains in ten years following the first introduction of their successful Class 381 EMUs in 1973. Class 381s were designed for fairly low speeds and the tilt is limited to five degrees – new designs are now being introduced with increased tilt capability.

Apart from these trains, and the Swedish X2000, at present the prospects for tilting trains rest mainly on the competing Fiat and Talgo concepts. Austrian Federal Railways has tried both and opted for the Fiat version, to be built in Austria as six-car electric sets.

German Railways also tried both, and actually opted for both, seeing uses for each system. The Fiat technology is to be applied to two-car diesel sets which, initially, will be used on the curved, hilly lines of Bavaria. A new 300km/h (187.5mph) Talgo Pendular train will be completed in 1996, the same year that ETR470 Pendolinos commenced operation between Italy and Switlzerland.

Radial wheelset steering

The increased cornering speeds achieved by the use of X2000's active hydraulic tilt system could cause severe track and wheel wear. A special feature of the new Swedish X2000 tilting train is its self-steering capability. Radial wheelset steering reduces wear by incorporating into the bogies the large rubber chevrons which are part of the primary suspension. The system has been used on Swedish State Railways' Class X10 suburban units.

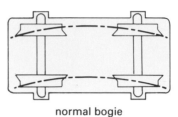

normal bogie

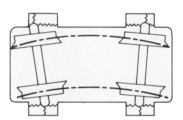

bogie with radial wheelset steering

High speed trains in Japan

Japan was the country that pioneered high speed train services in the 1960s. Since then the concept has been developed further with lighter and more powerful trains and brand new sets for regauged and narrow gauge lines.

In October 1964 the Japanese National Railways (JNR) completed the world's first high speed railway, between Tokyo and Osaka – the New Tokaido Line, a 515km (320 mile) route. It was built to standard gauge which meant there could be no inter-running with the rest of the 3ft 6in (1067mm) gauge JNR system. After the first year's operations – run at reduced speeds while the track settled in – full advantage was taken of its 210km/h (130mph) capabilities, and journey times for the limited-stop Hikari trains came down to 3 hours 10 minutes. Traffic boomed, and the number and length of the trains were increased.

The New Tokaido Line was the first section of the Shinkansen, or New Network, and its purpose was to provide more capacity between the coun-try's capital and its second city, as the existing narrow gauge lines were saturated. In 1972 the first westward extension – the New Sanyo Line – was opened, and three years later it stretched for 1069.1km (664.3 miles) from Tokyo to Hakata on the island of Kyushu.

Another seven years passed before the next additions to the high speed network came into operation, with the opening of the Niigata and Tohoku Shinkansen, running north and north-west from Tokyo. It was intended to extend the Tohuku line through the Siekan Tunnel to the island of Hokkaido, but this has not yet been achieved, and at present only narrow-gauge trains run through the 53.85km (33½ mile) tunnel. (This is longer than the Channel Tunnel.)

▼A Series 200 train streaks through the Japanese countryside. These trains have modifications to help them to cope with cold and snowy conditions. Door mechanisms are heated to prevent them from freezing and electrical equipment is mounted within the bodywork, rather than from the floor, to protect it from snow.

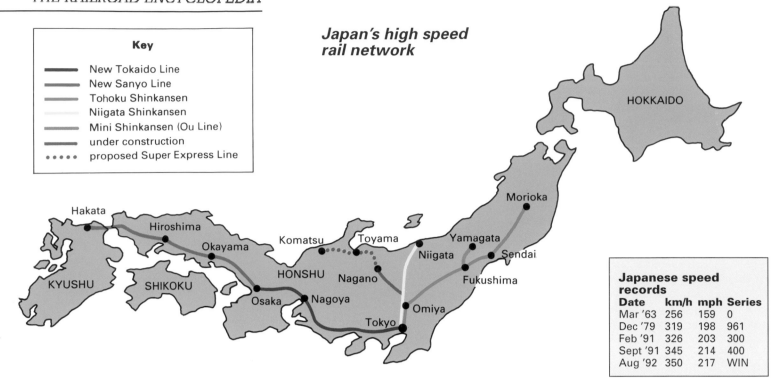

Japan's high speed rail network

Key

━━━ New Tokaido Line
━━━ New Sanyo Line
━━━ Tohoku Shinkansen
━━━ Niigata Shinkansen
━━━ Mini Shinkansen (Ou Line)
━━━ under construction
••••• proposed Super Express Line

Japanese speed records			
Date	km/h	mph	Series
Mar '63	256	159	0
Dec '79	319	198	961
Feb '91	326	203	300
Sept '91	345	214	400
Aug '92	350	217	WIN

At first, the Tokaido and Sanyo Shinkansen were operated by the blue and white Series 0 train-sets, which became known as the Bullet Trains. These were formed from two-car sets of a number of different types, but each set had its own pantograph and all axles were powered. A grand total of 3216 of these cars was built but, with each of them running some 400,000km (250,000 miles) each year, any individual vehicle has had a maximum operational life of no more than 15 years, and the fleet numbered only 1005 in April 1992.

For the lines north of Tokyo the green and white Series 200 trains were introduced. They looked similar to the original Tokaido sets, although there were some important differences. Aluminium bodies replaced steel ones, and thyristors took the place of tap-changers and silicon rectifiers. Special arrangements were also required to cope with the severe winter conditions where they operated.

In addition they used the 50Hz power supply that was standard in that part of the country. The Tokaido and Sanyo Shinkansen use a 60Hz system, which prevented through running even after the northern lines had been laboriously threaded through the centre of Tokyo to the Central station in 1991. Originally the Series 200 sets were 12-car trains, but, like the Series 0 type, they were later extended to 16 cars. Unlike them, because of their higher power ratings, two of the additional cars were trailers.

Speed restrictions
In the late 1950s the outline design for the New Tokaido Line envisaged a maximum speed of 260km/h (162mph), but this was thought to be too ambitious to gain the support of the World Bank. It was duly trimmed to 210km/h (130mph), which was to be the maximum speed for all Shinkansen trains for over 20 years. There were two reasons – commercial and environmental. Steady growth of

traffic provided a clear indication that the Shinkansen were competitive with other modes of transport, but experience showed that the trains were expensive to operate and took a heavy toll on the track.

At a very early stage too the noise problem started to make itself felt. The New Tokaido Line had been built through the most densely populated part of Honshu without much in the way of environmental protection. More protective measures had been taken when the Sanyo Line was built, but, even so, speeds at the western end were restricted by noise considerations.

By the mid-1980s the competitive situation had begun to change, with the development of many more internal air services, so there was pressure to increase speeds. First off the mark was the Tohoku

▼A Series 400 set of the East Japan Railway. These six-car sets operate on lines regauged to standard gauge. One of them is seen here on a Niwasaka – Sasakino working.

▶With the small fin above the cab, the pointed nose, and the design of the cab windows, these original Series 0 Shinkansen sets, seen at Tokyo, look more like aeroplanes than trains.

Shinkansen, which had been built with extensive noise protection walls along its route. In 1985 a 25kV power line was provided along the roof of some of the Series 200 trains, similar to those on the French TGVs. This enabled them to run with only three pantographs in operation, permitting the line speed to go up to 240km/h (149mph). As well as the problems that result from the use of multiple pantographs at high speed, they are one of the main sources of noise, so the fewer there are, the quieter the trains.

Weight and noise

There is also a close relationship between train weight and the noise from the wheels on the rails, and in the last decade a lot of work has gone into reducing the weight of the Shinkansen trains on the Tokaido and Sanyo Lines. In 1985 the Series 100 sets, with their more streamlined appearance, began to replace the original Series 0 designs on the faster services between Tokyo and Osaka.

Although also built of steel, they were 45 tonnes lighter, despite including two doubledeck coaches in each set. Their acceleration was better, and, without any change in maximum speed, in 1985 they were able to trim a nominal two minutes off the fastest journey times. A year and a half later the maximum speed on the Tokaido Line was raised to 220km/h (137mph), and the journey time was cut to less than three hours, giving an overall average of almost 180km/h (111.7mph).

Separate speed advances

In 1987 the loss-making, monolithic Japan National Railways was split into six regional passenger companies. Although all the shares are still held on behalf of the government by the JNR Settlement Corporation, along with the former debts, these railways are considered to be private companies, with the freedom of operation that this implies. Although each serves a separate geographical area, the split has prompted quite a lot of rivalry over speed, especially between the three companies – West Japan, Central Japan and East Japan Railways – which took over the Shinkansen lines.

The first speed-up took place in 1988 on the Niigata Line, which followed the Tohoku's lead by lifting some speeds to 240km/h (149mph). Two years later 275km/h (172mph) was permitted, but only in the downhill direction between Yuzawa and Urasa. Initially just two trains a day were allowed to do this, although the number was later increased to three. It was clearly an attempt at one-

Coping with snow

In some parts of Japan the Shinkansen experience heavy snowfalls, with maximum accumulations of over 4m (13ft) on the Niigata Line. Special precautions are needed to counter this, which include hot-water sprays on the lineside supplemented by jets directed at the blades of points. All the Series 200 trains are provided with integral Russel ploughs, and they have been designed to deal with all types of snow. All the underfloor equipment is shrouded, and special arrangements are provided to stop snow getting into the interior of the train through the cooling and air-conditioning intakes, or into the driving motors.

◀ The controls of West Japan Railway's WIN 350 train are surprisingly simple. This experimental train was used in trials and sports a variety of different equipment to help determine the specification of the production Series 500 trains, which will enter service on the Shin Osaka-Hakata line in 1996-7.

Japanese Railways maximum service speeds			
Date	km/h	mph	Line
pre-1964	120	75	3ft 6in gauge
Oct 1964	210	130	Tokaido Shinkansen
Mar 1985	240	149	Tohoku Shinkansen
Nov 1986	220	137	Tokaido & Sanyo Shinkansen
Mar 1988	240	149	Joetsu Shinkansen
Mar 1990	275	171	Joetsu Shinkansen
Mar 1992	270	168	Tokaido Shinkansen
Jul 1992	130	81	Ou Line*
1996	300	187	Hakata Shinkansen
(* after conversion to standard gauge)			

upmanship by the East Japan Railway, bearing in mind the limited opportunity it provided to gain operating experience at the higher speed.

It was on the busy Tokaido Line that the most significant leap forward took place in 1992, when the Series 300 sets developed by Central Japan Railway went into service, running at 270km/h (168mph) for considerable distances. At first there were only two trains a day in each direction, and their 2½ hour schedules lifted the overall speed to 206.2km/h (128.1mph). These Nozomi (Hope) trains made only one intermediate stop instead of two made by the Hikari services.

Starting from March 1993 these morning and evening business expresses were supplemented by a regular hourly Nozomi from Osaka and Tokyo, some running through to and from Hakata. (West Japan Railway owns five of the 20 sets now in service.) Visually, the Nozomi sets are a complete break from previous designs. The familiar Bullet Train front-end was replaced by a drooping nose and fairings over the bogies. The roof height is 40cm (16in) lower, and there are prominent anti-noise fairings round the pantographs. The weight has also been reduced dramatically, a 16-car set scaling only 396 tonnes compared with the 876 tonnes of Series 0 trains of similar length and capacity.

Exclusive designs

Although West Japan Railway has bought a number of the Series 100 and Series 300 sets, they are planning their own high speed design, for which they have produced the experimental WIN 350 (West Japan's Innovation for Operation at 350km/h). This six-coach set began trial running in May 1992, and four months later set a new Japanese speed record of 350km/h (217mph). Three experimental bogie designs were used, each of them a third lighter than those on the Series 100 trains, and fitted with active suspension. The cabs at the two ends of the set have completely different profiles, to test aerodynamics and noise levels. The experience which was gained with WIN 350 has been used to design the Series 500 sets for commercial operation over West Japan Railway at speeds of up to 350km/h (217mph), noise limits permitting.

East Japan Railway has its own development train, STAR 21 (Super Train for Advanced Railway towards the 21st century). It too includes a number of alternative features, including three types of body construction, two methods of controlling the motors, two front-end shapes, eight types of bogie, and several designs of pantograph shield. Some cars have individual bogies, while others are articulated together, like the TGVs. It is intended later to install more power to push the speed to 430km/h (267mph).

Narrow gauge

Although the existing Shinkansen trains are having to fight noise problems, the economic benefits they bring are prompting other parts of the country

▼A Series 300 set of the Central Japan Railway. These trains entered service in 1992 and run at speeds approaching 273km/h (170mph) for considerable distances.

Fastest Tokyo – Osaka journeys*				
Date	hours	mins	km/h	mph
pre-1964	6	30	85.6	53.2
Oct 1964	4	0	128.9	80.1
Nov 1965	3	10	162.8	101.2
Mar 1985	3	8	164.5	102.2
Nov 1986	2	52	179.8	111.7
Mar 1988	2	49	183.0	113.7
Jun 1995	2	30	206.2	128.1

* The old route is 556.4km (345³/₄ miles) long, compared with the Shinkansen distance of 515.4km (320¹/₃ miles)

▲The experimental WIN 350 set has fairings round the pantographs to reduce unwanted aerodynamic noise. The other end of the six-car train is differently shaped.

to demand their own high speed lines. These have become increasingly expensive to construct, so two different hybrid systems have been developed to obtain some of the advantages more cheaply.

The first of these involves the Mini Shinkansen, six-car Series 400 units, which are small enough to operate over former 1067mm (3ft 6in) gauge lines which have been regauged. East Japan's Ou Line was the first to be converted in the summer of 1992, connecting Fukushima on the Tokohu Shinkansen with the city of Yamagata. From Tokyo to Fukushima, one service an hour has a Series 400 set coupled to an ordinary Series 200, running at up to 240km/h (149mph). At the junction station they uncouple, and, while the full-size train continues to Sendai and the north, the Mini Shinkansen follows the regauged tracks for the final 90km (60 miles) of its journey. These have been realigned to permit speeds of up to 130km/h (81mph), which is slightly faster than previously permitted, but the trains are powerful enough to maintain this up gradients as steep as 1 in 25. On the Joetsu Shinkansen a Series 400 set achieved a new Japanese speed record of 345km/h (214mph) in September 1991.

The second type of hybrid line is the so-called Super Express, and involves the construction of a new narrow gauge line to Shinkansen standards of alignment and loading gauge. Until the route is connected with the standard gauge high speed net-

work at some future date, useful increases in speed – up to 200km/h (125mph) – are possible with narrow gauge stock, until there is justification for the track to be widened for through running by Shinkansen sets. The Seikan Tunnel has already been constructed on this principle. In 1998 the Winter Olympics are to be held at Nagano, and this will be served by a new full Shinkansen branch off the Joetsu Line at Takasaki, but the Super Express system could be adopted for the continuation along the north coast to Komatsu.

Plans for a maglev link

Although the Japanese railways have achieved such a success with high speed conventional railways, Central Japan Railway is still looking at the possibility of a maglev (magnetic levitation) link between Tokyo and Osaka, which might result in a 500km/h (311mph) commercial service early in the 21st century. In case the technology should prove too difficult or too expensive, work is also being carried out to develop the Series 300X trains, which would be capable of whatever speeds in the range 300-350km/h (186-217mph) would be permitted by the noise limits along a new Shinkansen route linking the two cities.

Within a quarter of a century, Japan's first high speed line, used by a single type of train, has become a much more complicated system as its popularity with the travelling public has risen steadily. Now as many as 11 trains an hour enter and leave Tokyo Central over a pair of tracks, and the faster trains on the Tokaido and Tohoku Line have load factors of over 90%.

As well as setting an example for the rest of the world, the pioneers of the Shinkansen have provided Japan with a remarkable system, on which there has never been a passenger fatality.

▼The East Japan Railway has its own development train, which includes a number of alternative features. In particular, some of its carriages have two bogies in the usual way whereas some are articulated together.

Train names
(Listed in order of increasing average speeds for each Line)

Tokaido and Sanyo Lines
Kodama (Echo)
Hikari (Light)
Nozomi (Hope)

Tohoku Line
Aoba (Green Leaves; also name of castle at Sendai)
Yamabiko (Echo)

Yamagata/Ou Line (Mini Shinkansen)
Tsubasa (Wing)

Niigata Line
Toki (Crested Ibis)
Asahi (Morning Sun)

As road congestion and pollution worsens in conurbations throughout the world, the ability of high speed trains to provide fast city centre to city centre journey times will become progressively more attractive. A Series 100 Shinkansen leaves Tokyo for the south.

Maglev: riding on air

Magnetic levitation systems bring a promise of wheel-less trains, riding above the track, to provide 310mph city to city links. But the technology for high speed maglev has proved far from simple – it could be a while before science fiction becomes science fact.

Run on a magnetic cushion which is created when a string of magnets is energized under a train to provide lift, magnetic levitation (maglev) has always seemed like the high tech equivalent of the genie's magic carpet.

Though the idea was first considered in the US in 1907, research on high speed maglev trains is now concentrated in Japan and Germany. Each country opted for a different system. Japan chose to develop the technology of magnetic repulsion, a system using electromagnets in the train and track which are designed to generate similar poles. When the current is turned on they repel one another, forcing the train into the air above the track.

Germany's Transrapid train uses magnetic attraction. It runs on a T-shaped concrete track with the magnets fixed underneath and the vehicle wrapped around the horizontal section. The electromagnets in the undercarriage of the train and the lower surface of the track are arranged with opposite poles facing one another so that each attracts the other when the current is switched on. Activation pulls up the train magnets. Computers constantly modify the strength of the current fed to the electromagnets so that the two sets never touch – the train hovers less than half an inch above the track surface.

Both the German and the Japanese trains use linear induction motors to propel themselves forward, with another set of magnets riding an electric current in the track.

Trials and tribulations

Transport engineers began to take the maglev concept seriously in the 1960s when linear motors started to move off the drawing board and on to test tracks. Experiments in Canada investigated the possibilities of linking the cities on the Toronto – Montreal corridor with a maglev line. Meanwhile, BR's Railway Technical Centre at Derby developed its own research programme.

As the tests progressed it became obvious that the apparently simple maglev concept was very difficult to put into practice. The problems were diverse, ranging from magnetic drag to trains which oscillated from side to side. These difficul-

◀ By the turn of the century the Japanese Shinkansen bullet trains will have reached full capacity. A new line, the Chuo Linear Express, is planned, operated by maglev trains reaching 310mph (500km/h). This prototype, MLU002, carried 44 passengers and worked on the repulsion principle.

ties took time and money to solve – soon the Germans and the Japanese were the only players left in the high speed maglev game.

The German Transrapid team was jointly funded by the German Ministry of Research and Technology (BMFT) and a consortium of seven companies. The team built a single line test track at Emsland near Hamburg with a loop at each end so that a complete circuit 24 miles (38km) long could be made.

The test track and first vehicle, No TR06, were ready in 1984. During the first year it covered 931 miles (1500km); once some early problems were solved, No TR06 was averaging 6831 miles (11,000km) a year.

Passengers first used the test train in 1988 during an international railway trade fair. But in September of that year faults were discovered on the Emsland track. All the bolts used were unable to withstand the dynamic forces exerted when a train passed. New mortar had to be used to secure longer, thicker bolts; repairs closed the track for further testing until July 1989.

Meanwhile, a new test train – No TR07 *Europa* – had arrived at Emsland, featuring an improved aerodynamic form and more effective brake and on-board computer systems. When testing resumed *Europa* soon reached its design speed of 248mph (400km/h) and on 18 December 1989

▶Japan's MLU002 used superconducting magnets mounted on the train with the same polarity as the U-shaped guideway. The repulsion caused by like polarities levitates the train about 4in (10cm) above the guideway. MLU002 was destroyed by fire in October 1991, but work continues.

▼Japan Airlines developed their own maglev trains in the 1970s and 1980s. When government funding was lost, the project was sold to a team of former employees, who continue their research. The latest, HSST 2015, is seen on exhibition at Yokohama.

touched 270mph (435km/h), the world record for a manned maglev.

In 1994 the German government gave the go-ahead to a Hamburg-Berlin Transrapid maglev proposal. However, its realisation remains in doubt, not least because the forecast of 15 million passenger journeys has been considered optimistic.

The flying bullet

While German technicians were busy at Emsland, Japanese engineers were already working hard on their 4¹/₃ mile (7km) track at Miyazaki on the southern island of Kyushu. It was here that the Railway Technical Research Institute conducted the tests which set the world speed record of 321mph (517km/h) for an unmanned maglev vehicle.

But the Institute was not just interested in hitting the headlines. Its programme was designed to iron out the problems of magnetic repulsion technology so that a train could go into commercial

▼In Germany, Transrapid 06 has recently been superseded by Transrapid *Europa*. It works by magnetic attraction, rather than repulsion. In December 1989 a manned ride in *Europa* reached a record 270mph (435km/h).

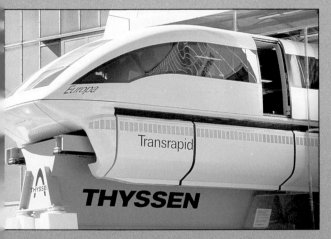

use. The first track at Miyazaki was an inverted T shape but that was abandoned in 1980 for a flattened U. In the second configuration the repulsion magnets were set in the floor of the track while those involved in propelling the train forward as part of the linear motor were attached to the side walls.

Japanese designers built two trains to test the track. The first, MLU001, consisted of three small cars with electromagnetic coils spread along the length of the train. The later test vehicle, MLU002,,was a single car with the coils concentrated in bogies at either end.

The coils used to propel the Japanese system are made from special superconducting materials. Each coil is fabricated from niobium-titanium alloy wire which is immersed in liquid helium to create the very low temperatures necessary to make it work.

The Japanese team discovered that repulsion levitation produces magnetic drag at low speeds. So retractable wheels, similar to those fitted to aircraft, had to be installed to support the train as it accelerated. Another drawback was that a single layer of propulsion coils on the side walls produced an uneven magnetic field. A new design will use coils in two overlapping layers which should overcome the problem.

All these modifications will be incorporated into the 27 mile (43km) Yamanashi test track being built near Kofu, a city about 62 miles (100km) west of Tokyo. The site is situated on the line of a proposed Tokyo to Osaka high speed relief line.

Experiments have so far been fairly successful – though a problem with a rubber tyre caused MLU002 to catch fire in October 1991. Despite this setback it is probable Japan will have its first maglev main line in 2005.

A British success

While the Germans and the Japanese were preoccupied with high speed maglev systems, BR's

Poles apart

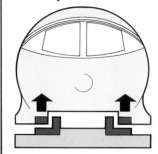

The Japanese system uses magnetic repulsion. Magnetic fields in the track meet those in the train and a repulsive force keeps the two apart. Superconducting magnets with like poles lift the train 4in (10cm).

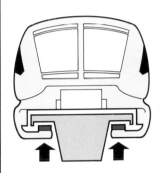

The German system – and that used for Birmingham Airport – uses magnetic attraction. Electromagnets on the train's undercarriage wrap under laminated iron rails below the guideway. The undercarriage rises towards the rail and lifts the train.

research centre at Derby was investigating a low speed maglev design. During the late 1970s the West Midlands County Council was planning a new passenger terminal at Birmingham International Airport. An anticipated 15% of people using the new terminal would arrive at the adjacent Birmingham International station.

The council decided that BR's maglev design was the ideal system to connect the station to the new terminal. With British Rail acting as technical advisers, GEC Transportation Projects were asked to organize a consortium to build the 681yd (623m) line. The designers decided to build two parallel but independent tracks with one vehicle shuttling back and forth on each. The cars are entirely computer controlled and do not need staff on board. Their movements are programmed to coincide so that each starts simultaneously from opposite ends of the line.

Although the British version is a low speed maglev, the system works in a similar way to Germany's Transrapid, with T-shaped track and a wrap around undercarriage on each vehicle. Electromagnets raise the cars 6in (15cm) above the track surface.

Birmingham Airport's maglev system went into operation on 7 August 1984 and proved a success with passengers. Each car made 32 trips an hour with every journey taking 100 seconds. As the time spent on board was so short, most passengers were expected to stand – only six seats were provided on each vehicle. Each 19ft (6m) long car was designed to take 40 passengers but over 50 squeezed in on occasions.

Because the only moving parts on the vehicles

Linear motors

Once lifted above the track a maglev train is propelled forward by a linear induction motor. This makes use of the reaction between magnetic fields of like and opposite polarities.

Coils on the train generate a magnetic field, the poles shifting along the train. The field creates electric currents in the reaction rail, which generates its own magnetic field. The two fields then interact so that the floating train is pulled along the track.

Power for the Birmingham Airport trains comes from transformers supplying 600V DC to two trackside conductor rails. There is also a 48V DC on-board battery.

Such systems save energy and require a minimum of maintenance, as no moving parts are needed to power the trains. They also produce little noise or vibration.

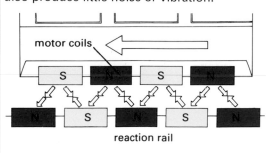

motor coils

reaction rail

were the doors, the airport found the system easy to maintain. Electronic monitoring equipment incorporated in each car warned staff of any developing fault; the average time taken to get the car back into service after a breakdown was just 13 minutes.

The success of Birmingham's low speed maglev was so complete that Frankfurt Airport authorities decided to build a similar system, linking its Eastern and Central Terminals, with a possible extension to the nearby underground station.

The civic authorities in Las Vegas were also impressed – they commissioned a $1^1/_{10}$ mile (1.8km) low speed maglev line with four stations linking a large conference centre and a market place in the city centre. This line is so quiet that one station is built inside a library. Both systems were completed in 1992-3.

These low speed systems seem to be the way of the future, not the high speed systems which have absorbed so much money – they might possess all the glamour but what is less certain is their ability to run reliably day in day out and make enough profit to pay back development costs.

▲Birmingham Airport had the world's first commercial maglev system. Working by magnetic attraction, it offered a top speed of 34mph (54km/h) – very much slower than the high speeds hoped for in Japan and Germany.

With no moving parts apart from the doors, wear and tear were minimal. Brake pads were fitted for an emergency, but the trains used the linear motor to stop. Trains were unaffected by rain, snow and ice, were virtually maintenance free and automatically report any faults.

However, the cost of spare parts proved excessive and the Birmingham maglev closed on 19 June 1995.

◄ A Canadian pioneer maglev was built to test plans to use magnetic levitation technology along the Toronto – Montreal corridor. The experiment revealed some of the problems of the system, such as vibration and magnetic drag.

Light rail systems

The latest link in the urban transport chain, light rail is an economical way of moving people quickly over short distances, sidestepping traffic jams and attracting passengers back to the public sector.

Light rail is a public transport system based on vehicles the size of a single deck bus which are joined together in pairs of up to four cars. They are powered by electricity and run on lightweight railway track. Each two-car vehicle travels at an average speed of 20-30mph (32-48km/h) and holds up to 250 passengers with the majority standing. Like trams they are relatively cheap to build and their routes avoid the heavy construction work necessary for most underground railways.

The track is normally segregated from road traffic which, by avoiding traffic jams, allows light rail to go faster than trams. The separation from road traffic also means that light rail systems are easy to automate using technology similar to that installed on underground rail lines. This lowers running costs. Few lines are more than ten miles (16km) long and stops are usually about half a mile (800m) apart.

Advanced tram systems evolved into light rail in continental Europe during the 1960s and 1970s.

The UK missed out because it had all but abandoned tram technology, with London seeing its last service disappear in 1952. Birmingham followed suit in 1953 and Sheffield dug up its tram tracks in 1960. Only Blackpool held out against what most urban authorities of the time saw as the march of progress.

Tyne and Wear Metro

Newcastle, Gateshead and other towns along the River Tyne were the first in Britain to realize that the unlimited provision of new roads would turn their city into a concrete jungle. Their foresight means that the north-east of England has the most mature light rail system in the country.

The light rail system run by the Tyne and Wear Passenger Transport Executive is 36.25 miles (58km) long and is organized into five lines. Most of the system was converted from an old British Rail loop which ran along the north side of the Tyne to Whitley Bay before doubling back to

▼Light rail systems fit between trams and underground railways in the transport infrastructure of large cities and combine the best features of old and new technologies. Specially fabricated 71yd (65m) concrete spans carry London's Docklands Light Railway across the former West India Docks. Wherever possible, use is made of former disused or underused railway lines – in the case of the City arm to Tower Gateway this accounts for two-thirds of the 7¹/₂ route miles (12km).

Newcastle. A second line headed north-west from Newcastle towards the city's airport. In the building of the Metro these lines were joined by new tunnels which linked up under Newcastle city centre. Here they joined another former BR line which followed the river east to South Shields.

The first trains ran in August 1980. By introducing a system segregated from other traffic, the transport executive provided a high frequency service which avoided city centre congestion and ran on time. No point on the system is more than 25 minutes from the middle of Newcastle.

Public use

The changes to the Tyne and Wear transport system made it very attractive to the public. The population of the area fell between 1974 and 1985 and unemployment increased as local heavy industries such as shipbuilding declined. A study of the Metro system by the Department of the Environment and Newcastle University estimated that these social and economic factors should have produced a 10% drop in public use of the system. Instead, the number of journeys on public transport in the area grew from 282 million in 1974 to 316 million in 1985 – a 12% increase.

Unfortunately for the Tyne and Wear area some transport initiatives by central government have not helped the public system. The 1985 Transport Act, which restructured the British bus industry, had a profound effect on travel in the area. By emphasizing competition and commercial initiative, the act discouraged the co-operative spirit which had helped integrate bus and light rail services. Single through tickets which covered bus and rail were abandoned. Some feeder services to the Metro stations were discontinued.

Simultaneously, the changing British tax struc-

ture put more money in pockets, which encouraged car ownership. As a result the use of public transport dropped, although the Metro held its share of the passengers. Not surprisingly, traffic congestion increased in Newcastle city centre and on the Tyne bridges.

Docklands Light Railway

The success of the Tyne and Wear Metro encouraged passenger transport authorities throughout Britain to develop light rail schemes of their own. But the process of designing the system, public consultation and persuading the government to back the idea took years. Only the London Docklands Development Corporation (LDDC), which was created in 1981, had the power and enough support from Whitehall to override the lengthy process and translate an idea quickly into practice.

The LDDC was established to redevelop approximately eight square miles (20.7sq km) of derelict land that extended east from the city of London. The success of Tyne and Wear and other light rail systems around the world in encouraging new developments close to stations led the LDDC to believe that the installation of a brand new light rail line would assist the task of regeneration in the area.

London Transport had already concluded a study which showed that an automated light railway running from a site close to the Tower of London to the southern end of the Isle of Dogs would cost only £58 million. An extension eastwards of the Jubilee line had previously been abandoned because its estimated cost was £325 million.

The government jumped at such a cheap solution which used old railway viaducts and track, following the Tyne and Wear pattern, for much of its length. As the idea developed and new office blocks and flats began to sprout in Docklands during the 1980s, a north-south spur connecting with underground lines and BR at Stratford was agreed. The final cost of the line, which opened in 1987, was £77 million.

▼Unlike other light rail systems Manchester's Metrolink isn't entirely segregated – on the two mile (3.2km) street level section the trains, which share space with other traffic, are designed to run through the city centre at a maximum speed of 30mph (48km/h). However, when travelling on their own segregated tracks these cars can attain a maximum of 50mph (80km/h).

1001

▲An effective light rail system must be linked to other parts of the public transport network. Bus services were rerouted to feed the Tyne and Wear system and initially this reduced the number of private vehicles heading for the centre of Newcastle and Gateshead. Some of the buses displaced from the inner city routes were used to introduce express services into suburban areas not served by the Metro. The light rail trains were quickly carried over the river on the purpose built Queen Elizabeth II Bridge. Unfortunately, bus deregulation and the resulting competition for passengers hindered the move towards an integrated transport policy.

▶After the boom years of the 1980s, the proposed development of the Isle of Dogs – in particular the Canary Wharf complex, the world's largest commercial development – heightened the need to expand the light rail system. Compared to other transport systems, light rail is flexible and relatively easy to expand even through heavily built up areas. A light rail system can cope with tight curves – up to 44yd (40m) radius – and gradients of up to 1 in 17.

▼**Perhaps the most surprising convert to the cause of light rail is that ultimate bastion of the car – Los Angeles. After decades of building expressways which turned the sprawling city into an expensive tangle of bumper to bumper traffic jams covered by a layer of smog, the first light rail line began operation in 1990.**

Unfortunately the LDDC had seriously under-estimated the attractions of the railway to potential users. Traffic of 22,000 passengers a day had been anticipated by the end of 1991. But 33,000 people were already using the system every day by the end of 1989.

With up to 50,000 people working in the area, the original railway would have been swamped. However, Docklands Light Railway (DLR) had difficulties extending the capacity of its system because much of the trackwork was single line and supported by a narrow viaduct. The solution was to double the size of each train and to extend the length of all the platforms to accommodate the new dimensions. This work and the excavation of tunnels at the western end of the line to connect the line to Bank underground station cost £250 million to which the developers Olympia and York contributed £68 million.

Despite this work and an extension east through more derelict land to Beckton, DLR cannot now cope with the anticipated numbers of passengers generated by the development of the Isle of Dogs. Light rail is limited to a maximum of 20,000 passengers an hour because of the strength of its track and the dimensions and number of its cars. This means that an extension to the Jubilee line has had to be built at a cost of over £1 billion.

Manchester Metrolink

While both Tyne and Wear and DLR are segregated systems, the third British light rail system – Metrolink – connects two former BR lines with a street level section through the heart of

The European experience

In mainland Europe many light rail and tram systems, such as this one in Stuttgart, are being extended. However, European town planners see light rail systems as only part of the answer to inner city transport problems. In Germany greater emphasis is given to pedestrianization, and whole areas of a city are paved over – unlike the one or two streets in a British city. As a result the Germans have found that fewer cars lead to a pleasanter shopping environment which increases the number of pedestrians, improves the quality of life and encourages trade in the area.

Manchester. In that respect it resembles many systems in continental Europe.

The first phase of Metrolink, which opened in 1992, is 19.5 miles (30km) long with 25 stations. Work has started on a similar scheme in Birmingham, using rail routes.

Apart from the obvious problems of light rail cars mixing with other traffic at street level, one problem that remains unresolved will arise in the event of an accident. If an incident occurs on the former BR lines the investigation will be the responsibility of the Railway Inspectorate. But if it occurs at street level will the police take charge? And what happens if the accident occurs as a metrocar leaves a ramp?

Signs of the future

Proposals for many other light rail systems are being discussed by planning and passenger transport authorities throughout Britain. The relative cheapness of the technology and the cost of construction is attractive to local government at a time when its budgets are being squeezed. But whether all of these new found enthusiasts realize the limitations of light rail's carrying capacity and its unsuitability for distances longer than 10 to 15 miles (16-24km) is open to question.

Major cities around the world have confronted these problems and are busy installing or updating light rail. Germany and Japan have always favoured the new technology and have the most comprehensive networks. France has now followed their lead; various systems have been adopted in cities as diverse as Grenoble, Lille and Paris.

Other systems are in the course of planning and construction. It would appear that light rail is now the apple of every city planner's eye from Salford to the Hollywood hills.

Vancouver's SkyTrain

Vancouver's automated SkyTrain urban rail system, which opened for the Expo'86 world's fair, has many innovative features, such as linear induction motors, steerable bogies and moving-block signalling. Though expensive and still controversial, the SkyTrain system is being expanded.

FACT FILE

Demand: 115,000 passengers a day. Over 7000 in a single direction in the peak hour
Frequency: every 2¹/₂ to 3 minutes in rush hours, and every 5 minutes at other times, including evenings, weekends and holidays
Length: the entire system became 28.8km (18 miles) long when a 4.3km (2.68 mile) extension to Surrey Town Centre was opened in March 1994.

The residents of Vancouver, British Columbia, Canada's premier west coast city, have long recognized the importance of innovative, excellent transport in developing the community. The city opened its electric tramway on 26 June 1890, and saw the completion on 8 October 1891 of one of North America's earliest interurban tramways from the city 12 miles south-eastwards to the former colonial capital of New Westminster. The original interurban later became known as the Central Park line. Vancouver became the hub of Canada's largest electric railway system, controlled by the British Columbia Electric Railway (BCER), which was British-owned until 1928.

Expo'86, the world's transport fair, was held to honour Vancouver's centenary in 1986. Moving people between the fair venues and from New Westminster was SkyTrain, Vancouver's automated light railway. Owned by BC Transit, the provincial transport agency, SkyTrain marked a return to urban rail in the city. Vancouver had succumbed to the once-fashionable rails-to-rubber transport trend. The Central Park line to New Westminster ceased in 1953, the last city trams ran in 1955, and the last interurban ground to a halt in 1958.

SkyTrain versus LRT

Vancouver soon longed for the old trams, and in 1971 a study was published recommending their return in the modern guise of light rail transit (LRT). The short-lived left-wing New Democratic Party (NDP) provincial government in the 1970s brought over a tram from Hannover in Germany to run on the diesel-only remnants of the Central Park line. However, the NDP was defeated in a general election, and the tram was later sold to Fort Edmonton Park, Alberta, without ever seeing service in British Columbia.

While LRT was favoured by local officials

▼A Mark I SkyTrain set crosses the Fraser River from New Westminster to Surrey on BC Transit's SkyBridge. The 616m (2000ft) long span, which opened in March 1990, is the world's longest cable-stayed transit-only bridge.

The first phase of SkyTrain was opened for regular service on 3 January 1986. It follows the old Central Park line for much of the distance on tracks attached to an overhead concrete guideway – which gives the system its name. It enters Vancouver's city centre in a former CP Rail tunnel, built by the railway to bring serviced locomotives and passenger carriages to its Vancouver terminus, which has also been modified for SkyTrain use. At the other end of the system, the light metro has now been extended across the Fraser River to Scott Road, in the suburb of Surrey, and will be completed to Surrey Town Centre station in 1994.

SkyTrain is wheelchair-accessible with lifts at most stations, which will total 19 when the line is finished. Tickets are sold from vending machines or from shops, while security is provided by closed-circuit TV, intercoms, public-address systems and emergency telephones backed up by roving BC Transit police. SkyTrain is well co-ordinated with BC Transit's bus routes and with its SeaBus catamaran ferries that sail from SkyTrain's ex-CP Rail terminal in Vancouver, across the Burrard Inlet to North Vancouver.

The technology

Like the original 1891 interurban line, SkyTrain is noted for its use of several transport innovations. These were packaged together by the Urban Transportation Development Corporation (UTDC) of Kingston, Ontario, now owned by Bombardier, and sold as the Intermediate Capacity Transit System (ICTS). BC Transit contracted with the British Columbia Rapid Transit Co (BCRTC), a private company, to operate it. The only other ICTS installations are in Detroit, Michigan and in

▲A worker makes adjustments to the linear induction motor (LIM) on a SkyTrain carriage bogie. The equipment is maintained at BC Transit's SkyTrain shops in South Burnaby. The yard where the trains are stabled is fully automated.

because of lower construction costs, the then-ruling right-wing Social Credit government forced Vancouver to accept the new technology, because the system would solve the transport problems posed by hosting the world's fair. SkyTrain cost $854 million (Can) to build, which was higher per mile or per passenger carried than tramway styled LRT systems being constructed at the same time in Calgary and San Diego.

Victoria

Vancouver's SkyTrain may not be the only urban rail system that BC Transit could be running in the future. The agency has suggested that a 17km (10.2 mile) Light Rapid Transit (LRT) from Victoria, the provincial capital, to its western suburbs could be built for $300 million (Can) on an abandoned ex-CN Rail line, with a branch built later to the University of Victoria.

Victoria in British Columbia is the province's second largest city, with an area population of 287,000 that is expected to grow to 400,000. It had western Canada's first tramway, which opened on 22 February 1890, and closed on 5 July 1948.

If studies back LRT, Victoria could then become the smallest North American city with urban rail transit. As a first stage, the province is now considering plans for a tramway in the city centre.

The SkyTrain network

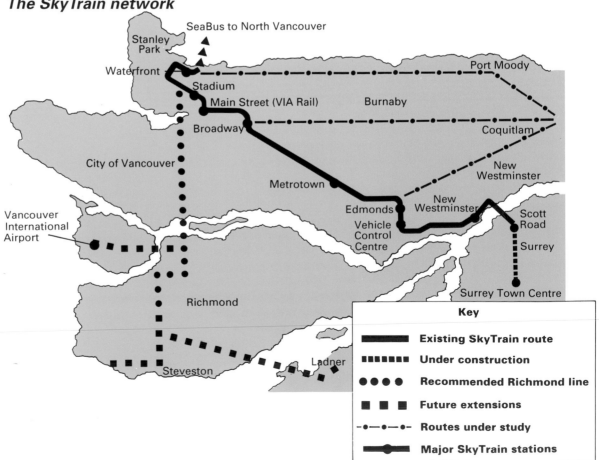

Key

▬▬▬	**Existing SkyTrain route**
▰▰▰	**Under construction**
●●●●	**Recommended Richmond line**
■ ■ ■	**Future extensions**
–•–•–•–	**Routes under study**
▬●▬	**Major SkyTrain stations**

Toronto, Ontario. While Toronto's was the first, opening in 1985, BC Transit's is the biggest. Like Vancouver's system, the decision to build Toronto's ICTS was also politically motivated. The Province of Ontario, which established the UTDC, had wanted a showcase for the technology.

The UTDC design features automated trains of bus-sized cars powered by linear induction motors (LIM) on steerable-axle bogies. The trains are controlled by a moving-block signalling system devised by SEL Canada. The 130-car fleet, whose design is classed as Mark I, are permanently connected into 65 pairs. Two- and four-car sets are the norm, but six-car trains have been run – most notably during Expo'86, but rarely since. Full automation allows BC Transit to run shorter, but more frequent, and therefore more convenient trains without additional crewing costs.

SkyTrain is the first major system to use the LIM, which splits a three-phase AC motor between the railway vehicle and the track. A pair of parallel third and fourth rails, mounted in a rack beside the tracks, supply and return 650V DC current that is converted to AC on the trains. SkyTrain's moving-block system is a derivative of the LZB system, used initially on German railways and first applied to an urban rail system in Berlin in 1971. UTDC was the first to adopt it for an

unstaffed train system. Movement is controlled by computers at SkyTrain's Vehicle Control Centre in suburban Burnaby and on board the trains themselves.

SkyTrain's systems are now being updated and refined. The line's capacity can be increased to 350,000 passengers per day. It handled almost 35 million people in 1995, an increase of about 60% since 1987. SEL and BCRTC have been developing new high-capacity software and an auto-restart

▲**SkyTrain operations and security are monitored from a facility at BC Transit's South Burnaby shops. The screens nearest the operators are for the trains, while the displays above are of closed circuit television scans of stations.**

▼**Near SkyBridge and next to the road bridge is a swing span used by the Burlington Northern, CN Rail, and the Southern Railway of British Columbia. The Southern Railway is successor to the British Columbia Electric Railway.**

Linear induction motors

The LIM works by splitting the rotor and the stator parts of a normal electric motor.

The stator is mounted on a bogie while the rotor becomes a reaction rail mounted on the track. When an AC current passes through the stator, magnetic fields are created between it and the reaction rail. The force created by the magnetic fields then moves the train along.

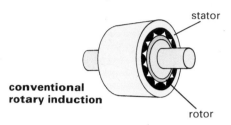

stator

rotor

conventional rotary induction

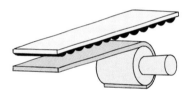

linear induction motor (LIM)

stator

rotor

▲The Surrey Town Centre route under construction. Much of SkyTrain's route is elevated, with precast guideway beams being lifted on to T-shaped supports. Tracks are then laid directly on to the guideway with noise-deadening resilient mounts.

system. When the central computers that control SkyTrain fail, which happens occasionally, the trains have to be moved manually to restart points. The auto-restart, which will use a network of guideway transducers, will get operations back to normal much faster.

BC Transit and UTDC have also been developing a new series of cars, the Mark IIs. They would be longer than the Mark Is and carry nearly double the load. The Mark IIs, coupled in three-car sets, would have a maximum capacity of 435 passengers per train, as opposed to 300 currently in four-car sets, for roughly the same length of train. The Mark II and the auto-restart project, however, are on hold pending funding, though money has been allocated for the software upgrade.

Expansion plans

SkyTrain is being planned to extend from Vancouver city centre 14.6km (8¾ miles) southwards to Richmond at an estimated cost of $788 million (Can), with future extensions to Ladner, Steveston and Vancouver International airport. BC Transit estimates that the Richmond line could attract 16,000 to 21,000 passengers each way in the peak hour within 20 to 25 years. In October 1992 an advisory committee recommended a route that would be segregated from road traffic, and that SkyTrain be selected as the preferred mode of transport.

In contrast to the original decision to build SkyTrain, the committee openly examined other modes, such as LRT, and found that SkyTrain had a higher capacity and lower operating and construction costs compared with trams on the selected route. Before the committee had completed its work, the NDP won back power but has since refused to commit funding for the proposed line because of the current recession.

Another similar panel has been appointed to look at mode and route options north-eastwards to Coquitlam, another planned SkyTrain destination. One of the choices is to run suburban trains on CP Rail from Vancouver to Port Coquitlam via Port Moody, which last saw a regular passenger service in October 1978.

▼Waterfront Station is SkyTrain's Vancouver terminus. It is reached by an ex-CP Rail tunnel that curves through the city centre. The planned Richmond route will leave the station then loop under the present tracks before heading south.

Driverless trains

Automatic trains still sound like the stuff of science fiction, but the Post Office's Mail Rail has been running without drivers for over 60 years. London has two automatic passenger lines, and on the Continent rubber-tyred driverless trains give a very smooth ride.

▼One of the original Class P86 Docklands Light Railway cars – made by Linke Hofmann Busch in 1986 – makes its way to Island Gardens. In 1992 the P86 cars were sold and SELTRAC automatic control progressively installed.

Although trains run along a track and don't need anyone to steer them, doing away with the driver is still difficult. Not only has the whereabouts of the train got to be known accurately, but the power and braking must be capable of being varied automatically to give the right speed at every point.

It was impossible to consider the idea of driverless trains in the days of steam, as the controls of these locomotives were too complicated to automate. It is not easy even with diesel power, but the simplicity of electrical circuits has made electricity the choice for virtually all automatic trains.

During much of this century various small steps were made towards automation. Many of the cab signalling systems developed from the 1900s onwards, such as the GWR's Automatic Train Control and BR's Automatic Warning System,

would stop the train at the approach to any danger signal unless the driver resumed control. The Automatic Train Protection devices in use on the Continent and currently being introduced in Britain cannot be overridden by the driver, but restarting trains still has to be done manually.

From the early days of electric multiple units (EMUs) some degree of automation was used with the power controls. Initially, notching out the starting resistances was entirely under the control of the motorman but, once the principle of the accelerating relay had been discovered, it was possible to automate this process. This still left the driver to decide whether to run in series, parallel or weak field, and then move his controller to the appropriate notch. After that the equipment looked after the whole process for him.

The use of such a system was possible only

where the performance of every train was virtually identical, regardless of its length. For electric locomotives which have to haul variable loads, manual notching had to be retained until quite recently.

Driverless operation was used only where all the trains were of the same type and ran to more or less identical timings. Thanks to thyristors, however, the controls of many modern electric locomotives now permit the driver to select a speed and then the equipment maintains this, uphill and down. InterCity Class 91s use this equipment, nicknamed cruise control.

The Post Office railway
Because early automatic trains could not ensure reliability, the first such trains were not used for carrying passengers. For over 60 years the Post Office has operated a 10km (6½ mile) driverless railway beneath the streets of London.

Trains on the 60.9cm (2ft) gauge tracks are powered from a centrally positioned third rail, which can be charged at either 440 or 150 volts DC, and their position is determined by low voltage track circuits between the running rails. These also cut off the current from the section of conductor rail immediately behind the train, protecting it from the one following.

The current for the motors passes through a large solenoid on the power unit which, when energized, holds the brakes off against a strong spring. As soon as a train enters a dead section, not only is the power cut off, but the brakes go on sharply as the solenoid is de-energized. The resulting stop is somewhat sharper than would be acceptable for a passenger train.

The fastest schedules have seen non-stop trains travelling from Liverpool Street Station to Paddington in only 13 minutes – much quicker than could be achieved on the capital's roads. There is still considerable human intervention in

▲In the USA, on the Black Mesa & Lake Powell Railroad, large driverless electric locomotives once hauled long mineral trains. However, difficulties with the railway unions means that the railway now has drivers again. Over the past two decades, a number of these automatic mineral railways were built, sometimes running long distances.

▶In France, Lille's VAL railway has no staff aboard – it is supervised from a main control room. The railway works on the electronic loop system and, to make sure everything is running smoothly, cameras observe events at every station. VAL trains run on rubber tyres.

▶ Once the train operator presses the twin start buttons, London's Victoria line trains accelerate and brake automatically. Trains respond to coded impulses transmitted through the track. There are no lineside signals – except starters at junctions and stations. Block sections are marked by special headway posts. As well as the signal brake command spots, coast commands are provided to reduce energy consumption.

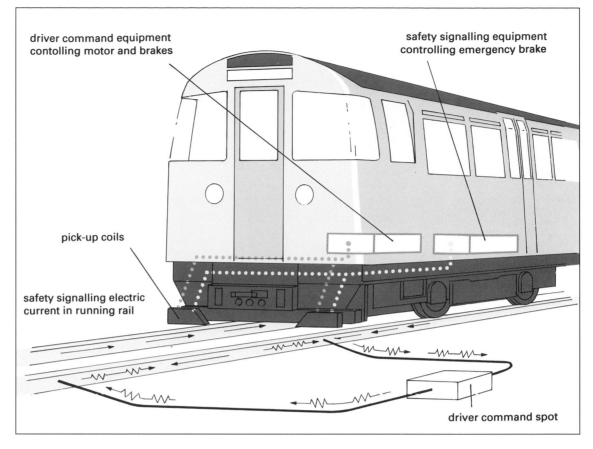

driver command equipment contolling motor and brakes

safety signalling equipment controlling emergency brake

pick-up coils

safety signalling electric current in running rail

driver command spot

▼One of the first systems in the world to have completely automated trains was San Francisco's Bay Area Rapid Transit (BART). In practice they were operated with someone in the cab supervising their running.

the operation of the system, quite apart from loading and unloading, but plans have been announced for major investments to make it more automated.

The Victoria line

London Underground's Victoria line uses antennae to pick up information from track circuits, telling the train about the state of signals, as well as other information. The system is known as Automatic Train Operation (ATO). A 180 second impulse code on the track circuit current keeps the train below 35km (22mph), while a 420 code allows it to accelerate to full speed. If the impulses

are lost completely, the train stops immediately.

This safety system has to be supplemented by a driver command system, acting at certain 3m (10ft) long spots on the track. Approaching a station, the first of these cuts the power to the motors to make the train coast and the others then tell the brakes when to come on. Between them they slow the train progressively until it stops at the right place in the station.

The Paris Metro

Another way of making all the trains on a particular line run at the same speed and make the same stops is the so-called 'wiggly wire'. This is used on the Paris Metro. It is a very different type of communication, consisting of a wire in a continuous zigzag a few inches wide, mounted between the tracks, parallel to the rails.

An aerial in the leading vehicle senses the current in the wire every time it passes over it, and the controller then speeds up or slows down the train so that the same number of wires are crossed every second. By changing the pitch of the zigzags, the train automatically follows the speed profile required. A separate system brings the train completely to a halt in the platform or at a stop signal.

German high speed lines

A different type of control system uses a series of loops. A pair of insulated cables runs along the track, one usually lying in the centre of the sleepers, while the other is clipped to the foot of one of the rails. At intervals they change places across one of the sleepers – this forms the end of each loop. For the past 25 years this system has been

▶ **Canada has an automatic railway in Vancouver, popularly known as Sky Train. In August 1990 BC Transit System's automatic car No 037 makes its way across College Place, Vancouver.**

Never-Stop railway

A driverless railway was installed at the British Empire Exhibition at Wembley in 1924 to convey passengers to the site. Called the Never-Stop railway it consisted of a number of separate coaches with 'toast-rack' seating. Each vehicle had a lug underneath it, which engaged in a slot in a horizontally rotating shaft running the full length of the line. As the shaft rotated, the lug propelled the coach forward. In stations the slots were close together so that the vehicle moved slowly enough for people to get off.

Mail Rail

The Post Office's automatic railway – Mail Rail – has been running under the streets of London for over 60 years. It has recently been modernized. Here a refurbished unit is being loaded; behind it a newer train, made by Greenbat in 1979, waits its turn. The automatic operation of the line is controlled by track circuits. As a train moves along power is shut off in the section behind it.

installed on all German lines where speeds in excess of 160km (100mph) are reached.

The start of each section equipped with the loop system is marked by a lineside sign with the initials LZB, standing for *Linienzugbeeinflussung* (literally, line for influencing trains). Each time the antenna on the train crosses the end of one of these loops, a signal is sent to its own computer – as well as those in the control centre. In addition, other information can constantly be exchanged between the train and central control.

Docklands Light Railway

The loop system can also be seen on the Docklands Light Railway (DLR) where the loops are only 25 metres (27yd) long. It is necessary to pinpoint the train's position more accurately than this, so revolution counters are fitted on two of each train's axles which locate it within 6m (20ft).

The line was built to use the fixed block system, in which no two trains are ever allowed to get closer than the distance required for the rear train to stop from its highest speed. To increase the number of trains operated on the line, the SEL-TRAC moving block system has been installed. This always allows a 45m (50yd) safety zone between trains, but does not used fixed block sections.

Each DLR train carries a Train Captain. In addition to checking tickets, the captains open and close doors at stations and press a button when the train is ready to go. Should the automatic system break down, the train can be driven at slow speed by the captain under instructions from the control room.

The VAL

Elsewhere in Europe there are driverless trains which do not have any staff aboard. In Lille the VAL (*Vehicule Automatique Legére* – light automatic vehicle) system has been operating since 1983. Using rubber-tyred vehicles to deal with the 1 in 10 gradients and reduce vibration and noise, these metro trains can average more than 48km (30mph) over some of the longer stretches between stations.

In the control centre there are 24 large television monitors in a curve across the front of the control room, and these can be switched to any of the 252 cameras installed. If an alarm sounds, the screens on the desk in front of the four controllers immediately provide menus telling controllers what other displays they can select to deal with the problem. A notice inside each car warns passengers that their conversation can be overheard in the control room.

The stopping time of trains at stations is fixed by the controllers within quite a small range (typically 17-23 seconds), and even in the rush hour the regularity of arrivals at the main city is remarkable.

▶ Japan, not surprisingly, operates a number of automatic metro systems. Since the Portliner trains are operated completely by computer control, Train Captains have little to do – as this picture shows.

▼After successful trials of Automatic Train Operation on the Woodford – Hainault line in 1964, the Victoria line was fully automated from its opening in 1967. The Victoria line uses Metro-Cammell 1967 stock. A driver travels in the cab, but only to operate the doors. Provision is made for emergency manual control, during which trains are limited to 16km (10mph). Trains carry automatic fault diagnostic equipment in the cab.

Although driverless from the outset, London's Docklands Light Railway was built with grossly inadequate capacity in a short-sighted attempt to save money. Rebuilding the network with the SELTRAC automatic train control system to increase capacity has been both disruptive and costly.

Amtrak: America's passenger railway

Set up to run America's unprofitable express trains over tracks it didn't own, with a ramshackle and motley assortment of worn out carriages, the future for Amtrak did not seem too rosy. But it has surmounted most of its problems and earned respect for its achievements.

Data for 1995
Route mileage: 24,500 (40,232km); 346 miles (555km) electrified at 11kV 25Hz AC and 13kV 60Hz AC catenary
Trains run per day: 250 intercity, 553 commuter (1992)
Annual passenger journeys: 22 million intercity, 20.3 million commuter
Locomotives: 281 diesel-electric and electro-diesel, 65 electric
Carriages: 1700

Providing efficient intercity passenger services in a large, sprawling country like the United States of America is not easy. The high standard of living and low petrol prices make car ownership highly attractive, while the distances of more than 600 miles (966km) that separate many cities and holiday resorts make air travel a necessity.

Given these conditions, the National Railroad Passenger Corporation, better known as Amtrak, does well, carrying some 22 million passengers in 1994. It is a private corporation but receives financial support from the US government, which also owns its assets.

Amtrak was created by the US government in 1970 to relieve the privately owned US railways of loss-making passenger trains. With a mandate to provide and improve passenger services, but at a profit, it took over most of the country's intercity routes on 1 May 1971. The company inherited an assortment of old locomotives, carriages, stations and servicing facilities painted in a motley assortment of liveries. Train crews at that time were provided by the railway companies.

The only modern trains Amtrak had were rakes of Metroliner EMUs. Designed for 150mph (250km/h) but rarely running at more than 110mph (177km/h) on the Northeast Corridor route between New York and Washington DC,

▼In summer 1993 a Swedish X2000 high speed tilting train was demonstrated in the USA. It is seen leaving Chicago on a demonstration trip to Dwight, Illinois, propelled by two Amtrak diesels. In trials on the Northeast Corridor it was able to run under its own power.

▲The basic Amtrak network. In April 1993 the company launched its first regular transcontinental train by extending the Sunset Limited express to run from Los Angeles to Miami. The journey takes 58 hours.

they were built in the late 1960s as part of a US government railway demonstration project. For a couple of years Amtrak struggled on, with few observers giving it much chance of survival. Then with the 1973 energy crisis, trains were looked at with renewed interest. Passenger numbers soared as the queues at petrol stations grew.

This was the turning point for Amtrak, and it began to replace and renew its fleet. By 1982 all of its carriages were either new or had been

rebuilt. Amtrak also installed a ticket and reservations system controlled by computer. New stations and workshops were built or rebuilt from existing facilities.

In 1976, Amtrak was given the 455 mile (732km) Boston – Washington railway, with its branches from Philadelphia and Harrisburg, in Pennsylvania. Also acquired was the line from New Haven, Connecticut, to Springfield, Massachusetts. This had belonged to the bankrupt

▶An Amtrak Superliner dining car is loaded with fresh victuals. The contrast of the old fashioned trolley and the smart new carriage has been symbolic of Amtrak itself, although that is now changing.

▲One of Amtrak's Turboliners enters Chicago station past rakes of Amtrak carriages. These trains were supplied by French builders in the mid-1970s and were based on the SNCF RTG sets. The 'Turbopower' lettering on the side refers to the fact that these trains are powered by gas turbine engines, rather than by turbo-charged diesel engines as might be expected.

Penn Central Railroad. The US government (Congress) allowed Amtrak to spend $2500m to rebuild these lines so that it could run trains between New York and Washington, taking two hours 40 minutes, and between New York and Boston, taking three hours 40 minutes. Amtrak also rebuilt the line from Philadelphia to Atlantic City, which opened in May 1989, only to close in 1995. The tracks were shared with NJ Transit, a state-owned commuter rail agency.

In 1983 Amtrak started employing its own train crews, first on the Northeast Corridor and later throughout the country. By 1993 the Corporation was employing about 24,000 people.

In 1987 Amtrak managed to earn enough revenue to pay all of its operating costs. When capital costs are taken into account, revenue covered 48% of costs in 1981, and 72% in 1990, with the Corporation hoping to break even by 2000. An operating subsidy of $185m was agreed for 1995, but the figure is expected to fall each year. However, a trust fund has been set up to cover long-term investment.

Amtrak operations today

Amtrak operates 250 trains a day over 24,500 route miles. This does not include the commuter trains it runs under contract to local transport authorities. It carries small parcels and mail as well as intercity passengers.

Most of its services run over the rails of the private railways and tolls are paid for the use of the track. These are due for revision in 1996. It also offers the railway companies incentive payments to ensure the punctual operation of its trains.

In addition, Amtrak has its own tracks, not just in the Northeast Corridor but also a stretch from Porter, Indiana, to Kalamazoo, Michigan, for its Chicago to Detroit and Toronto trains. Like the railway companies, it has its own permanent way equipment. Amtrak also works trains over tracks owned by state governments for commuter services.

Amtrak's system is basically that which it began with in 1971 with a few gains and losses. Its trains reach 45 of the 48 mainland states, plus the District of Columbia. While it must comply with Congressional criteria on whether to abandon services over routes it had taken over in 1971, it has fewer constraints on lines added since then.

Individual states have been important in helping Amtrak to expand its operations. Under Section 403(b) of the law that created Amtrak, states are allowed to request additional services if they agree to finance up to two-thirds of the losses.

Some states go further than that. The state of New York, for instance, spent more than $150 million to improve track, buy equipment and add trains on the New York – Albany – Buffalo line, known as the Empire Corridor. Yet by far the largest investor in Section 403(b) has been the State of California. As a result, Amtrak's Los Angeles – San Diego service has trebled from three return journeys per week in 1971 to nine in

Amtrak's commuter trains

Amtrak is not just the USA's intercity passenger carrier but is also one of the country's largest suburban railway operators. It runs trains out of Boston, Massachusetts, New Haven, Connecticut, Baltimore, Maryland, Washington DC, and in the San Francisco area and southern California under contract to regional transport authorities.

Amtrak's sole purpose in 1970 was to run intercity trains. The law specifically excluded commuter train operations. In 1983, however, the state of Maryland asked Amtrak to run its services from Baltimore and later Perryville to Washington on the Northeast Corridor.

Thanks to contracts to operate new commuter networks such as those in Los Angeles and south of Washington DC, Amtrak will soon carry more commuters than intercity travellers.

The state of Maine has been working with Amtrak to reinstate a service between Boston and Portland by way of Dover, New Hampshire (115 miles/185km), with three trains a day. The market is both commuter and intercity.

America's other intercity trains

Amtrak is not the only intercity passenger train operator in the USA. Two other railways, the Alaska Railroad and the Long Island Rail Road (LIRR), also run express trains. A train is generally regarded as intercity if it travels more than 90 miles (145km), although Amtrak does operate shorter routes such as from New York to Springfield in Massachusetts.

The Alaska Railroad runs a daily express train on its main line between Anchorage and Fairbanks, 356 miles (573km), in the summer and a weekly stopping train in the winter. It runs all year between Anchorage and Whittier, plus a seasonal daily train to Seward.

Alaska's trains are very popular with tourists. In 1991 the railway attracted 471,217 passengers, an 8% increase over 1990. It recently bought six new carriages from C Itoh of Japan.

The LIRR is North America's busiest commuter railway. It has a network of electrified routes funnelling under the East River into New York City's Penn station. However, the railway also operates diesel-hauled trains from Hunterspoint Avenue, in Queens, to Montauk, a distance of 115 miles (185km). Passengers from Manhattan go by underground or ordinary LIRR train to its main transfer point at Jamaica to use this service.

The Montauk line is extremely well used. It serves the Hamptons, which are up-market suburban communities. Its trains are also made up of the only non-Amtrak first class carriages in the USA, the LIRR's Sunrise Fleet parlour cars. One-way journey times to Manhattan of more than three hours mean that it attracts very few commuters from the outer ends of the line.

Some local authorities operate trains whose distance or markets put them into the intercity category, even though their timetables are designed primarily for use by commuters.

▲The twice-daily Amtrak express from Washington to Miami, hauled by an F40PH diesel, passes through Winter Haven in Florida, the station for Disney World at Orlando. The F40PHs were intended for short haul commuter traffic, and had to be modified to suit electrically heated doubledeck trains. They are more often seen in multiple.

1993. The San Joaquins – a generic name for all trains using the stretch of track between Oakland and Bakersfield – have expanded from one train each way from Oakland to Bakersfield in 1979 to four in 1992. In December 1991 a service of three trains a day was introduced from Roseville and Sacramento to Oakland and San Jose.

California is increasing its commitment to intercity railway services by paying for extra trains and has bought 40 doubledeck carriages and nine new 3000hp GM locomotives for Amtrak.

An important addition to the Amtrak system is a network of special Thruway coaches which accept Amtrak tickets and connect with certain trains. They allow Amtrak to serve destinations where it is either not possible, or not worthwhile, to provide direct train services.

Since its inception, Amtrak has built new stations in more than 30 cities and renovated another 25. It hopes to carry out a $315 million plan to move from Penn station in New York City, which is underneath Madison Square Garden, to the neo-classical US Post Office building across the street, which is now redundant and much more attractive. It straddles the railway tracks so providing platform access will be relatively easy.

Rolling stock

Amtrak has 1962 carriages. The mainstay of its modern rolling stock is made up from 492 Amfleet I and 150 Amfleet II carriages, restaurant cars and lounge cars acquired between 1973 and 1981 from the Budd Co. The Amfleet I design was derived from the Metroliner EMUs; the Amfleet IIs differ in that they have larger windows and a single vestibule.

Its premier midwestern and western trains are worked by doubledeck Superliners. Amtrak ordered 284 of them from Pullman-Standard in 1975, followed by a further 140 from Bombardier in 1991.

A third category of stock is the 104-strong Horizon fleet. They were built by Bombardier in 1989-90 and are used on short-distance trains feeding Chicago and on the Capitols and San Joaquins. The Horizons are built to a design first used for suburban carriages in Boston, New York and Philadelphia.

Amtrak also has 13 five-car Turboliners derived from the French RTG, though they are being phased out. Seven of these trains are allocat-

▶ A push-pull train from Detroit arrives in Chicago. The cylinder-like driving trailer was converted from an ordinary Metroliner carriage built in 1967. The use of driving trailers makes for much greater operational flexibility on relatively short runs by the avoidance of running round at busy locations such as Chicago, where Amtrak shares facilities with other operators. The other three coaches are Horizons, based on a suburban carriage design.

▲An Amtrak express stands in San Diego station in California. The large Santa Fe sign behind the train is a reminder that Amtrak trains operate largely by virtue of their running powers over railway companies' lines. Unlike in Britain, many American stations, such as this one, have rail-level platforms.

modern long distance carriages developed by Amtrak. Fifty sleeping cars to this design have been ordered, but anticipated contracts for restaurant cars, lounge cars and day coaches have been frozen.

Most of Amtrak's trains are hauled by a stud of 210 3000hp Bo-Bo General Motors F40PH locomotives which were delivered between 1976 and 1988. General Motors (GM) also supplied Amtrak with 54 of its main electric locomotive, the Swedish-designed 7000hp Bo-Bo AEM-7 class in 1980-81 and 1988.

Between 1993-5, three batches of new locomotives were delivered: 20 Dash 8-32BWH, built by General Electric in 1993; 44 Genesis I streamlined locomotives with 4000hp AC motors; and 10 Genesis II electro-diesels for New York.

Amtrak's future

The prospects for Amtrak's future look promising. Electrification of the line from New Haven to Boston and track improvements to allow speeds of 155mph (250km/h) will give a New York – Boston travel time of less than three hours in contrast to the 1993 time of nearly four hours. Amtrak tested the Swedish X2000 and the German ICE in 1993. In 1996 an order was placed with Bombardier/GEC Alsthom for a fleet of 18 high speed tilting trains made up of two power cars and six coaches.

ed to the Empire Corridor and are fitted with third-rail pick-up shoes so they can run over electrified lines to Penn station in New York.

The oldest batch of equipment is Amtrak's Heritage Fleet of long distance carriages dating from the 1950s. Over 800 were acquired from the railways and converted to electric heating between 1978 and 1983; they will all be replaced eventually by modern Viewliner coaching stock – new,

Steam speed records

In 1804, when Richard Trevithick's pioneering locomotive made its journey along the Penydarren tramroad, its inventor operated the controls by walking along the track in front of it. In a letter the following day, Trevithick recorded that 'The engine while working went nearly five miles pr hour' – no more than a brisk walking pace. This was perhaps the first ever steam speed record.

When *Locomotion* ran from Shildon to Stockton 21 years later, it could only outdistance riders on horseback because marshes alongside the line impeded the horses. At full speed the locomotive could just manage 15mph.

At the Rainhill Trials in 1829, Stephenson's *Rocket* achieved 29mph. This was eclipsed in tragic circumstances the following year, when *Northumbrian* reached 36mph as it conveyed the dying MP William Huskisson to Eccles after he had been run over by *Rocket* at Parkside.

The contestants' achievements at Rainhill were carefully recorded. Later, it became difficult to establish accurate claims as speeds increased and railways spread throughout the world.

Unlike world speed records on land and in the air, there are no international standards for railways. For example, the effect of a strong following wind has never been taken into account and on almost every occasion a record breaking train was appreciably assisted by gravity. This applies equally to the TGV's present world record of 320.2mph as to *Mallard*'s 126mph in 1938.

Speed records were usually obtained by stop-watch measurements from mile or kilometre posts. In some cases the speed claimed at the time was later adjusted after the information had been examined further.

The performance of the Milwaukee Road's Hiawatha expresses in the 1930s was accurately measured and the 112mph record by the streamlined Atlantic No 2 in 1925 was adequately proved.

During the 1930s, there was considerable rivalry over maximum speeds between the LNER and the LMS. In 1937, the LMS claimed a maximum of 114mph on the press run of their Coronation Scot streamliner train. This would have beaten *Silver Link*'s record but the figure was not confirmed by a number of experienced recorders on the train. This left *Coronation* sharing the record of 112mph with the LNER A4 and Milwaukee Atlantic.

By 1936 the German Pacific No 05.002 reached 124.5mph and in 1938, *Mallard* achieved an historic all-time record for steam of 126mph.

Date	Wheel arrgt	Name/No	Country	Railway	Speed mph (km)
Feb 1804	0-4-0	Trevithick's Penydarren Locomotive	GB	Merthyr tramroad	5 (8)
Sep 1825	0-4-0	*Locomotion*	GB	Stockton & Darlington	15 (24)
Oct 1829	0-2-2	*Rocket*	GB	Liverpool & Manchester	29 (46)
Sep 1830	0-2-2	*Northumbrian*	GB	Liverpool & Manchester	36 (58)
Nov 1839	2-2-2	*Lucifer*	GB	Grand Junction	57 (92)
June 1845	2-2-2	*Ixion*	GB	Great Western	61 (98)
June 1846	2-2-2	*Great Western*	GB	Great Western	74 (119)
May 1848	4-2-2	*Great Britain*	GB	Great Western	78 (125)
June 1854	4-2-4WT	No 41	GB	Bristol & Exeter	82 (132)
1889	4-2-0	No 604	France	Est	89 (143)
Mar 1897	4-2-2	No 117	GB	Midland	90 (145)
May 1904	4-4-0	*City of Truro*	GB	Great Western	100 (161)
Nov 1934	4-6-2	*Flying Scotsman*	GB	LNER	100 (161)
Mar 1935	4-6-2	*Papyrus*	GB	LNER	108 (174)
May 1935	4-4-2	No 2	USA	Milwaukee	112 (180)
Sep 1935	4-6-2	*Silver Link*	GB	LNER	112 (180)
May 1936	4-6-4	No 05.002	Germany	Deutsche Reichsbahn	124.5 (200)
July 1938	4-6-2	*Mallard*	GB	LNER	126 (202)

▲ All the fully authenticated world records achieved by steam locomotives are the maximum speed attained, rather than averages. Some top speeds, like *Mallard*'s, were sustained only for a few yards.

◀ Although a record of 74mph was achieved by a GWR locomotive in 1846, it was not until 1931 that the company ran trains at such average speeds in everyday service. The Cheltenham Flyer was the first train in the history of railways to average regularly over 70mph. On 14 September 1931, the express sweeps through Tilehurst, Berkshire on its way to London.

Diesel speed records

The internal combustion engine has been used by railway traction since the early 20th century. Because the available power of engines was low, new diesel locomotives were intended only for light duties, particularly on branch lines where operating costs were causing concern, or for shunting. World records were set up for this form of traction, but the speeds achieved were so far behind contemporary achievements of steam that no one bothered to take any notice.

After World War I, internal combustion engines became smaller and better ways were found to transmit power to the wheels of a locomotive or train. By the 1930s, with more efficient diesel motors becoming widely available, high speed trains were developed. These mounted the first serious challenge to steam's speed supremacy.

It is not the highest speed reached that matters to the ordinary traveller, but how long the journey takes – high *average* speeds, although slower than the peak speeds, have more commercial importance. The difference between the two speeds is shown by the Burlington Railroad's high speed run with its three-coach, stainless-steel, streamlined Pioneer Zephyr in May 1934. The maximum of 112.5mph earned the Zephyr the world speed record, but it also ran the 1015 miles from Denver to Chicago non stop at an overall average of 77.6mph. At the conclusion of its run, the train was displayed at an exhibition alongside its rival, the Union Pacific M10001, which was to achieve the next world record of 120mph later that year.

Although the North American diesel streamliners quickly made their mark on the railway scene, all other world speed records with diesel power have been achieved in Europe. In 1972, the Spanish Talgo record was attained with a diesel-hydraulic locomotive, later overtaken in the UK using HSTs with electric transmissions. Ironically, the 1986 and 1987 diesel records were made by HSTs during bogie trials for the forthcoming East Coast electric InterCity 225 trains.

There have also been a number of record-breaking oddities powered by internal combustion. In 1933 a German railcar, propelled by an airscrew, reached 143mph, but there are no reports on the effect that the slipstream had on waiting passengers as it passed through a station. In 1966, the New York Central mounted a pair of jet engines on top of a railcar, generating a speed of 183.9mph – and much noise. Gas turbines have also been successfully used in a number of trains propelled through their wheels.

Date		Train	Country	Speed mph (km/h)
Dec	1932	VT877 railcar	Germany	102.5 (165)
May	1934	Pioneer Zephyr	USA	112.5 (181)
Oct	1934	Union Pacific M10001	USA	120 (193)
Feb	1936	Leipzig railcar	Germany	127.4 (205)
June	1939	Kruckenberg set	Germany	133 (214)
May	1972	Talgo 353-005	Spain	137.9 (222)
June	1973	HST prototype	GB	143.2 (230.5)
Sep	1985	HST	GB	144 (231.7)
Nov	1986	HST	GB	144.9 (233)
Nov	1987	HST	GB	148.5 (238.9)

◀ Since 1932 there have been 10 fully authenticated world speed records for diesel-powered trains. By the 1930s, mechanical methods had replaced stop-watches to record top speeds accurately, and most diesel records benefited from this new technology.

▲In May 1934 the Burlington Railroad's Pioneer Zephyr reached 112.5mph and earned the world railway speed record. The three-coach, stainless-steel, streamlined train also ran the 1015 miles from Denver to Chicago non stop at an overall average of 77.6mph.

Electric speed records

The first electric locomotive was built by R Davidson in 1842. Battery powered, it reached 4mph (6.4km/h) on the Glasgow – Edinburgh line, but the design was far too crude to be a rival for steam traction.

It was not until 1879 that Werner von Siemens produced the first recognizable electric train, drawing current from a conductor along the track. Although this machine was only a miniature gauge model in a Berlin exhibition, within 22 years a Siemens & Halske locomotive had topped the 100mph (160.9km/h) mark on the Marienfelde – Zossen Germany military railway. The same test track was used in 1903 to set up three more records, the fastest being no less than 130.6mph (210.1km/h), a speed never surpassed by steam.

The current collection methods used for the Siemens & Halske tests involved three different contact wires, mounted one above the other on masts alongside

▼Early electric traction records were achieved during primitive experiments, but since 1954 this form of motive power has dominated railway speed records. Over the last 40 years the pace has been set by the TGVs and ICEs of France and Germany.

the track. The vehicles sprouted a series of collectors which badly infringed the normal loading gauge and there was no way the contact wires could be continued through a junction. For this reason these trains have always been considered as oddities.

It was not until the late 1930s that the speed capabilities of orthodox electric trains started to rival steam, with a speed of 126mph (202.7km/h) being achieved by an Italian streamlined railcar in 1939. Since 1954 this type of motive power has held all the absolute railway speed records, Spanish and British diesel records being well behind the contemporary electric achievements.

Over the past 40 years, honours have been shared by the French and German railways, with their TGVs and ICEs. The friendly rivalry between the two countries stimulated German efforts to push the speed of their prototype ICE beyond the TGV's 1981 record. Seven months later, the French engineers marginally regained the lead during a test run with the prototype TGV for the new Atlantique line, but did not claim it officially.

The French were saving their efforts for a series of trials planned for the new line after it had been completed. A long

downhill stretch to the bridge across the river Loire provided a magnificent racing stretch. Between December 1989 and May 1990 no less than five new world records were set, culminating in a final speed of 320.2mph (515.3km/h).

The Japanese railways do not figure in the world record table. From 1965 their Bullet trains set new world records for commercial services, being the first to set schedules of more than 100mph (160.9km/h) start-to-stop. They have nevertheless achieved a number of national railway speed records. The new Series 300 set up a figure of 202.4mph (325.7km/h) on the Central Japan Railway in February 1991 and in March, on the East Japan Railway, the new Series 400 reached 214.4mph (345km/h).

So rapid are current world developments that a speed of 205mph (329.9km/h) was reached early in 1992 on the new Spanish AVE before the line between Madrid and Seville had been completed.

In Britain the railway speed record is still held by the APT-P, which attained 162.2mph (261km/h) between Beattock and Lockerbie in December 1979 – but the Class 91 came very close in September 1989 with 161.7mph (260.2km/h) descending Stoke Bank.

Date	Train/locomotive	Country	Speed mph (km/h)
1901	Siemens & Halske loco	Germany	101.0 (162.5)
Oct 1903	Siemens & Halske railcar	Germany	126.0 (202.7)
Oct 1903	Siemens & Halske railcar	Germany	128.5 (206.8)
Oct 1903	AEG railcar	Germany	130.6 (210.1)
July 1939	ETR200 multiple unit	Italy	126.1 (202.9)
Feb 1954	CC7121	France	151.0 (243)
Mar 1955	BB9004	France	171.5 (276)
Mar 1955	CC7101	France	202.6 (326)
Mar 1955	BB9004	France	205.7 (331)
Feb 1981	TGV33	France	230.5 (370.9)
Feb 1981	TGV33	France	236.4 (380.4)
Apr 1988	ICE prototype	W Germany	240.5 (387)
Apr 1988	ICE prototype	W Germany	249.2 (401)
Apr 1988	ICE prototype	W Germany	251.0 (403.9)
May 1988	ICE prototype	W Germany	252.8 (406.8)
Dec 1988	TGV88	France	253.7 (408.2)
Dec 1989	TGV325	France	275.0 (442.5)
May 1990	TGV325	France	317.3 (482.3)
May 1990	TGV325	France	317.4 (510.6)
May 1990	TGV325	France	320.2 (515.3)

▲High speed electric networks are growing all the time throughout Europe. The Spanish AVE (*Alta Velocidad Espanol*) runs at over 220km/h on the standard gauge line from Madrid to Seville, known as a NAFA. Other new electric locomotives on the line will be built to a design led by the German firm Siemens – who set the early speed records in 1903.

Index

Page numbers in **bold** type indicate complete articles.
Page numbers in *italic* type indicate illustrations.

ACKNOWLEDGEMENTS

Photographs: 8, 9(t) Science and Society Picture Library; 10 MH (Hugh Ballantyne); 12 RAS; 13 NRM; 14-15 RAS (F.R.Hebron); 16, 17, 18-19 HE; 20 Geoff Rixon; 21 MH; 22 NRM; 23 MH (Colour-Rail); 24-25 MH (Jim Jarvis); 26 UPR; 27 MH (Jim Jarvis); 28 HE; 29 Milepost 92Ω; 30 MH (Colour-Rail); 31 H-D Ltd; 32 MH (Colour-Rail); 33 RAS; 34 MH (Jim Jarvis); 35 HE; 36 MH (Jim Jarvis); 37-40 HE; 41 MH (Jim Jarvis); 42-44 HE; 45 Steamscenes (Nils Huxtable); 46 Bob Caflisch; 47 HE; 48 MH (Jim Jarvis); 49-54 HE; 55 UPR; 56-58 HE; 59, 60 MH (Jim Jarvis); 61-63 HE; 64 Ullstein Bilderdienst; 65 RAS; 66 MH (Hugh Ballantyne); 67 John Westwood; 68 Anthony J Lambert; 69, 70 MH (Hugh Ballantyne); 71 State Authority of New South Wales; 72 MH (Hugh Ballantyne); 73 HE Collection (H.J.Sturton); 76 Jim Neubaue; 77 HE Collection (H.J.Sturton); HE Collection (C.J. Felstead Collection); 77 HE; 78 SNCF; 79 NRM; 80(t) George Carpenter; 80-81(b) SNCF; 82-85 William A Raia Collection; 86-88 HE; 89 MH (Jim Jarvis); 90-91 HE; 92-95 MH (Jim Jarvis); HE; 96-101 HE; 102 Steamscenes (Nils Huxtable); 103 HE; 104(t) Steamscenes (Nils Huxtable); 104(b), 106 HE; 107-110 SNCF; 111 NRM; 112 MH; 113(t,b) ILN; 113(c) Sylvia Cordaiy Picture Library; 114, 115(t) ILN; 115(b) Mary Evans Picture Library; 116 ILN; 117-121 CPR; 122 Corbis UK; 123 H-D; 114 (tl) Society for Cooperation in Russian and Soviet Studies; 114(b) PF; 114-115 PF; 126 H-D; 127 PF; 128(t) Topham; 128(b) H-D; 129 CPR;

130(t) NRM; 130-131(b) CPR; 131(t) CPR; 132(t) MH; 132(b) NRM; 133,134(t) Rank Organization; 134-135(b) MH (J.S. Whiteley); 135(t), 136(t) Rank Organization; 136(b) MH (P.M. Alexander); 137 Kobal Collection (Paramount Studios); 138-140 IWM; 141(t) IWM; 141(b) MH; 142(t) PF; 142(b) IWM; 143 SPL (Taheshi Takahara); 144 SNCF; 145(t) Peter Semmens; 145(c) SNCF; 145(b) GEC Alsthom; 146(t) Central Japan Railways; 146(b) Deutsche Bundesbahn; 147(top inset) Milepost 92Ω; 147(t) InterCity; 148 HE; 149 SNCF; 150(t) RHPL; 150(b) SNCF; 151 RENFE; 152 SNCF; 152(b) Central Japan Railways; 153 Zefa; 154(b) RAS; 154-155 Asea Brown Boveri; 155 RHPL; 156 (inset) InterCity; 156-157 MH (Peter J Robinson); 157 (inset) Milepost 92Ω; 158 RENFE; 159 ICL; Norihasha Matsumoto (Yuuji Oikawa); 161(t) The Image Bank; 161(b) West Japan Railways; 162(b) Central Japan Railways; 162-163(t) West Japan Railways; 163 East Japan Railways; 164 Quadrant; 165 SPL; 166 (inset) Frank Spooner; 166-167 The Image Bank; 168(t) SPL; 168(b) RHPL; 169 Tony Stone Images; 170(b) GEC Alsthom; 170-171 Tyne and Wear PTE; 171 LRTA (M.R.&J.Taplin); 172(t) LRTA; 172(b) Los Angeles County Transport Commission; 173-176 BC Transit; 177 Eric Hayman; 178(t) Jim Winkley; 178(b) David Haydock; 179, 180(t) Jim Winkley; 180(b) Post Office; 181(t) Rex Features; 181(b) Brian Morrison; 182 Quadrant (Jim Winkley); 183 HE; 184 RHPL; 185,186

Jim Winkley; 187(t) RHPL; 187(b) HE; 188 H-D; 189 Jim Winkley; 190 RENFE.

Illustrations: 9(b) Geoffrey Wheeler; 11 Science and Society Picture Library; 12-13 Maltings Partnership; 14(t) NRM; 16-17 SAL; 19(t) William Gardener Collection; 20-21 Stuart Black; 23(t) NRM; 24-25 SAL; 27(t) UPR; 30-31 SAL; 32 NRM; 34-35 SAL; 36(t) HE Collection; 38-39 SAL; 40(t) HE Collection; 42-43 SAL; 44(t) HE Collection; 46-47 SAL; 48(t) Electro-Motiv; 50-51 SAL; 52(t) Collection of B.L.Bulgrin; 54-55 SAL; 57(t) NRM; 60-61 SAL; 62(t) George Carpenter Collection; 64-65 John Holroyd; 66(t) Nuremberg Museum; 70-71 John Holroyd; 72(t) State Authority of New South Wales; 74-75 SAL; 76(t) Ronald Wright Collection; 78-79 SAL; 81(t) SNCF; 82-83 SAL; 88-89 SAL; 90(t) HE Collection (R.S.Curl); 92-93 SAL; 94(t) Harold Edmonson Collection; 98-99 SAL; 100(t) HE Collection; 102-103 SAL; 105 UPR; 108-109 Stuart Black; 110(t) GEC Althsom/SNCF.

Key: CPR=Canadian Pacific Railways; H-D=Hulton-Deutsch Collection; HE=Harold Edmonson; ILN=Illustrated London News; IWM=Imperial War Museum; MH=Millbrook House; NRM=National Railway Museum; PF=Popperfoto; RAS=Rail Archive Stephenson; RHPL=Robert Harding Picture Library; SAL=Salamander Books; UPR=Union Pacific Railroads.